MEGHAN MARKLE

EXPOSED

By Christopher D Spivey

Version PBMM2018.06.08

CONTENT

Introduction

Who is Meghan Markle?
Now that may sound like a daft question since nigh on the whole population of the planet will know that Meghan Markle is an American actress who is married to Prince Harry – a member of the British Royal family.
Indeed, if you believe the world's press, then Meghan's story truly is a real-life Princess fairytale.
However, by the same token that makes you akin to a zombie:
Someone who appears to be alive but is brain-dead.

After all, fairytales just don't happen... No ifs, no buts, they don't happen.
You see, Meghan Markle, like her deceased mother-in-law, Princess Diana is a construct – a made up persona.
Or put another way, Meghan doesn't exist outside of newspaper reports, faked photos, forged documents and a series of actors who appear in public as and when is necessary.

Furthermore you would not believe how easy it is to pull off a deception of such great magnitude.
In fact, the deception is made all the easier because it is so unbelievable which is reinforced by the Nazi master of propaganda, Josef Goebbels who said:
"The bigger the lie, the more it will be believed"

A truer word never spoken from a man who was also a creation...
Indeed, NOTHING from before the dawn of the 20th century is as we have been led to believe.

However, for you to fully understand who - or what - Meghan Markle is, I will have to show you along the way, how the world of the monster-elite really works.
Therefore, read on with an open mind and hopefully by the time that I am finished you will see just how blatantly you have been mugged off.

Chapter 1
The Tom Tom Club

Now, what you need to bear in mind is that the idea of the construct, Meghan Markle marrying Prince Harry will have been formulated an awful long time ago and if I was to guess when, I would say probably back in the early 1990's.
However, if a person isn't a real person then that person's family cannot be real either, can they?
Of course they can't. So let's start there.

And straight away I can tell you that Meghan's half-brother, Thomas Markle Jr is definitely a wrong-un... And not because of the following infamous [fake] news story either:

THE Markle family have been thrust into the international spotlight thanks to actress Meghan's engagement to Prince Harry.
Here's what you need to know about Thomas Markle Jr, the half-brother of the Suits actress who, earlier this year, was accused of putting a gun to his girlfriend's head during a row.
50-year-old Thomas Markle Jr shares the same father as Suits actress Meghan, who is dating Prince Harry.
It's been reported that he's close to his half-sister but friends have disputed this, saying they have not spoken for some time.
When Meghan was born in 1981, Thomas Jr was living with his father, sister Samantha and step-mother Doria.

He recently moved to Oregon in the US after separating from a partner.
He was married for 11 years to Tracy Dooley, with whom he has two sons - Thomas and Tyler.
His ex-wife, Tracy, said he has alcohol issues.
He was arrested on January 12 in Oregon for allegedly holding a gun to a woman's head during a drunken argument.
He was later charged with menacing, pointing a firearm at another person, and unlawful use of a weapon.

According to court documents, he pointed the gun at Darlene Blount in an attempt to get her to leave.
He has since apologised and said he is "seeking help".
Source: The Sun Newspaper

You can see a photo of Thomas Markle Jr and Darlene Blout in Photo A However that is a total, total bollox story designed to give Meghan credibility in the same way that the persona, the Duchess of Cambridge AKA, Kate Gold-Digger-Smith was allocated a drug-dealing uncle named Gary Goldsmith (see photo B).

PHOTO A: Thomas Markle Jr & Darlene Blout – the bird he allegedly threatened with a gun

PHOTO B: Gary Goldsmith 'covertly' filmed cutting up Cocaine

And indeed it would seem that Goldsmith – like Thomas Markle Jr – *also likes threatening birds as evidenced in the segment below taken from the Daily Mail on the 17th of November 2017:*

Gary Goldsmith was spotted thrashing tennis balls days after he punched his wife with a 'left hook' and knocked her out, MailOnline can reveal today.
The Duchess of Cambridge 's uncle was in court on Tuesday where he admitted knocking Julie Ann Goldsmith unconscious during a drunken row outside their house on October 13.
He was due in court on October 31, after being charged with assault by beating but his defence lawyers went instead to ask for 'caution' for the offence could be considered - which was eventually rejected.

Exclusive pictures reveal that the following day, November 1, he was out playing tennis in his local park in London.
At times Kate's Uncle, whose sister Carole is her mother, looked tired and was seen holding his back and knee.

Two weeks later he was back in court where he admitted punching his wife, who was not in court.

He will be sentenced at a later date and could face a restraining order to stay away from his wife, suggesting they may no longer be together.

Gary Goldsmith struck his wife Julie Ann with a powerful 'left hook' which sent her tumbling onto the pavement after the pair attended a charity auction at a private members' club.

The businessman, who is the younger brother of Kate's mother Carole Middleton, will be spared jail after pleading guilty to assault by beating...

Course, Uncle Gary's wife, Julie Ann Goldsmith is played by the same actress who plays Julie's sister-in-law, Carole Middleton nee Goldsmith... Who is of course Gary Goldsmith's ' sister *' and Kate Gold-Digger-Smith's mother (see photo D).*

PHOTO C: Goldsmith and his wife – the bird that he punched In the head

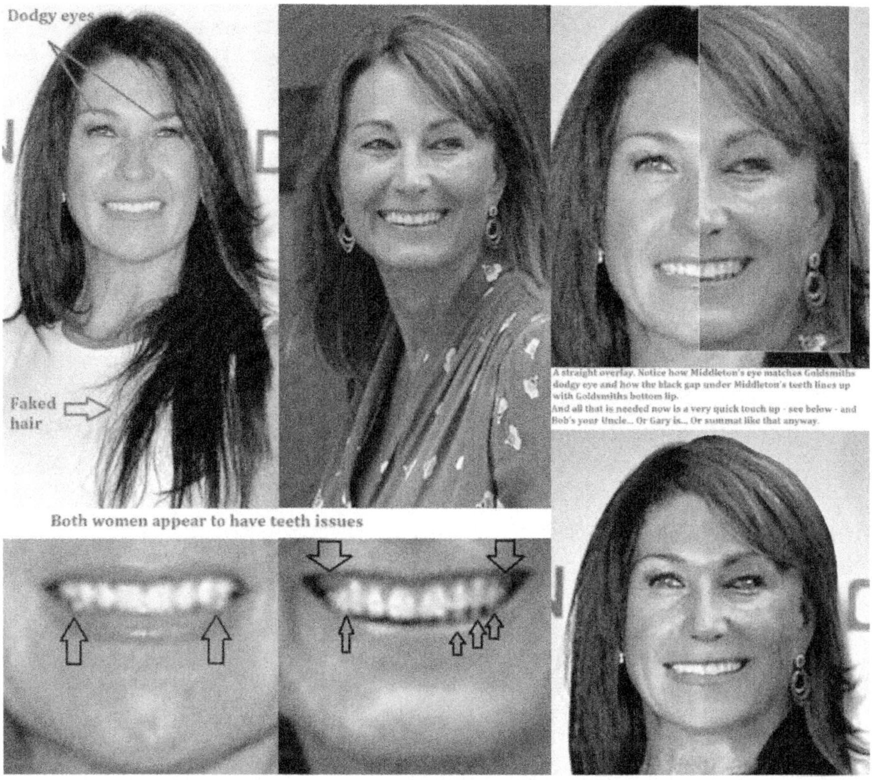

PHOTO D: Goldsmith & Middleton comparison

Moreover, I strongly believe Goldsmith-Middleton to also be a woman named Tracey Wilkinson, who - according to the National press - was supposedly murdered by her foster-son, Aaron Barley :

The following is taken from BBC report on the 4th of October 2017 in relation to Aaron Bailey and Tracey Wilkinson:

A homeless man who "destroyed a family" by stabbing to death a mother and son who had helped him has been jailed for life with a minimum of 30 years.

Aaron Barley admitted murdering Tracey Wilkinson and 13-year-old son Pierce on the first day of his trial on Tuesday.

Mrs Wilkinson's husband Peter was also stabbed six times in the attack at their home in Stourbridge in March.
Mrs Justice Carr told Barley, 24, he had "betrayed their trust in every way" and warned he might never be released.

Barley murdered the pair after a year in which he was given food, friendship and shelter by Mrs Wilkinson, Birmingham Crown Court heard on Tuesday.

Details of Barley's 21 previous convictions were read out in court, including an assault on his former partner.
The judge told Barley she had decided not to impose a whole-life tariff "principally because of your youth".
"You clearly represent a very significant risk of serious harm to members of the public," she said.

Prosecutor Karim Khalil QC said Barley killed Mrs Wilkinson, 50, in her bed and her son in his room before then attacking her 47-year-old husband as he returned home from walking their dog.

Mrs Justice Carr told the court of the "terror" Tracey and Pierce must have felt when Barley attacked them.

"One of them, at least, must have been aware of the stabbing of the other," she added.

The couple's daughter Lydia, 19, was away at Bristol University at the time of the attack.

PHOTO E: Tracey Wilkinson compared to Carole Middleton

However, this book is about Meghan Markle although I do discuss the Aaron Bailey fake news story in detail on my website (

www.chrisspivey.org) in one of the installments of my series of articles entitled: **"How the west was won".**

Indeed, in order for you to gain a greater understanding of what I am going to be telling you in this book, you would do well to read Part 1 of the aforementioned articles.

Nevertheless, what you have to understand is everything has to connect in the Satanic world of the ' elites *' AKA Monsters.*

So with that in mind, I will tell you that there is a high-class jeweler's in America called " ***Thomas Markle*** *", although the flash-bling-retailer is supposedly nothing at all to do with Meghan's dad or brother, both of who are obviously called Thomas Markle.*

You can see a photo of the Jeweler, Markle in photo F and if you are paying attention you will instantly notice that he is the splitting image of Uncle Gary Goldsmith.

And once you have familiarised yourself with that photo, take a look at photo G which is a comparison of Markle the jeweler and Uncle Gary Goldsmith. However, before you do be aware of the old adage that states everybody in the world has a double.

You see, I say that because it is total, total bollox and if true, one half of the world would look like the other half. Therefore, you won't be surprised to learn that the real odds of us having an exact double is 30 billion to one... Think about that for a minute.

Course, by the same token, the Monster-Minions have to 'doctor' ALL of their photos to stop people cottoning on to the fact that the likes of the Markle family are just actors who play many other roles - a necessary factor in order to keep the secret.

Indeed, you do not need to take my word for that as there is unlimited proof of the fact on my website.

Thomas Markle - Jeweler

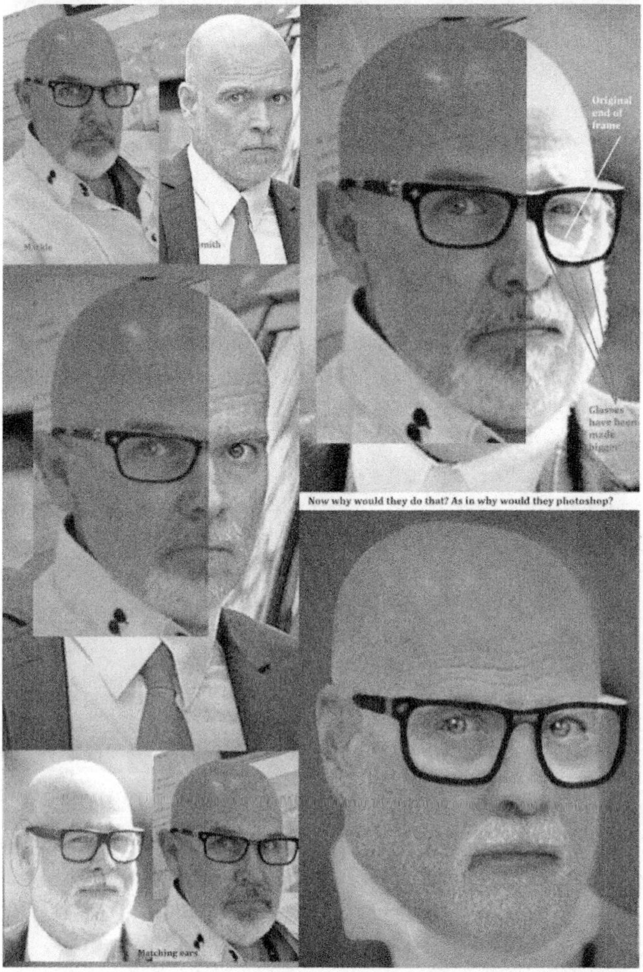

PHOTO G: Thomas Markle & Gary Goldsmith comparison

However, there is more... There is always more don't cha know. You see, I am also very suspicious about the bird in photo H.

Her name is allegedly Salice Sanders – a made up name if I ever heard one – *and she is doing a promotion for '* Thomas Markle *', the Jewelers.*

However, Sanders looks far too much like Meghan Markle to be a coincidence in my humble opinion (see photo I).

Indeed you have to remember what I have just said about the thirty billion to one doppelganger chance. On top of that, you have to take into account that Salice Saunders - who is taking part in a lottery on behalf of Thomas Markle Jewellery - looks exactly like Meghan Markle whose father is called Thomas Markle.

Now what would the odds of that be? I mean you have to bear in mind that I have changed no angles on the photos either - which when you think about it must make the odds fantastical!

But here, have a second opinion (see photo J).

So, straight away – before we have even got to Meghan herself – *there is a huge Elephant in the room.*

And then there is also photo K, which shows a woman looking remarkably like Meghan in appearance serving behind the counter at Thomas Markle Jewellery.

And whilst I am not stating for a fact that the bird in the photo serving behind the counter is Mental Meghan, it certainly looks like her and once again it is just a little too coincidental for my liking.

PHOTO H: Salice Sanders

Despite their faked noses and MM's fake chin they still look increadibly similar to one another.

PHOTO I: Meghan & Salice comparison

PHOTO J: Meghan & Salice comparison

PHOTO K: Meghan lookalike serving customers at T Markle Jewellery

Now, getting back to Meghan's half-brother, Thomas Markle Jr; and I can tell you that his jail mugshot matches the jail mugshot of John Wayne Gacy perfectly... And by " perfectly *" I mean, 100% spot-on perfectly.*

John Wayne Gacy was allegedly a serial killer from the 1970's although all the research that I have done suggests to me that like so many other serial killers from history - Gacy is just a made up persona.

The following is taken from Wikipedia:

John Wayne Gacy Jr. (March 17, 1942 – May 10, 1994) was an American serial killer and rapist. He sexually assaulted, tortured and murdered at least 33 teenage boys and young men between 1972 and 1978 in Cook County, Illinois (a part of metropolitan Chicago).

All of Gacy's known murders were committed inside his Norwood Park ranch house. His victims were typically induced to his address by force or deception, and all but one of his victims were murdered by either asphyxiation or strangulation with a makeshift tourniquet ; his first victim was stabbed to death. Gacy buried 26 of his victims in the crawl space of his home. Three other victims were buried elsewhere on his property, while the bodies of his last four known victims were discarded in the Des Plaines River.

Convicted of 33 murders, Gacy was sentenced to death on March 13, 1980, for 12 of those killings. He spent 14 years on death row before he was executed by lethal injection at Stateville Correctional Center on May 10, 1994.

Gacy became known as the "Killer Clown" because of his charitable services at fund-raising events, parades, and children's parties where he would dress as "Pogo the Clown" or "Patches the Clown", characters he had devised.

Gacy was born in Chicago, Illinois, on March 17, 1942, the only son and second of three children born to John Stanley Gacy (1900–1969), an auto repair machinist and World War I veteran, and his wife Marion Elaine Robinson (1908–1989), a homemaker.

Gacy was of Polish and Danish ancestry. His paternal grandparents (who spelled the family name as "Gatza" or "Gaca") had immigrated to the United States from Poland (then part of Germany). As a child, Gacy was overweight and not athletic. He was close to his two sisters and mother, but endured a difficult relationship with his father, an alcoholic who was physically abusive to his wife and children.

Throughout his childhood, Gacy strove to make his stern father proud of him, but seldom received his approval. This friction was constant throughout his childhood and adolescence. One

of Gacy's earliest childhood memories was of his father beating him with a leather belt at the age of four for accidentally disarranging car engine components that his father had assembled.

On another occasion, his father struck him across the head with a broomstick, rendering him unconscious. [His father regularly belittled him and often compared him unfavorably with his sisters, disdainfully accusing him of being "dumb and stupid".

Gacy, while regularly commenting that he was "never good enough"] in his father's eyes, always vehemently denied ever hating his father in interviews after his arrest.

Now look at photos L and M very closely.

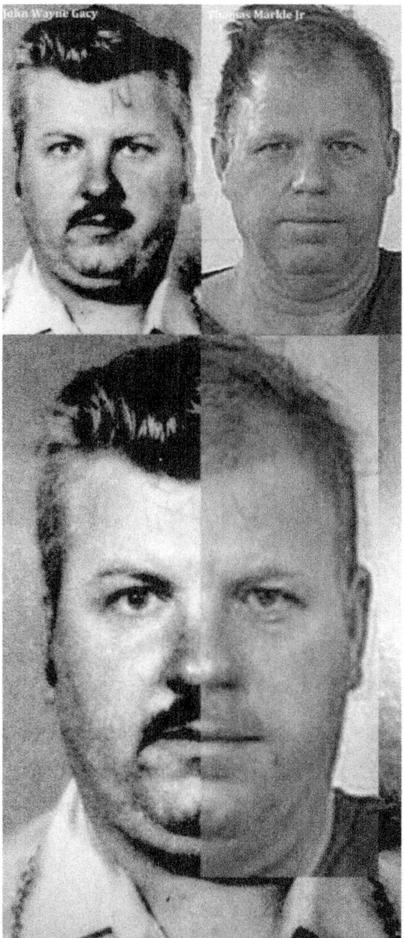

PHOTO L: Thomas Markle Jr & John Wayne Gacy comparison

PHOTO M: A second Markle/Gacy comparison

Now obviously what we have here is a Satanic Connection as it would be impossible for Markle Jr to be Gacy... Or at least it would be in theory.

Course, those of you not familiar with my work will no doubt think that it is just a coincidence whereas regular readers of my website, wwwchrisspivey.org will know different.

Indeed, in one of the series of articles that I have written entitled " How The West Was Won *" I prove beyond all doubt that Gacy and the alleged Kennedy assassin, Lee Harvey Oswald's mug-shot also come from the same source.*

Course, all articles on my website are free to read an as such you have no need to take my word for it.

Now I will say before going any further that of course the above sounds like bollox when taken on its own. Indeed, that is how the Monsters get away with what they do.

However, when you realize just how widespread this practice of theirs is and that everything has to connect with everything else (the bigger picture *), only then will you become aware that the chances of it all being coincidence are zilch.*

Course, since these actors are often following in their mother & father's footsteps (career wise) *it was necessary for me to also compare Thomas Markle Snr (Meghans 'father') with Gacy since –* in theory *– they really could be one and the same, if Markle Jr is the splitting image of his father when he was in his fifties... Understand?*

Of course you do.

Furthermore, to add to these amazing 'coincidences' it is a fact that both Gacey and Markle Snr have the same middle name of Wayne.

PHOTO N: Thomas Wayne Markle in comparison to John Wayne Gacy

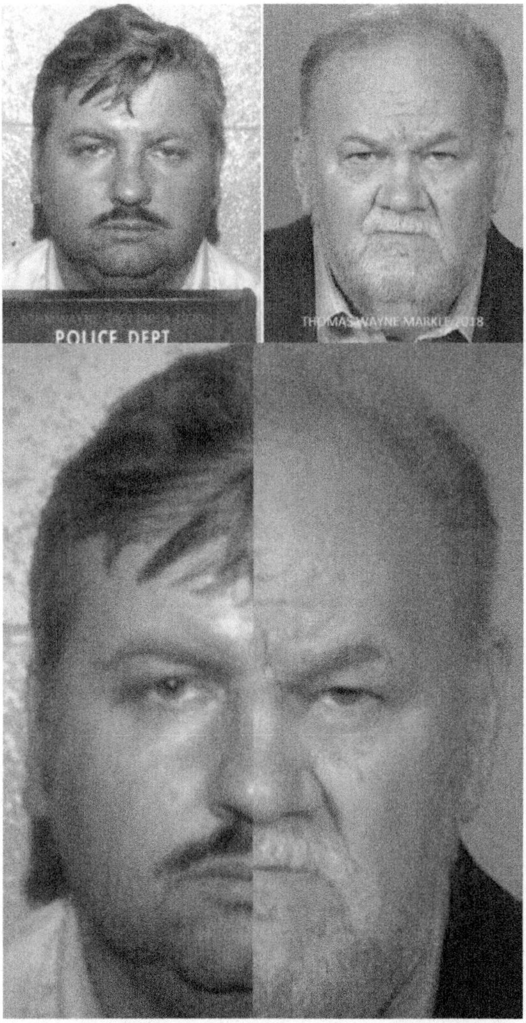

PHOTO O: Half and half Gacy/Markle comparison

And I have to say that to my mind, the pair being one and the same isn't beyond the realms of possibility, especially since their bio's give Gacy a birthdate of March 17th 1942 and Markle a birthdate of July 18th 1944.

Moreover, I would say that Markle Snr could quite well also be the [Satanic] film director, Guillermo del Toro - although Toro is - at least on paper -twenty years younger than Markle Snr.

Wikipedia has the following to say about the ***Mexican*** *film director:*
Guillermo del Toro Gómez (born October 9, 1964) is a Mexican film director, screenwriter, producer, and novelist.

In his filmmaking career, del Toro has alternated between Spanish-language dark fantasy pieces, such as the gothic horror films The Devil's Backbone (2001) and Pan's Labyrinth (2006), and more mainstream American action films, such as the vampire superhero action film Blade II (2002), the supernatural superhero film Hellboy (2004), its sequel Hellboy II: The Golden Army (2008), and the science fiction monster film Pacific Rim (2013).

His latest film, The Shape of Water (2017), has received critical praise and won the Golden Lion at the Venice Film Festival.

And of course, Thomas Markle Snr was in the film industry (strange then the lack of photos *) and he now lives in... Wait for it, wait for it...* ***Mexico*** *- a fact that most hard-of-thinking people would put down to coincidence.*

The following is from Wikipedia:

Thomas Wayne Markle Sr. (born 1945) is an American retired television lighting director and director of photography.

He received a Chicago / Midwest Emmy Award for work on the television program Made in Chicago in 1975 and was a co-recipient of two Daytime Emmy Awards for work on the television soap opera General Hospital, in 1982 and 2011.

Markle married student and secretary Roslyn Loveless in 1964; they had met the year before at an on-campus party at the private University of Chicago. They have two children, Samantha (1964) and Thomas Markle Jr. (1966). Markle and Loveless divorced in 1975.

He married Doria Ragland at Paramahansa Yogananda 's Self-Realization Fellowship Temple in Hollywood (Los Angeles) on December 23, 1979 by Brother Bhaktananda. The Markles had a daughter together in 1981, Rachel Meghan Markle (known by her middle name), who later became the Duchess of Sussex. Thomas and Doria Markle's marriage ended in divorce in 1987 or 1988.

Markle won $750,000 in the California State Lottery in 1990, but he ultimately lost the money, and in 2016 filed for bankruptcy over a debt of $30,000. He lives in Rosarito, Mexico.

Nevertheless, you can compare Markle and Toro in photos P & Q

PHOTO P: Thomas Wayne Markle compared to Guillermo del Toro

PHOTO Q: Half face comparison of Toro and Markle.

Now I will repeat that I can fully understand that this information is hard to believe for some of you, and as such, all I will say at the moment is; read on with an open mind and see how you feel by the end of this book, because there is a lot more evidence to come.

Certainly, Toro is very Satanic in his creations (see photo R) and has just won an Oscar for his film 'The Shape Of Water'.

The following segment is taken from an article published in 2018 in Variety Magazine:

Guillermo del Toro won his first Oscar on Sunday night, nabbing the best director trophy for his sci-fi/fantasy/romance picture " The Shape of Water."

"I am an immigrant, like many, many of you, and in the last 25 years, I've been living in a country all of our own," he said, taking the stage following a standing ovation.

"Part of it is here, part of it is Europe, part of it is everywhere, because I think the greatest thing that our industry does is erase the line in the sand," the filmmaker said. "We should continue doing that, when the world tells us to make it deeper."

Del Toro then thanked Fox Searchlight for listening to a "mad pitch" and believing "the movie would be a sure bet."

"I want to thank the people that have come with me all the way," he continued, thanking a long list of contributors...

And could that Oscar possibly have been awarded to Toro for 'services rendered'?

PHOTO R: Toro's Satanic creations

PHOTO S: L-R - Thomas Markle Snr, Grandson Tyler Dooley, Thomas Markle Jr and Markle Snr's eldest Grandson, Thomas Markle the Turd.

Nevertheless, I feel sure that the diehard, " you-talk-bollocks-Spivey *" brigade and the Government-Paid-Trolls will still not be convinced of the Gacy/Markle connection, so let me silence their dumb-fuck attitude once and for all.*

Now to do that you need to first study the Photo S.

Strange photograph don't cha think? Actually, you probably don't because you will doubtlessly have not studied it the way that I have.

Therefore, let me tell you that it is photoshopped to fuck and very strangely off center. In fact the reason that the photo is copyright of the Daily Mail (hence forth known as 'The Chimp' and their shit-rag journalists copy-writers known as either the Monkey-Boyz, the Monkey-Kuntz or the Monkey Nutz *) is because they have knocked it up... It is not a real photo.*

Now why would they do that if all was above board & legit?

And the answer that you are looking for is " they wouldn't *"... Well done to those of you who answered correctly.*

So now let me show you the give-away, piss-poor workmanship involved in faking that photo.

And to do that you need to look at Photo T which shows the left-hand bottom half of the composite and where it has been photoshopped. You then need to look at Photo U which shows where it has been photoshopped and finally Photo V which is a close up of the right hand side.

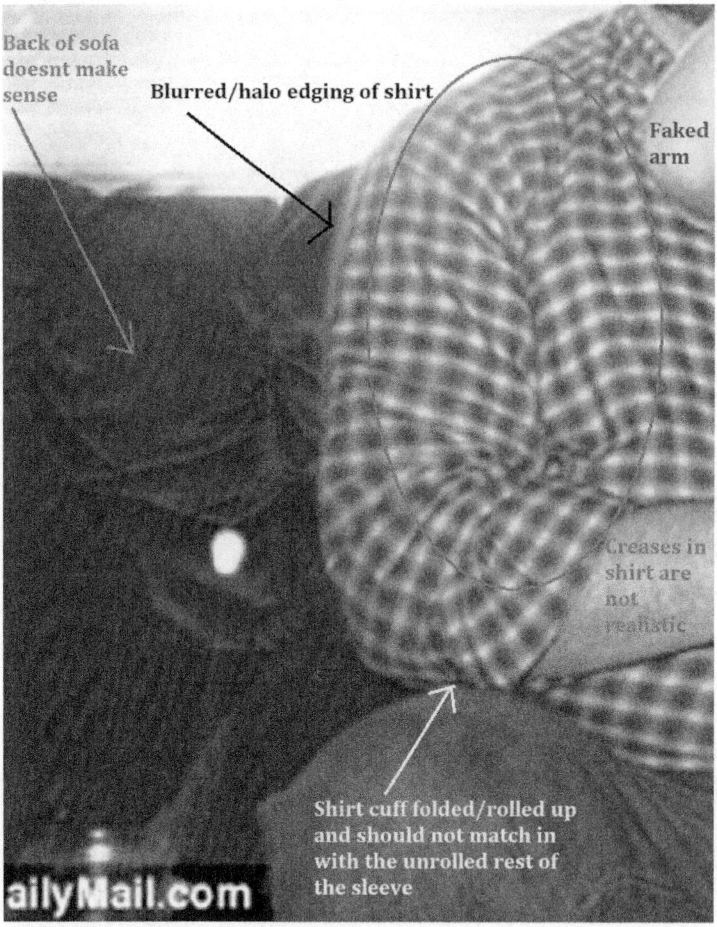

Photo T

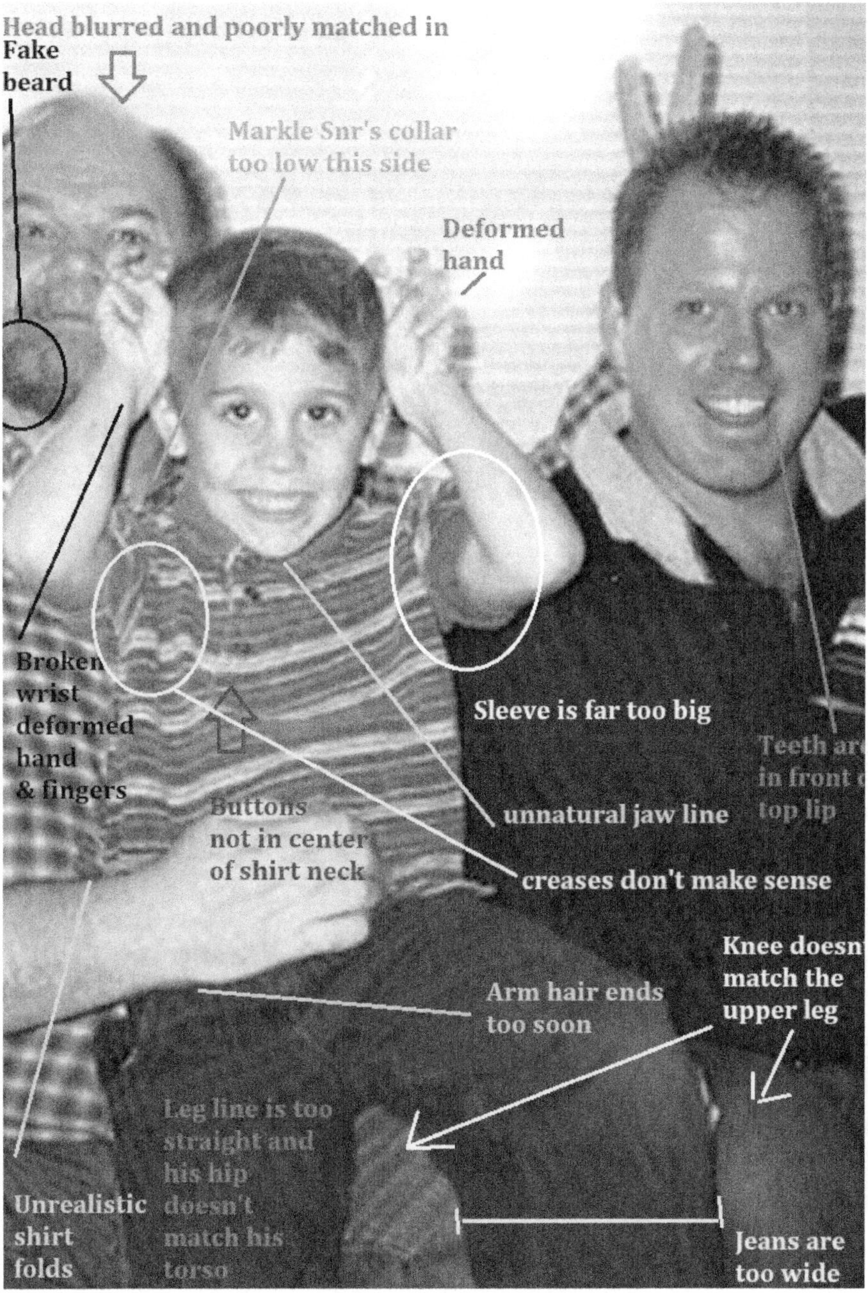
Head blurred and poorly matched in
Fake beard
Markle Snr's collar too low this side
Deformed hand
Broken wrist deformed hand & fingers
Sleeve is far too big
Teeth ar in front o top lip
Buttons not in center of shirt neck
unnatural jaw line
creases don't make sense
Knee doesn match the upper leg
Arm hair ends too soon
Leg line is too straight and his hip doesn't match his torso
Unrealistic shirt folds
Jeans are too wide

Photo U

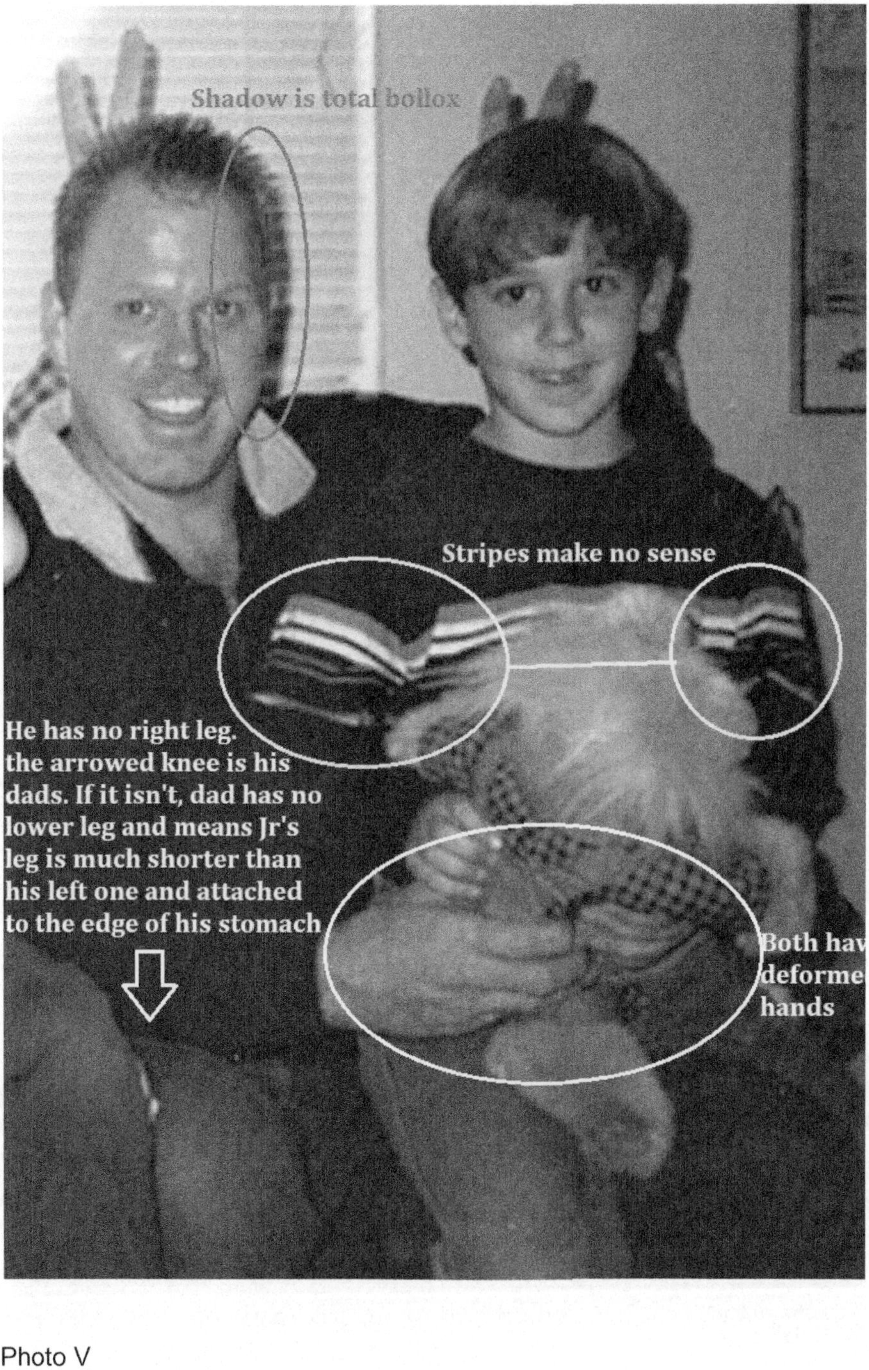
Shadow is total bollox
Stripes make no sense
He has no right leg.
the arrowed knee is his
dads. If it isn't, dad has no
lower leg and means Jr's
leg is much shorter than
his left one and attached
to the edge of his stomach
Both hav
deforme
hands

Photo V

The next generation of Markles and their complicated ties

Family together: Meghan Markle was an 11-year-old when she posed with her father Thomas Markle, and her two nephews Thomas Dooley (left) and Tyler Dooley (right), and her then sister-in-law, Tracey Dooley (far right). Tracey Dooley had married her brother Thomas Markle Snr, and had the two boys, making her an aunt while she was still in elementary school

PHOTO W: A screenshot of the 'Markle' family

Now you also have to ask yourself why – at his age - *Thomas the Turd has a teddy in the photo... Moreover, you have to ask yourself why Markle Jr also has hold of it.*

And I imagine that you are now thinking that I am being pedantic... Which I certainly am not.

You see, I think that the teddy is either a message of some kind that only the Monsters are privy to or else it is symbolizing something.

Now the reasoning behind my thinking is not just the fact that it is strange that a boy of Thomas' age is carrying around a teddy, but also because he is carrying teddies in every ' childhood *' photo that he is in... And every one of the teddies is different - like in Photo W for example.*

I should also point out that photo W is actually a screenshot that I took from a Chimp article, rather than using the actual photo. I did that because the Chimp caption beneath it is quite telling, especially since the photo comes courtesy of Thomas Markle Jr - Meghan's redneck brother..

You see, for that photo caption to exist it MUST have been Thomas Markle Jr who told the press recipients that his 'sister' Meghan was

11 years old when the photo was taken... Which would mean that Thomas the Turd-Dooley (who is gay apparently although that is not stated in the article that the screenshot is taken from *) is ONE year old in the photo and Tyler Dooley is at best, a newborn baby.*

After all, it is a well reported fact that Meghan is ten years older than Thomas the Turd and Eleven years older than Tyler. It would therefore appear that Markle Jr hasn't read the script properly.

Markle Jr also appears to have his children mixed up as that surely must be Thomas the Turd on the right (holding the doll *), and not Tyler as stated in the caption.*

And just to clarify the above, Gay Thomas the Turd Burglar observation; the Chimp article does not state that he is gay, but does state:

Eldest son Thomas is a 26-year-old store manager for Domino's Pizza and lives in Mammoth Lakes, California, with his husband Ronnie, 41.

Now it also clearly states in the above report that Thomas the Turd is the eldest of Markle's two boys at twenty-six years of age and his brother, Tyler is twenty-five.

However, as I was writing this exposé another Chimp article appeared on the 29th of December 2017, in which Thomas Markle Jr gives an interview to the Chimp hacks following a controversial statement made about his & his half-sister, Meghan's family, by Prince Harry.

And once again the same photo as Photo W accompanied the interview/article, which – like last time *– I have taken a screenshot of so as you can see for yourselves the accompanying text (photo X).*

Meghan's relatives have since slammed Harry's claim, saying Meghan had a 'really good' family 'who were always there with her. 'Childhood photos provided by her half-brother Thomas Jr show 11-year-old Meghan with her father Thomas Sr, her nephews, and sister-in-law

PHOTO X: Check out the Chimp's photo caption.

We are family: Thomas Markle Jr said his father will be 'extremely hurt' by Prince Harry's comments. He told DailyMail.com that Meghan Markle had enjoyed spending time at Christmas with her father (left), him (center) and her nephews including Tyler Dooley (right), having become his aunt when she was just 10

PHOTO Y: Check out the Chimp's photo caption.

'My dad really liked Christmas more than anything; that was his favorite holiday. He would put some fake presents under the tree once in a while - just some off the wall gift so you would have no idea why you got it or what it was or what it meant.'

Meghan became an aunt aged five when Samantha became a mother to her niece Ashleigh Hale, now 31, and again aged ten when Thomas Markle Jr had the first of his two children, Tyler, now 26, and Thomas III, now 25, with his now ex-wife Tracey Dooley.

Her nephews became part of her Christmas routine.

Thomas Jr said: 'She [Meghan] had more fun opening presents with my kids than opening up her own presents. She'd probably be the first one under the tree opening up presents.

'My dad was the glue for all that. I would have Christmas at my house with my kids, my dad would have a Christmas at his house, Doria would have a Christmas.

'One way or the other, we all made the rounds and saw each other. When we could, we got together for Christmas dinners. So as far as the family she never had goes, she probably had like four Christmases in one day - it would be a really busy day.'

Thomas Jr, who has not spent the festive season with Meghan for at least 15 years, spent his own Christmas at home in Grants Pass with fiancée Darlene Blount, 37, and her seven-year-old son.

PHOTO Z: Screenshot taken from a Chimp article

Yet despite the text being different on this one to the other one, the writer is still insisting that Meghan is 11 years old in the photo, which as I pointed out last time makes her nephew, Thomas the Turd one year old in the photo and her nephew Tyler a new born baby.

Furthermore, the article also included Photo Y, which once again is a screenshot taken from the article rather than the actual photo itself.

So, Thomas the Turd is definitely Tyler now... Although that isn't actually as blatant a mistake as you would first think - as you will find out shortly.

And keeping with that new article, I have also taken a screenshot of some of the text to show you which you can read in Photo Z.

Read it? Strange or what!

Although not half as strange as the following Chimp article released on the 4th of February 2018. However, before you read it let me remind you that Meghan is 10 years older than Thomas the Turd (who is sometimes Tyler) and 11 years older than Tyler (who is sometimes Thomas the Turd *).*

Moreover, according to Meghan's brother, Thomas Markle Jr who supplied the photos to the Chimp, his half-sister Meghan was 11 years old at the time which of course would have been impossible if you believe this shite.

We have also read how Meghan's Nephews - The Turd & Tyler - *became part of the Christmas routine in the Markle household... As told by Thomas Markle Jr. And as a last reminder, we also see Tracey Dooley* - mother to the Turd & Tyler an ex-bird of Markle Jr - *in some of the those photos supplied by Thomas Markle Jr...*
Are we all quite, quite clear on that?

We are? Good, then have a read of this old bollox from the Chimp and I have underlined the important bits for you:
Meghan Markle 's wedding is due to be a star-studded affair, with the Obamas, her Suits co-star Patrick J. Adams, and Serena Williams rumoured to be on the guest list.

But two relatives might not be in attendance after Ms Markle's half-brother Tom intervened, saying that he wants to ban his two sons from going.

According to their father, Thomas, 26, and Tyler, 25, haven't seen Ms Markle since they were babies - and he claims they're just trying to cash in on the Markle name.

Tom told the Sunday Mirror : 'Tracy [Thomas and Tyler's mother] and me stopped living as man and wife three months into the marriage because the relationship was such a disaster. She never wanted the Markle name when we were married and now suddenly she acts like she's still part of the family.
'I don't want her to have anything to do with us and the boys shouldn't go along with it. They shouldn't be at the wedding either.

'Both boys were always Dooleys as kids. I got sick of making the name an issue with Tracy and ultimately she had her way.

They're Dooleys. You cannot pick and choose when you're a Markle.'

Tom, who currently lives in a bungalow in Grants Pass, Oregon, with his fiancee Darlene Blount, shares a father with Ms Markle.

He divorced Thomas and Tyler's mother Tracy in 2000.

Tom added: 'It's got to stop. The boys were babies when they met Meghan last and Tracy has never even met Meghan, ever. 'I don't believe Tracy or my sons have the right to call themselves Markles. If this embarrasses Meghan then I am sorry, but Tracy can't go on claiming to be a Markle.'.. *Source: The Daily Mail, 4/2/18*

Now I am a bit kinda speechless!

Nevertheless, I will refer you back to photo W because it puts the icing on the cake in exposing this family as a fraud... That or it takes the right fucking piss.

You see, we now have Markle Jr saying that his sons have not seen Meghan since they were babies yet they clearly are not babies in photo W... A photo provided by the hypocrite himself.

Moreover, there are three things that you need to know about Photo W... Which I hasten to add is a photoshop. And again, why would they need to photoshop if everything was above board?

Nevertheless, those three things are:

Firstly, ' Grandpa Tom Wayne Markle *' is looking very much like the '* Clown, John Wayne Gacy *'.*

Secondly, the two boys are the same person.

Thirdly, the boys are taken from a photo of one of John Wayne Gacy's alleged victims. (see photo A1)

Photo A1

Now there is not a lot more that I can really do to prove to you that Markle Snr is John Wayne Gacy since the younger photos of Markle Snr are ALL very shite quality… Very strange for an award winning Hollywood, lighting director, who is portrayed in the press as being a recluse - at least he is according to the press:

Meghan Markle's dad, Thomas Markle, has yet to meet his future son-in-law.

This is because the retired lighting director lives in a cliff-top house in Rosarito Beach — around a 15-minute drive from the Mexican/US border.

After retiring from Hollywood in 2011, Mr. Markle moved to the stunning resort town in California Bay where his home now overlooks the Pacific Ocean.

Meghan Markle's half-brother and Thomas Markle's son, also called Tom Markle, told the Daily Mail that his father has grown

increasingly reclusive since the announcement of the engagement.

"Dad never liked the limelight, but since the news came out about Meghan and Harry he's become a total recluse," Tom Jr said.

"I haven't seen him in years. He hates the attention Meghan's romance has brought on to him. He loves her but hates the idea of being in the spotlight."

Regardless of Mr. Markle's reclusive status in northern Mexico, the father's love for his daughter is obvious. Since he divorced ex-wife and Meghan's mother, Doria Ragland, in 1988 when Meghan was five years old, the father and daughter have retained a close relationship and still speak regularly.

In an Instagram post on Father's Day 2016, Meghan Markle wrote: "Happy Father's Day, daddy. I'm still your buckaroo, and to this day your hugs are still the very best in the whole wide world. *Source: Business Insider, December 5th 2017*

However, that and other reports along the same line totally contradicted themselves when in an effort to portray the Markle family as rednecks, thus proving that the Royal family do marry commoners - which they most certainly don't - *some bright spark came up with the idea of a story that saw Thomas Markle accepting a share of £125,000 to pose for photos just before the wedding of Meghan and Harry took place.*

Meghan Markle's dad is 'deeply embarrassed' for posing for 'fake' paparazzi photos, his son has said. Thomas Markle, 73, will still be walking his daughter up the aisle as she marries Prince Harry on Saturday, but first he will apologise 'sincerely' to the couple, according to Thomas Jr.

Meghan's half-brother jumped to their father's defence and told the Mirror: 'People are quick to judge but they have no idea how much scrutiny we live under. 'Nobody can understand what it is like opening your curtains in the morning and being watched by these paparazzi to going to bed at night and still seeing them there.' Mr Markle's daughter Samantha also said she was to

blame for the 'staged' photos because she encouraged him to do put him in a 'positive' light. *Source: The Metro, 14th of May 2018*

And that report is just one of many all saying the same thing. Yet would a recluse, with a millionaire daughter, who was at the time marrying into one of the richest families in the world really pose for photos for a share of £125 Grand?

That makes no sense at all, especially since Meghan is meant to adore her father, and could afford to give him much more money than that, just to keeping him from causing her and Harry such embarrassment.

Indeed, would an award winning Hollywood lighting director really be so skint?

Moreover, you have to understand that the whole of the worlds press and other media outlets is ultimately under the control of SIX bloodline families and nothing gets published or broadcast without their say so.

Therefore, had the story not been a fraud to serve a purpose, then the House of Windsor would have had no problem keeping the old bollox under wrap.

Course, predictably - at least it is when you know what is really going on - *Thomas Markle had a [pretend] heart attack days before the wedding and didn't walk his daughter down the aisle.*

Nevertheless, the press needed to ram home the point that the Markle's are a family of rednecks, and as such, after publicly apologising for embarrassing his 'daughter'*, Markle then went and did the same thing again:*

Meghan Markle 's father Thomas was reportedly paid £7,500 for a bombshell interview on Good Morning Britain in which he broke his silence about missing the royal wedding.

In an extraordinary TV appearance, Thomas Markle apologised for the staged paparazzi photos and revealed details of how Harry asked for permission to marry Meghan.

According to the Daily Mail, he accepted £7,500 for the TV appearance. Kensington Palace officials are believed to have been kept in the dark about the interview until it went live.

The newspaper reported that Good Morning Britain presenter Piers Morgan confirmed that Meghan's father pocketed "a few thousand pounds" but insisted his "ultimate motive was not money." *Source: Evening Standard, 19th of June 2018*

Now interestingly enough, the total prat, Piers Morgan is a fully paid up useful-idiot-tool of the Establishment and there is most likely a hidden meaning to his claim that Markles " ultimate motive was not money *".*

And indeed why would it be when £7,500 is pocket money to Meghan and Harry and once again could have easily been kept out of the news had they wanted it to be.

Nevertheless, to further prove that ALL of Meghan's photos from her youth are fakes, take a look at photo A2

Still, returning now to photo A1, in which I claim that Thomas the Turd and Tyler Dooley are the same boy. And if you go to photo A3 you will see exactly what I mean.

Thomas Snr in this photo

And Thomas Snr in this photo...

Are both taken from the same source photo

Photo A2

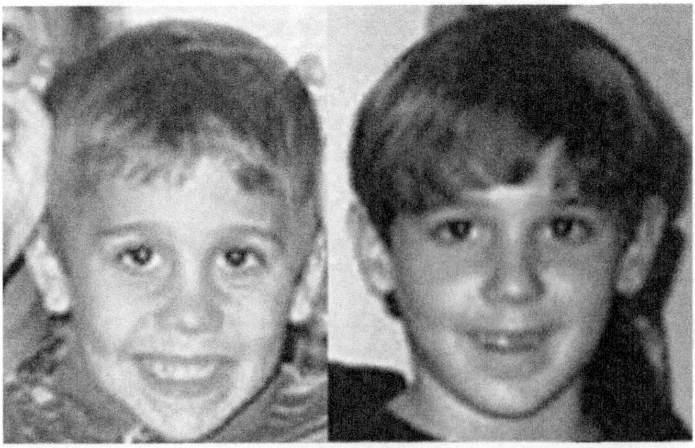

Both boys have got fake jaws from the top lip down. The bollox shadow supposedly given off from Tom the Turd's head makes him appear to have a wide mop of hair. Both have had their eyes widened and in Tyler's case he appears to have invisible hooks attached to ropes hooked into his bottom eyelids, with invisible imps pulling down. Moreover, Tom has had his top teeth "stained" and bottom ones blanked out. His 'fake' ear has also been turned upside down.

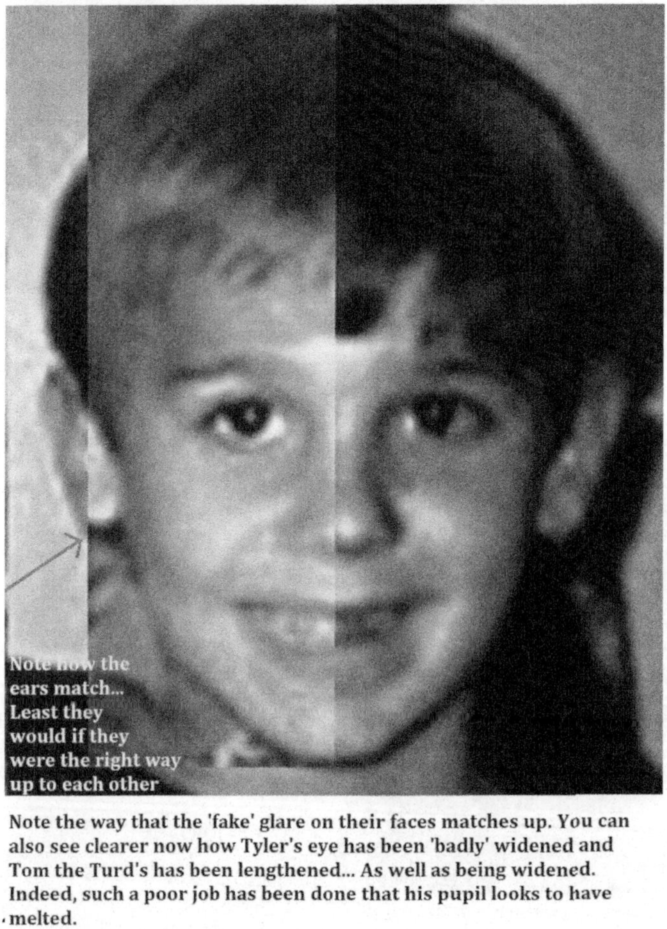

Note how the
ears match...
Least they
would if they
were the right way
up to each other

Note the way that the 'fake' glare on their faces matches up. You can also see clearer now how Tyler's eye has been 'badly' widened and Tom the Turd's has been lengthened... As well as being widened. Indeed, such a poor job has been done that his pupil looks to have melted.

PHOTO A3: Thomas & Tyler comparison

As well as the other anomalies that exist in this fake photo, is the coffee table. I mean look at the hight of it on the left side end compared to the right side end!

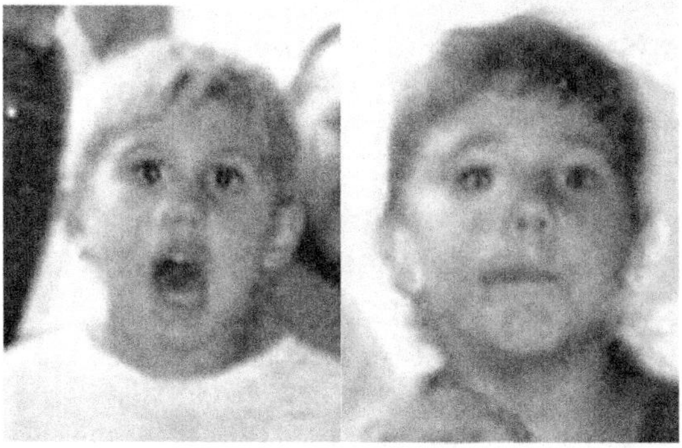

Photo A4

PHOTO A5: The boys are back to being 'twins' again and Meghan got fat as fuck

Course, that is not to say that two separate boys do not exist. It just means that in this particular hybrid photo, the same boys head has been used to represent both brothers.
Indeed, in an effort to give the Markle more credibility - not to mention more controversy - it was reported in the press just prior to the wedding that Tyler was selling Cannabis - albeit legally:

It is just a few weeks away now and the Markle family must be bursting with excitement as Meghan's marriage to Prince Harry approaches.

But the arrangements are not the first thing on the mind of Meghan's nephew Tyler Dooley – he's more focused on the millions of dollars' worth of marijuana he is helping to grow.

The 25-year-old boasts of his pride at being a 'pioneer' in an industry that is now legal in the United States. *Source: The Daily Mail, 17th April 2018*

Now in regard to my comment " that is not to say that two separate boys do not exist *", if you look at photo A4 in the last photo batch, you will see that the two young fellas are clearly different in looks - although the difference is probably artificially created since Thomas the Turd looks as though he is having a stroke.*
In fact, that is the more likely explanation given the fact that in the photo A5 taken/knocked up immediately after or before photo A4, the boys are back to being identical twins… It's a miracle!

" Cut the crap Spivey and just fukin' tell em ".

Okay. Cheeses sliced!... Can't a man even build up a bit of suspense anymore?
Now, if you are paying proper attention you will already have sussed what has been done to the two boy's (boy) faces in the photographs. However, for the benefit of those who haven't, let me show you and also say: Up ya fucking game because this is serious shit that is going on here with the Monsters...
They ain't doing it for fun.

Okay, you now need to go to Photo A6 and study the photos closely. And when you have, even the dumbest of you should be able to see how – at least – *some of the boy's face was made into two boys faces.*

But don't worry if you can't, ya blind tinkers because I am going to show you anyway… I don't half look after yous lot.

Now for me to do that you need to look at Photo A7. And in that batch of photos you will see that Tom does in fact now looks a lot more like his ' father *'. However, I do have to say that I believe Tyler has a lot of the former child-actor, Macaulay Culkin in him. (see photo A8)*

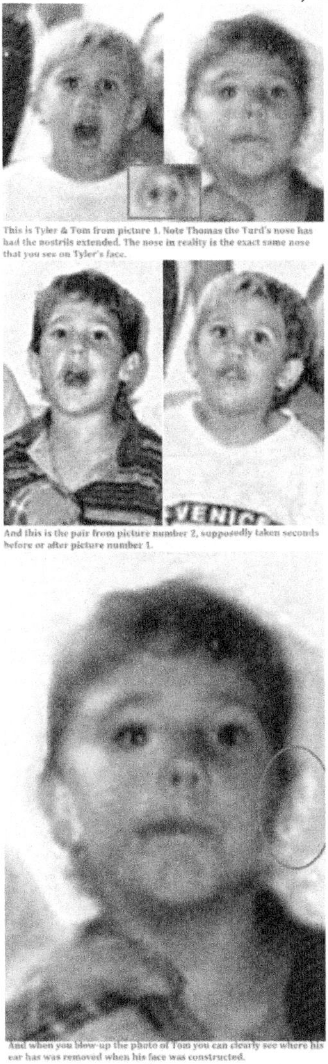

This is Tyler & Tom from picture 1. Note Thomas the Turd's nose has had the nostrils extended. The nose in reality is the exact same nose that you see on Tyler's face.
And this is the pair from picture number 2, supposedly taken seconds before or after picture number 1.
And when you blow-up the photo of Tom you can clearly see where his ear has was removed when his face was constructed.

Photo A6

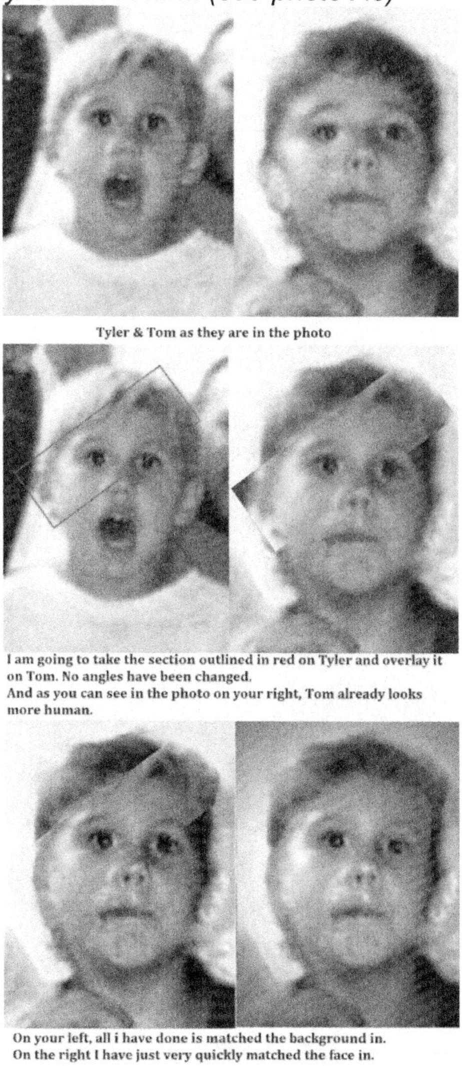

Tyler & Tom as they are in the photo
I am going to take the section outlined in red on Tyler and overlay it on Tom. No angles have been changed.
And as you can see in the photo on your right, Tom already looks more human.
On your left, all i have done is matched the background in.
On the right I have just very quickly matched the face in.

Photo A7

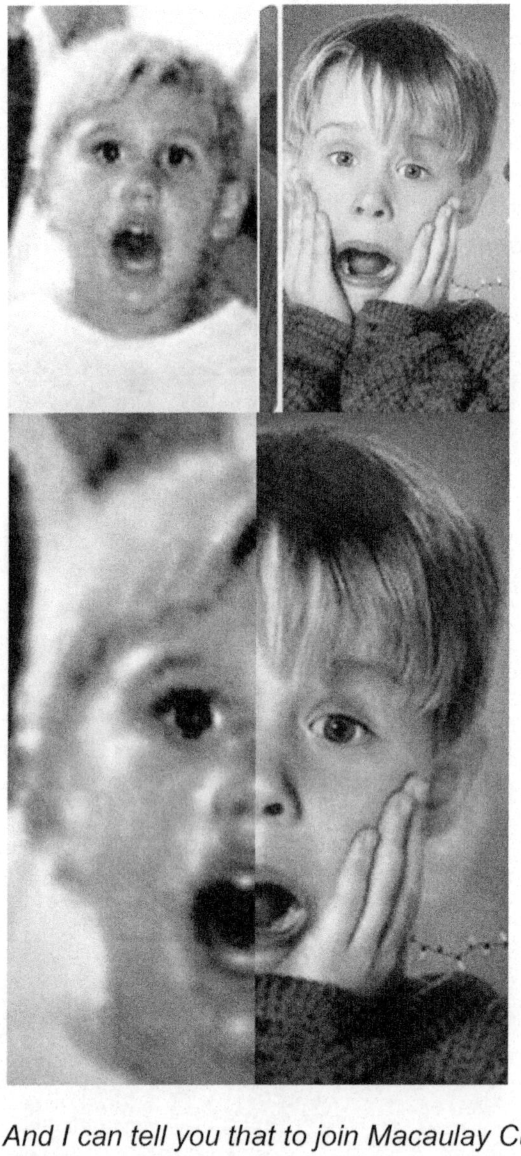

Photo A8

And I can tell you that to join Macaulay Culkin's face with Dooley's, I didn't need to change any angles... Just sayin'.

Course, it would again be easy to pass off the fact that the two half photos join so well as being coincidence, but study the photos carefully. How similar are they? That certainly is not a coincidence.

But why would the Monsters want to connect Culkin to this charade?

Well, at the risk of becoming boring I will tell you once again that EVERYTHING has to connect to everything for the Satanic-Monster-Majik to work. Now it doesn't matter if you believe that to be bollox or not, or even if you don't believe in Satanic Majik, because the real issue here is that the Monsters totally believe in it.

However, if you are having trouble swallowing that I would once again suggest that you go to my website, www.chrisspivey.org and carefully read Part 1 of my article "How The West Was Won".

You see, in that long article - that will cost you nothing to read - I explain why the Monsters believe that their Satanic Majik works as well as why everything has to connect to everything else for it to work.

Indeed the so called 'elites' have been practicing this Majik for centuries and if you don't partake then you are not in the club.

Nevertheless, to get back on track, check out Photo A9.

Now no angles of the photos have been changed whatsoever and I see no point in touching in Tom's face, being as if you cannot see how the faces have been made up by repeatedly over-laying pieces from two or three source photos (including Macaulay Culkin's) then mate, you just don't want to see it.

And indeed, this fakery carried on with the Dooley boys into their adult photos – well it would have to wouldn't it since they do not really exist (see photo B1).

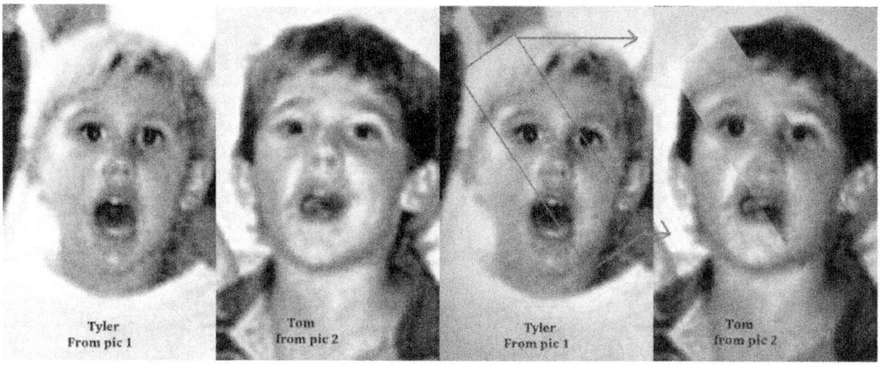

PHOTO A9: The section of Tyler's face marked in red outline has been overlaid onto Thomas the Turd's face and overlays perfectly.

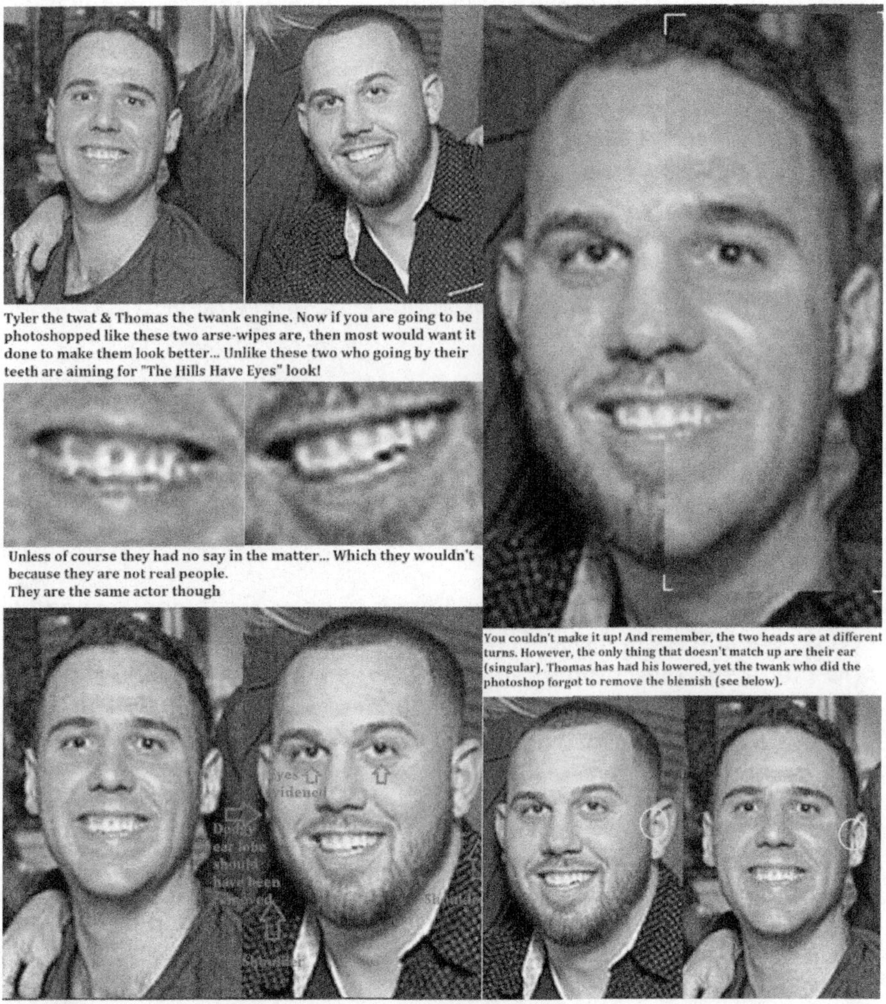

Tyler the twat & Thomas the twank engine. Now if you are going to be photoshopped like these two arse-wipes are, then most would want it done to make them look better... Unlike these two who going by their teeth are aiming for "The Hills Have Eyes" look!
Unless of course they had no say in the matter... Which they wouldn't because they are not real people.
They are the same actor though
You couldn't make it up! And remember, the two heads are at different turns. However, the only thing that doesn't match up are their ear (singular). Thomas has had his lowered, yet the twank who did the photoshop forgot to remove the blemish (see below).

PHOTO B1: Comparison of the Dooley brothers in adulthood.

So, we now have Meghan's nephews as fakes, as well as Meghan's father and brother... Course, as I say, the Chimp and the other shit-rag purveyors of bull-shite would have known that from the start.

Now, swiftly moving on and we have that third anomaly on photo A1, namely; the Dooley brothers being the John Wayne Gacy victim, Michael Marino (remember that name for later on and check out Photo B2).

Now the Dooley brothers looking exactly like Marino obviously reinforces the Satanic connections that I have already shown you since they couldn't possibly be Marino because if the Gacy story is to be believed then Marino was murdered long before Tom and Tyler were even born - which takes us to Chapter 2

Now at first you would think not. However when you look at the bags under Marino's eyes and then study Tom the Turd's it becomes clear that his eyes have been artificially opened using Marino's bags as guidelines. As for the nose? Well that is just a question of shadows.

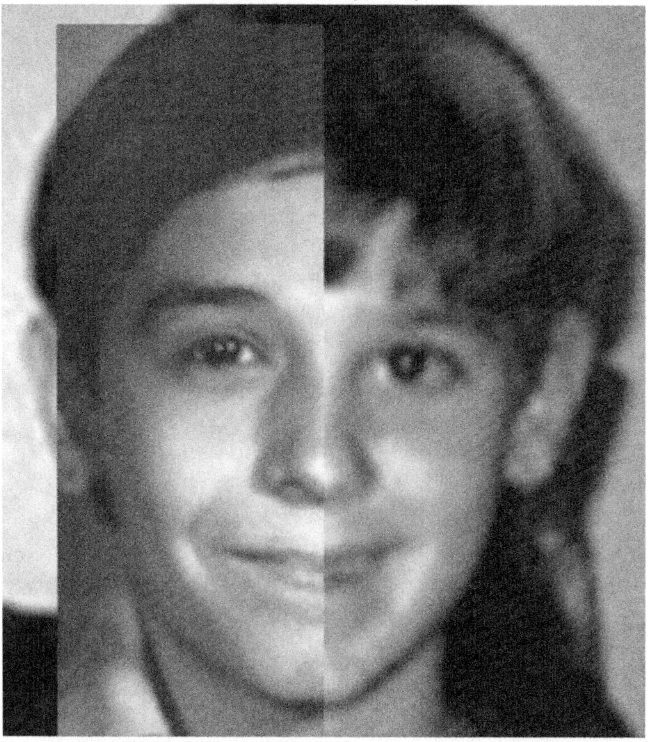

Now check out how the hair matches, the ears match and how the mouth connects despite Marino's being closed - as well as the chin shadow.

PHOTO B2: Comparison of Tom the Turd and Michael Marino.

Chapter 2
The President Connection

Now I am a long way done from proving to you that Meghan's father, brother and nephews are nothing more than made up personas. However, the John Wayne Gacy connection needs exploring further because his story connects to former American Presidents, Jimmy Carter, Ronald Reagan, George H Bush and George W Bush.

So let me start by telling you that Gacy was very well acquainted with former first lady, Rosalyn Carter - the wife of Jimmy Carter: The following segment is taken from Wikipedia:

Gacy was a staunch supporter of the Democratic Party, eventually becoming a Democrat precinct captain. In this capacity, he met and was photographed with Rosalyn Carter, wife of Democrat president Jimmy Carter. Carter posed for pictures with Gacy and autographed the photo "To John Gacy. Best Wishes. Rosalyn Carter"...

Anyone else find that a tad too coincidental?

In fact it is the same old bollox as always and very much in the same way that George Bush Snr knew John Hinkley Jr, who attempted to [fake] assassinate, the then US President Ronald Raygun – Bush being Raygun's Vice-President at the time (see photo B4).

The following is taken from www.goodreads.com:

Surprisingly, World Vision crops up again with Ronald Reagan 's attempted assassin, John Hinckley, Jr., whose father, John Warnock Hinckley, Sr., was president of World Vision United States. The gunman's father was also a multi-millionaire Texas oilman and President and Chairman of the independent oil and gas exploration firm Vanderbilt Energy Corporation. Considering he belonged to such a wealthy and prominent family, it seems rather odd that John Hinckley, Jr. was always portrayed by the media as some kind of vagabond who did nothing but stalk Jodie Foster and read Catcher all day.

What was also rarely if ever reported was that Hinckley Sr. was a major financial contributor to the failed 1980 Presidential campaign of the Vice President, George H. W. Bush, the man who would have become President sooner had Reagan been killed in the assassination attempt.

But the Bush-Hinckley family ties don't end there. Oh no, not by a long shot...

Hinckley's older brother, Scott, had a dinner date scheduled at the home of Neil Bush, the Vice President's son, the day after the assassination attempt on Reagan. A March 31, 1981 news headline by Associated Press confirmed this: Bush Son Had Dinner Plans With Hinckley Brother Before Shooting.

George H.W. Bush's other son, George W. Bush, also admitted to journalists that he may have had dealings with Scott Hinckley who was Vice-President of Vanderbilt Energy, but could not remember either way.

Obviously this is all very circumstantial, but then again...What are the odds that the family of the convicted shooter of the President were intimately tied to the Vice President's family and were also Texas oil tycoons who part-financed the Vice President's unsuccessful presidential campaign against the President?

And why were so few of these facts ever reported by the mainstream media?

Exactly!

And obviously George W Bush later followed in his father's footsteps by becoming the 43rd President of the USA. But here is a thing: George W Bush has been married this long time to wife Laura.

But I'll bet that you have never noticed how alike the former First Ladies, Rosalynn Carter and Laura Bush are, have you?
Am I the only one who finds that suspect?
Well if I am, then shame on you... I mean as suspects go, they don't come much more suspect than Rosalyn Carter. In fact check out photos B6 and B7 for starters

PHOTO B3: Rosalyn Carter meets John Wayne Gacy

The Houston Post

Good morning!

It's Tuesday, March 31, 1981

25 cents

Reagan wounded

BEST COPY AVAILABLE

Press aide clinging to life; 2 law officers also injured

Bush's son was to dine with suspect's brother

Post exclusive

More inside

Reagan's surgery

www.whitehouse.org

Proof the Bush's & Hinkley's were friends

PHOTO B4: A rare newspaper report of the Bush/Hinkley connection.

PHOTO B6: Rosalyn Carter with an unidentified boy who looks very much like Thomas the Turd

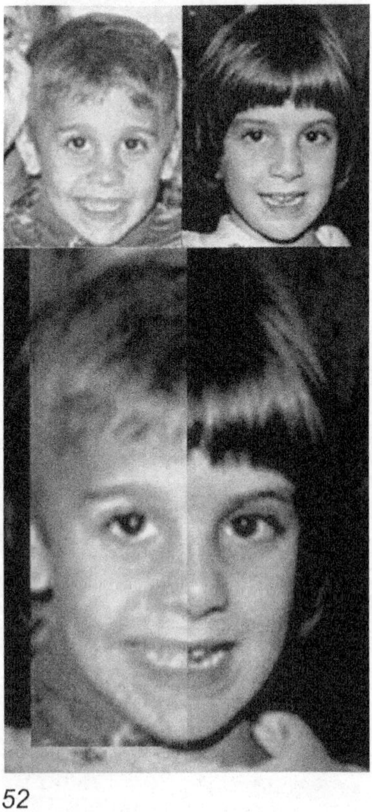

PHOTO B7: Comparison between the unidentified boy and Tyler Dooley

How damning is that... Not to mention insidious.

After all, besides the blatantly obvious fraud, the unidentified boy is in a photo taken in the 1970's... Long before Tyler & the Turd were even thought of.

And of course, if you have read my article on the Raygun fake assassination attempt found on my website and entitled ***"Reagan*** *", you will already know that Jeb Bush –* son of George Bush Snr & brother of George W Bush – *provided the face for John Hinkley Jr (* the would be Raygun assassin - see photo B8 *).*
And when you have looked at that photo, you need to ask yourself if all acquaintances are 30 billion to one doppelgangers.

Nevertheless, the following is taken from that article of mine:

Certainly Hinckley didn't shoot him anyway, because it would have been an impossible shot in the first place - even for a fluke:

Hinckley fired a Röhm RG-14.22 long rifle blue steel revolver six times in 1.7 seconds, missing the president with all but one shot. The first bullet hit White House Press Secretary James Brady in the head. The second bullet hit District of Columbia police officer Thomas Delahanty in the back of his neck as he turned to protect Reagan.

Hinckley now had a clear shot at the president, but the third bullet overshot him and hit the window of a building across the street.

As Special Agent In Charge Jerry Parr quickly pushed Reagan into the limousine, the fourth bullet hit Secret Service agent Timothy McCarthy in the abdomen as he spread his body over Reagan to make himself a target. The fifth bullet hit the bullet-resistant glass of the window on the open side door of the limousine.

The sixth and final bullet ricocheted off the armored side of the limousine and hit the president in his left underarm, grazing a rib and lodging in his lung causing it to partially collapse, and stopping nearly 1 inch (25mm) from his heart.Parr's prompt reaction saved Reagan from being hit in the head.

Ricocheted off the bullet proof glass indeed!

And as for the bullet that actually hit Reagan, well Fuck me, I don't know how it did since the President was already spread across the backseat with Jerry Parr all over him like a rash and the pair looking to the world as if they were having a dry hump.

Indeed, to add a bit of realism to the old fanny Reagan is quoted as saying that he hadn't realised that he had been shot and thought the pain in his ribs had come from Jerry Parr as he suspiciously looked like he tried to bum him...

It is in fact no wonder that Hinkley spent next to no time in prison for the attempted murder of an American President.

PHOTO B8: John Hinkley with an inset comparison photo of Jeb Bush

PHOTO B9: Olga Sweet of New Canaan presents former President, Jimmy Carter with a portrait that she painted of him, watched by husband, Robert and sons William and James.

PHOTO C1: Same as B9 but with added inset photos

Swiftly moving on and now you need to have a butchers at photo B9. Study it closely and then look at the next photo C1.

Okay, I have had to allocate the people in the inset photos a number each because of their many ties to each other – mostly Satanic connections I hasten to add - *are so wide spread that to not do so would become really confusing for you.*

Moreover, all these ties lead to other ties with other people, places & events, because at the risk of repeating myself too many times: Everything has to connect to everything in the Satanic lives of the elite.

So, let's start with the 'artist', Olga Sweet ***(numbered B in the photo)*** *... And she is not a particularly good one either in my book. Nevertheless, according to her website - since she doesn't appear to have a Wikipedia page:*

Ms. Sweet's clients include the Duke of Argyll, Nacho Figueras (the celebrated Argentinian polo player and Ralph Lauren model), President Carter, Dr. Frances Fergusson (the President Emerita of Vassar College and former Chair of the Board of Overseers of Harvard University), Countess Mary Bagsster-Collins, Karl von der Heyden (the former CFO of PepsiCo, RJR Nabisco, and Heinz and former Co-Chair of the American Academy in Berlin), Pierre de Beaumont (the founder of Brookstone), Vassar College, and the Greenwich Polo Club.

Ms. Sweet's oil and graphite portraits have been auctioned at the benefits of UNICEF, the Junior League of New York City, Southampton Hospital, Southampton Animal Shelter, Bay Street Theater (of Sag Harbor), CTREE of the Hamptons (of which Georgina Bloomberg is Honorary Chair), the American Heart Association of the Hamptons, the Hadassah Medical Center (of Israel), the Neil S. Hirsch Family Boys & Girls Club of Palm Beach County (Mr. Hirsch is the owner of the Black Watch Polo Team), the American Heart Association of Palm Beach, the Naples Winter Wine Festival, the American Red Cross (of Greenwich), the YWCA of Greenwich, and other nonprofit organizations.

In recognition of her work, Ms. Sweet is often invited to do the Ceremonial Ball Toss and Presentation of Awards at the Greenwich Polo Club and the Bridgehampton Polo Club.

And as coincidence would have it, one of her paintings that kept coming up whilst I was looking into her was of Prince Harry (see photos C2 & C3).

PHOTO C2: I mean just look at it! It is shite and clearly not finished

PHOTO C3: So I had a bash at it myself

PHOTO C4: Olga holding her painting of Ignacio Figueras

And whilst my attempt to improve the photo of Harry (photo C3) is not a masterpiece, you can't polish a turd and it is still 100% better than Olga's bodge... Especially now that I have fixed the shoulder which she had drawn far too wide.

Now what we have in Photo C4 is Olga holding her painting of **Ignacio Figueras** – a model & polo player apparentl *y – who is stood next to her... I thought that I best clarify that fact since the portrait (sketch) is hardly a good likeness.*

Nevertheless, I have a strong feeling that art is not really Olga's thing. You see, I believe that she is Patti Davis (No2 in the Carter photo C1) - the drug-addled, wayward daughter of former US President, Ronald Raygun.

Ronald Wilson Reagan (February 6, 1911 – June 5, 2004) was an American politician and actor who served as the 40th President

of the United States from 1981 to 1989. Prior to the presidency, he was a Hollywood actor and trade union leader before serving as the 33rd Governor of California from 1967 to 1975.

Reagan was raised in a poor family in small towns of northern Illinois. He graduated from Eureka College in 1932 and worked as a sports announcer on several regional radio stations.

After moving to Hollywood in 1937, he became an actor and starred in a few major productions. Reagan was twice elected President of the Screen Actors Guild —the labor union for actors—where he worked to root out Communist influence.

In the 1950s, he moved into television and was a motivational speaker at General Electric factories. Reagan had been a Democrat until 1962, when he became a conservative and switched to the Republican Party. In 1964, Reagan's speech, " A Time for Choosing ", supported Barry Goldwater 's foundering presidential campaign and earned him national attention as a new conservative spokesman.

Building a network of supporters, he was elected Governor of California in 1966. As governor, Reagan raised taxes, turned a state budget deficit to a surplus, challenged the protesters at the University of California, ordered in National Guard troops during a period of protest movements in 1969, and was re-elected in 1970.

He twice ran unsuccessfully for the Republican presidential nomination, in 1968 and 1976. Four years later in 1980, he won the nomination, and then defeated incumbent president Jimmy Carter. At 69 years, 349 days of age at the time of his inauguration, he became the oldest president-elect to take the oath of office (a distinction now held by Donald Trump, since 2017). Reagan faced former vice president Walter Mondale when he ran for re-election in 1984, and defeated him in a landslide with the largest electoral college victory in American history.
Source: Wikipedia

And as you have just read, Reagan - sometimes referred to as 'Raygun' by no one except me - followed Jimmy Carter into the White House.

Course, daughter, Patti Reagan/Davis is not an artist – as in a painter *– and indeed she describes herself as being an "* actress *" and "* author *"... Although she was hardly Meryl Streep and when you are born into the Hollywood elite, drawing inspiration from your own life experience is always going to make for an interesting book to those saps obsessed with celebrity.*

Therefore it is hardly surprising that Davis is best known for being her father's daughter and for stripping off in Playboy Magazine. (see photo C5).

Indeed she could very well have someone's eye out with those nipples if she isn't careful.

Nevertheless, I'm being a tit so best we just go compare Olga Sweet with Patti Nipples Davis.

And once you have had a butchers, I am sure that you will agree that they are pretty spot on.

PHOTO C5: Davis on her Playboy photo shoot.

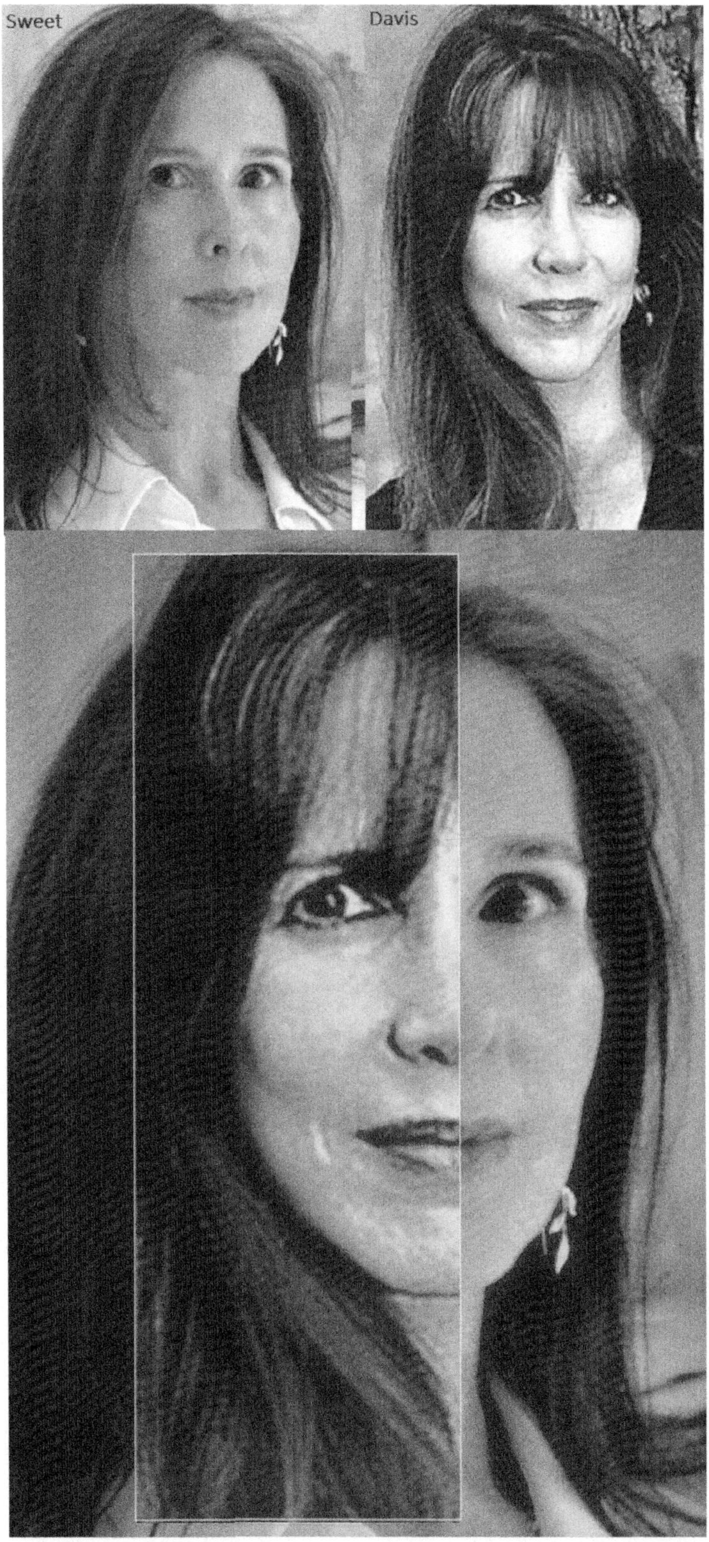

PHOTO C6: Patti and Olga comparison. The nose may look different but as I say, they have to change the features in photos else they would never get away with it.

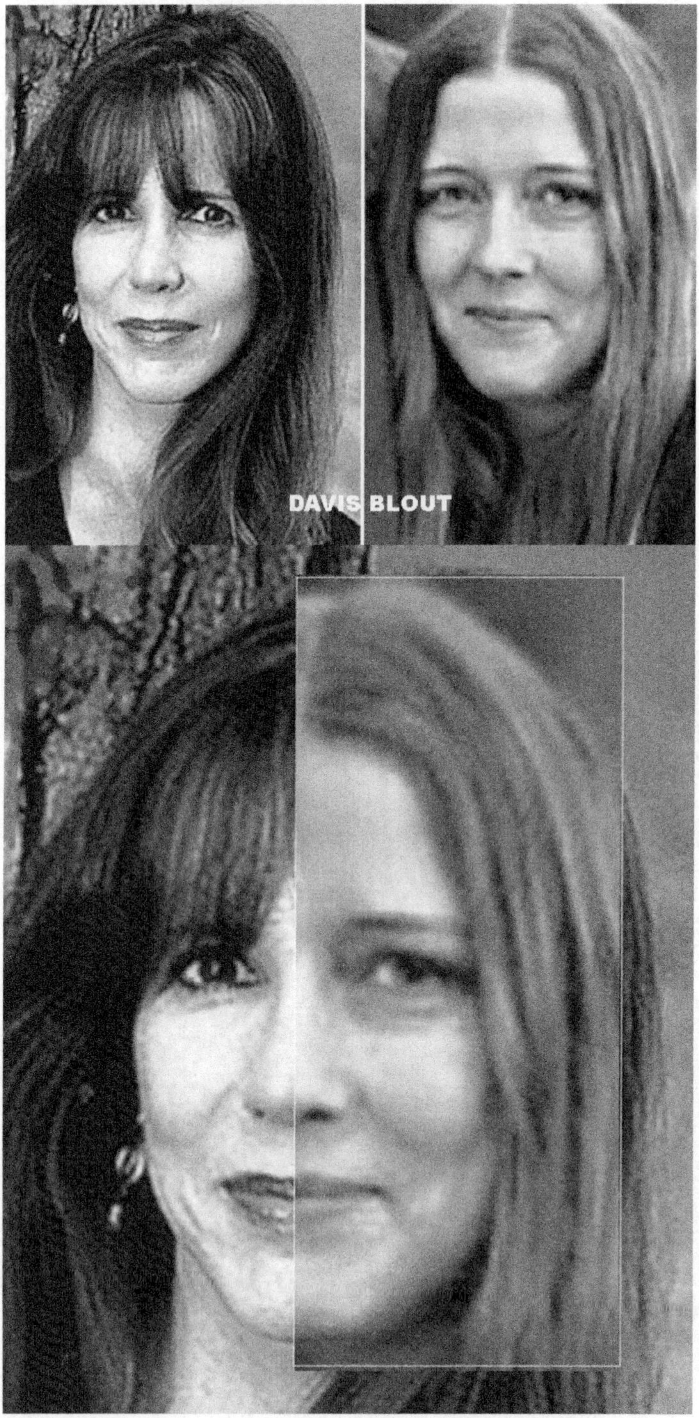

PHOTO C7: Blout/Davis comparison.

However, before you go forming an opinion, you need to keep an open mind until I have finished telling you who all those people in the Sweet/Carter (photo C1) photo are.

Now, Sweet 'n' Davis are also Darlene Blout – who you will remember is supposedly Thomas Markle Jr's bird... You know, the one that he put a gun to her head. Here, check-out this comparison of Davis & Blout (see photo C7).

Are you taking note of how well all of these overlaid half faces are matching in perfectly. Course, if you think that is just a coincidence and you can do it with all photos of people who look vaguely the same, then please be my guest and try it.

You see, you have to understand that this type of close-lookalike does not randomly continue to occur. I mean, sure everybody knows someone who looks a bit like someone else, but nowhere near to the degree that we see in ANYTHING connected to the Satanic elite.

And I cannot stress enough to you how important that 30 billion to one statistic is. Sadly, most people do not have any idea of how big a number a billion is, because if they did they would be absolutely outraged that when talking in terms of the rich nowadays we are talking in terms of multi-billionaires as opposed to not so long ago when the words multi-millionaire preceded the person in questions name.

In fact to put a billion into perspective, If you could count continuously in perfect rhythm, one number per second, without breaks for sleeping, eating, and you know LIVING... It would take ***31 years, 251 days, 6 hours, 50 minutes, 46 seconds*** *to count to a billion.*

Therefore, you are looking at 64 years to count to 2 billion if you did so continuously and if you took tea-breaks and sleep-breaks while doing so, even if you were born with £2 billion pound to your name, you would be dead before you could count it to make sure that it was all there.

And as such, the chances of finding someone who looks exactly like you in your life time is practically zilch, yet in the world of monsters, doppelgangers interact with each other on a daily basis! And as you will find out as we go along, that is far from a coincidence.

Now think about that for a moment or two and then look at the next photo batch of Hollyweird lookalikes (Photos C8-C12)

And you cannot tell me that the celebs in those photos looking so alike to other celebs isn't beyond weird.

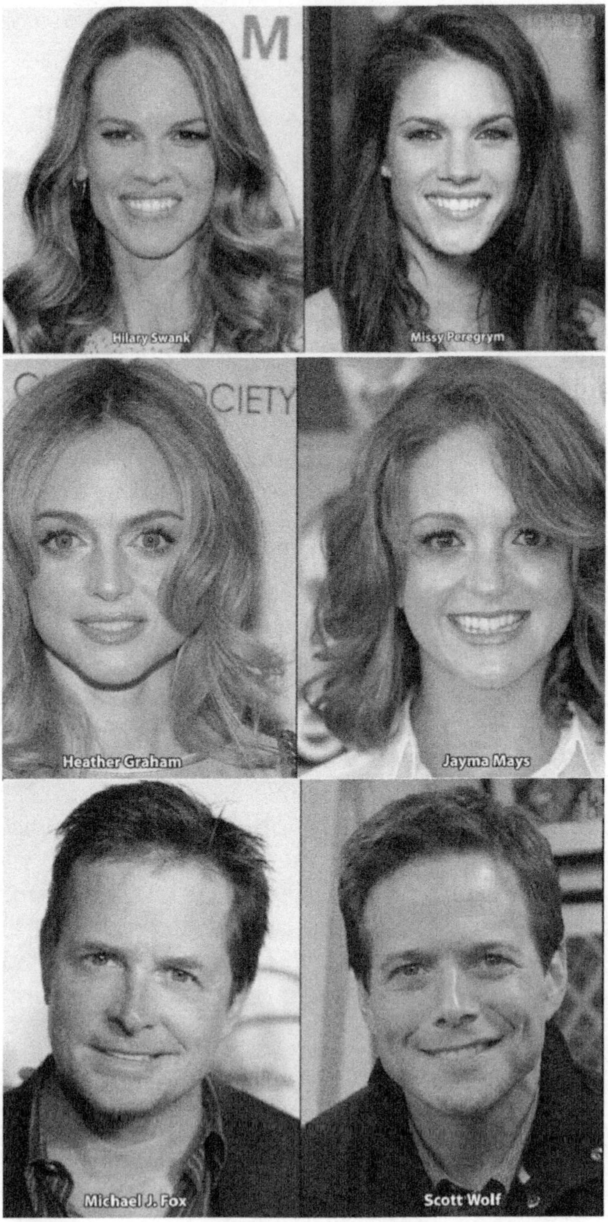

Photo C8

Lucy Hale
Selena Gomez
Jennifer Carpenter
Hope Solo
Ian Somerhalder
Rob Lowe

Photo C9

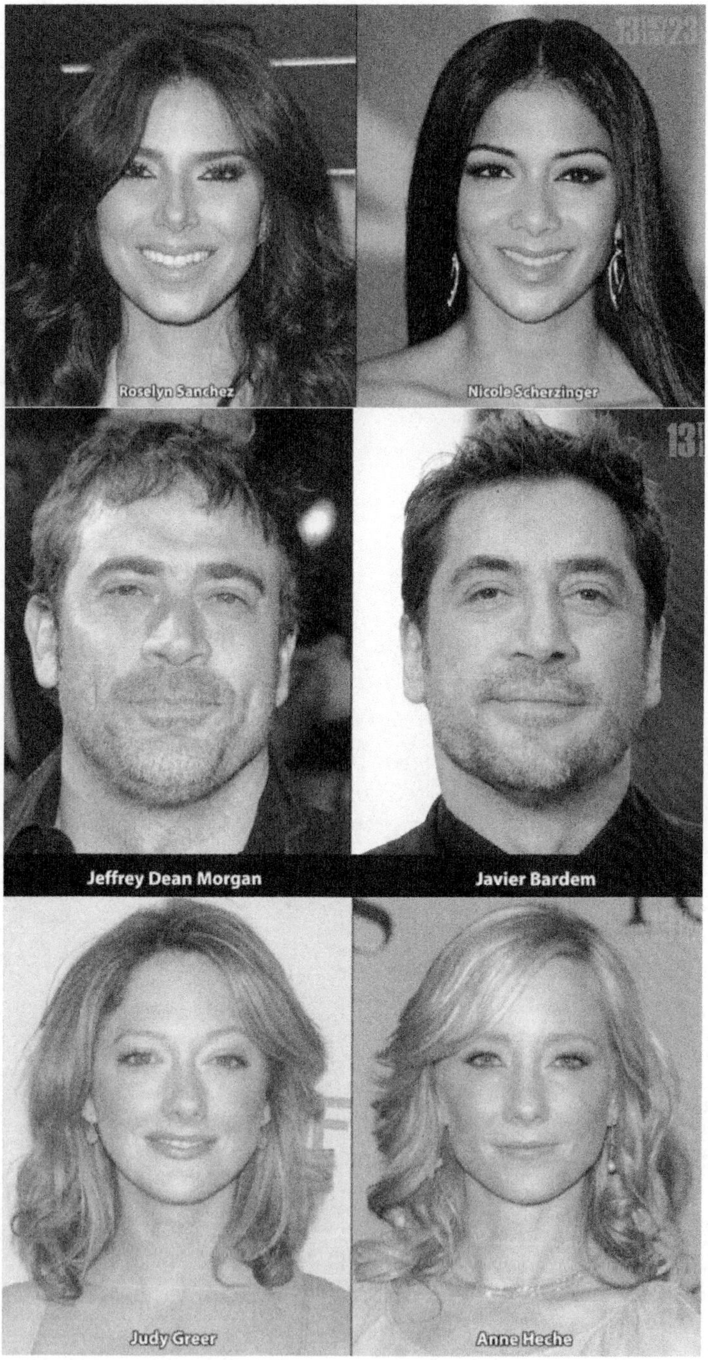
Roselyn Sanchez
Nicole Scherzinger
Jeffrey Dean Morgan
Javier Bardem
Judy Greer
Anne Heche

Photo C10

Helena Christensen
Cameron Diaz
Jessica Biel
Christy Turlington
Daniel Radcliffe
Elijah Wood

Photo C11

Linda Evangelista
Milla Jovovich
Brad Pitt
Benicio del Toro
Amanda Seyfried
Dakota Fanning
Kristen Stewart
Alicia Silverstone

Photo C12

Nevertheless, I did notice that in an effort to give the Markle's some legitimacy - by portraying them as a family of rednecks - *a story also appeared about Darlene Blout being arrested for beating up Thomas Markle Jr:*

Meghan Markle's future sister-in-law was arrested on New Year's eve in Oregon after an altercation with Thomas Markle, potentially dashing her brother's hopes to attend the royal wedding in May.

An law enforcement source with the Josephine County Jail told DailyMail.com that Tom's fiancée 'Darlene Blount was booked on January 1st. She was charged with fourth degree assault.'

Prince Harry 's soon to be sister-in-law was arrested just before the clock struck midnight on New Year, and was booked around 4:20am, after a boozed-up altercation with Tom.

Before ringing in the New Year on a sour note, Tom spent his Christmas at home in Grants Pass with Blount, 37, and her seven-year-old son.

He has not seen or spoken to his 36-year-old half-sister since 2011 but says he and Meghan are not estranged but lost touch after she moved to Toronto, Canada, to take up a role in Suits.

'She got to the point where she got busier and busier so it was really hard to nail her down,' he explained to DailyMail.com.

'It's not really that we grew apart, it was she was out there [in Toronto] doing her job – it was the biggest deal she got on TV so she had no time.

'But we spent a lot of weekends together with our grandmother [Doris Markle] before she left.'

He is now hoping that the Markle clan will one day be reunited for Christmas and says that while he doesn't expect an invitation to Meghan and Harry's May wedding, it would mean a lot to get one. *Source: The Daily Mail, January the 6th 2018*

And In turn, Sweet-Davis-Blout are also in all probability Tracey Dooley – mother to Tom-Tyler Dooley and Markle Jr's ex-bird (see photos D1 and D2)... Dooley, according to Markle Jr; has never met

Meghan despite the photos (seen earlier in this book) provided by Markle Jr telling a totally different story.

Mind you, you may have noticed that in photo D1, Tracey Dooley appears to have changed heads since she looks totally different to the Tracey Dooley that we saw earlier in the 'family' photos provided to the press by Thomas Markle Jr - in fact kinda like the same way that they replace characters in soap operas with a different actor: (photo D3).

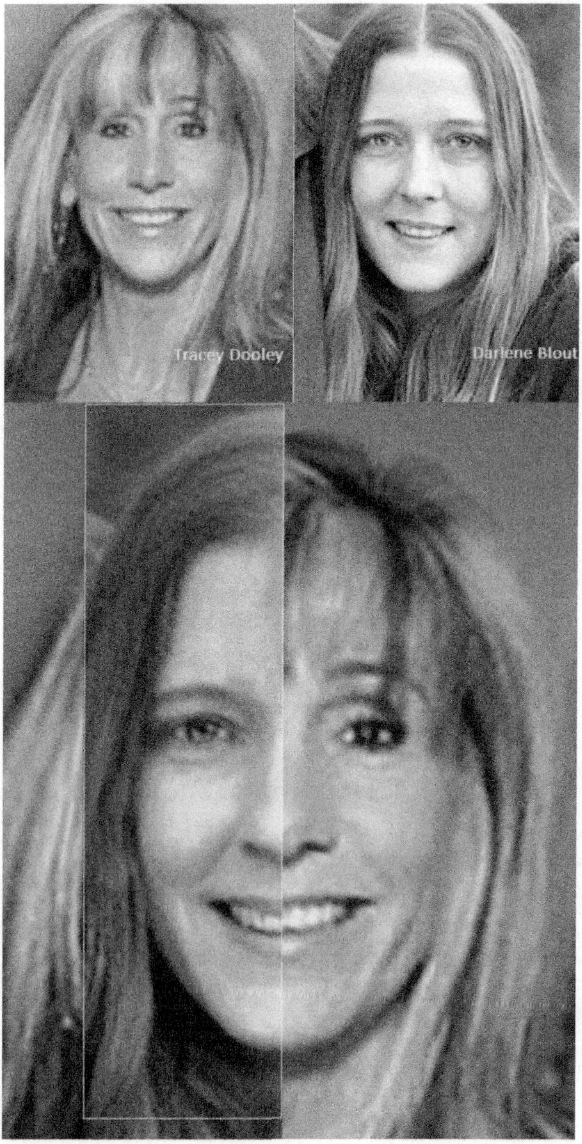

PHOTO D1: Tracey Dooley compared to Darlene Blout

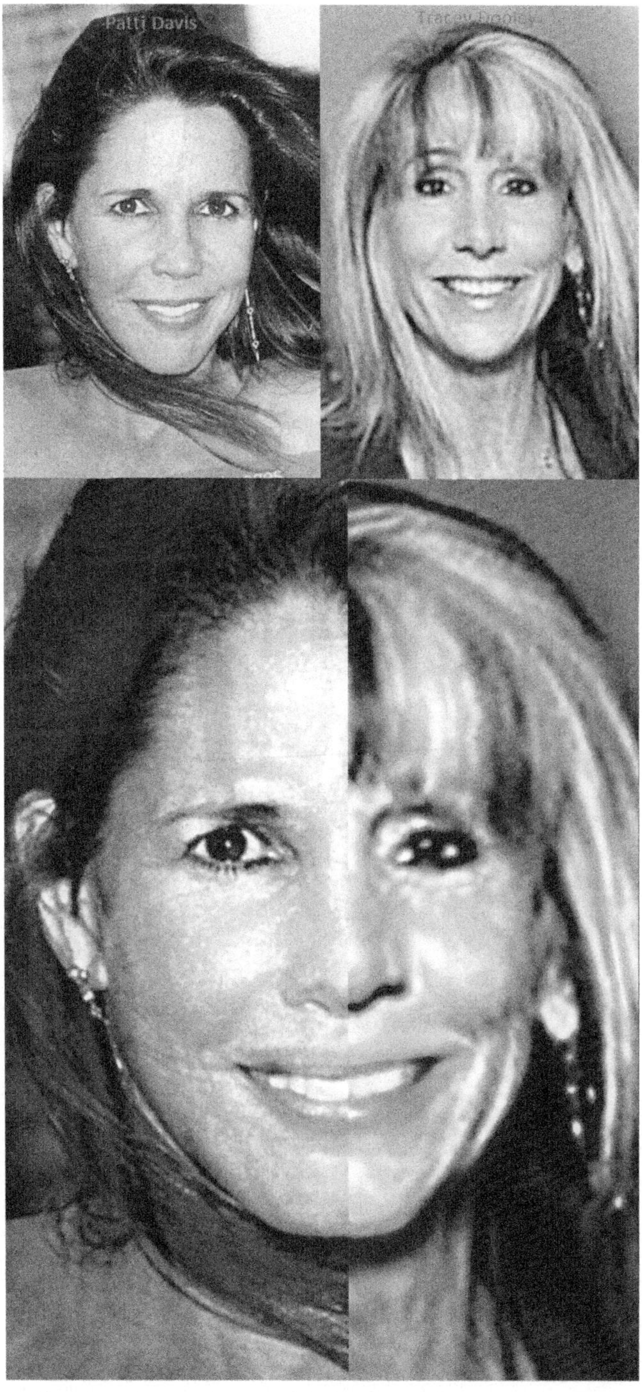

PHOTO D2:
Tracey Dooley
compared to Patti
Davis-Reagan

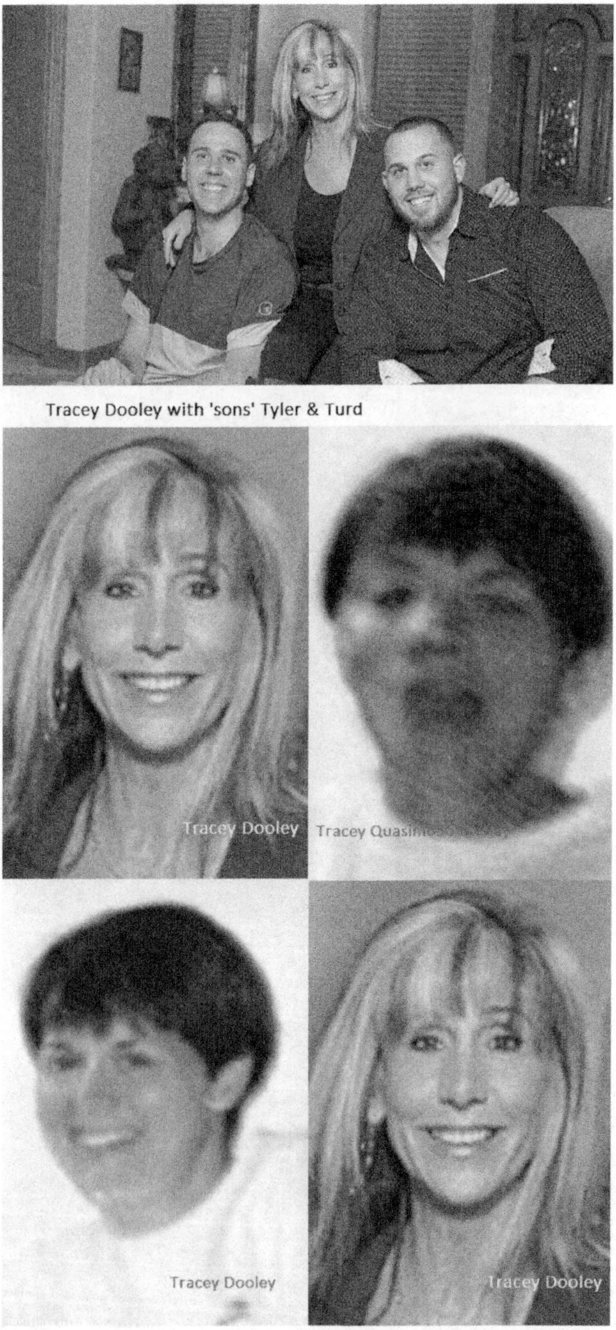

PHOTO D3: Tracey Dooley compared to other photos of Tracey Dooley.

Now as I say, Patti Davis-Reagan wasn't a very good actress but she did feature in a 1981 made-for-tv-movie called **" For Ladies Only "** -

a kinda low budget ***"Midnight Cowboy*** *" meets "****Boogie Nights****" production starring Gregory Harrison.*

Now Gregory Harrison also starred in the TV series "Trapper John" - a spin off from M.A.S.H which ran on CBS from September 23, 1979, *to* September 4, 1986 *and in which Patti Davies also briefly appeared.*

Harrison was born in Avalon, California, in 1950, the son of Ed, a ship's captain and poet.

Harrison served for two years in the United States Army during the Vietnam War era as a medic...

So straight away we see that Harrison's father was a high ranking naval captain and Harrison himself also served in the military. This is important information because you discover - time and time again - that so many of these actors taking part in these large scale frauds are connected to the military which in turn is connected to Military intelligence i.e the security services.

He was the title character on the 1977–78 science fiction series Logan's Run, after which he played the role of Levi Zendt on the 1978 NBC miniseries Centennial.

In 1979, after years of being a relatively unknown actor, Harrison finally won the role of surgeon, Dr. George "Gonzo" Gates on Trapper John, M.D., starring opposite Pernell Roberts on the medical drama spun off from M*A*S*H.

Harrison had guest starred on an episode of M*A*S*H the year after Wayne Rogers departed from his role as Trapper John on that series. Harrison remained as Gonzo on Trapper John until the middle of the show's seventh season, when he decided to leave for other ventures.

The series continued for several more episodes without Harrison, but concluded its run at the end of the 1985–86 season. Harrison had been a fan of Roberts' role as the eldest son of the Cartwright family on the series Bonanza (1959-1973). The two remained friends until Roberts' death from pancreatic cancer on January 24, 2010.

Harrison's later role as stripper John Phillips in the 1981 TV movie For Ladies Only made him a favorite with women and gay men in the 1980s. He spoofed that role in the 1986 miniseries Fresno where his character appeared shirtless at every opportunity. Harrison was a regular in the final season (1989–90) of Falcon Crest, opposite Jane Wyman, who was absent for nearly the remainder of the last season, due to her health problems and unhappiness with the direction her show was going. *Source: Wikipedia*

BINGO!

Jane Wyman was of course the first wife of American President Ronald Reagan, who along with his daughter Patti has already played a big part in this story.

Therefore, giving mind to the above connections and photos D4 & D5, it is pretty safe to say that Harrison and Davis know each other very well. Moreover, Gregory Harrison is our number 3 in the Carter photo C1 (reproduced for your convenience as photo D6).

PHOTO D4: Gregory Harrison and Patti Davis

PHOTO D5: Gregory Harrison and Patti Davis

PHOTO D6: Republished copy of photo C1

Reagan married the actress Jane Wyman on the 26th of January 1940 at the Wee Kirk o' the Heather church in Glendale, California, after they met whilst starring together in the film " ***Brother Rat*** *"... And what a Rat Raygun turned out to be.*

Course, once again we have an example of an Actor playing the role of a President.

Nevertheless, they had two biological chil dren; Maureen born in 1941 who later died in 2001 and Christine born in 1947 - but sadly, she only lived for one day.

The couple then adopted a third child, Michael who was born in 1945. The Reagans filed for divorce in 1948 after the couple had arguments about Ronnie's political ambitions and the divorce was finalized in 1949.

Wyman, also stated that their break-up was due to a difference in politics since Ronnie was still a Democrat at the time, whilst Wyman was a registered Republican.

Reagan later had the distinction of being the first divorced person to assume the nation's highest office when he became President 32 years later.

However, the couple reportedly continued to be friends until his death, with Wyman voting for Reagan in both of his Presidential campaigns and she is reported as stating upon his death that " America has lost a great president and a great, kind, and gentle man*".*

And according to Wikipedia:

Reagan met actress Nancy Davis (1921–2016) in 1949 after she contacted him in his capacity as president of the Screen Actors Guild. He helped her with issues regarding her name appearing on a Communist blacklist in Hollywood.

She had been mistaken for another Nancy Davis. She described their meeting by saying, "I don't know if it was exactly love at first sight, but it was pretty close." They were engaged at Chasen's restaurant in Los Angeles and were married on March 4, 1952, at the Little Brown Church in the Valley (North Hollywood, now Studio City) San Fernando Valley.

Actor William Holden served as best man at the ceremony. They had two children: Patti (b. 1952) and Ronald "Ron" Jr. (b. 1958).

Observers described the Reagans' relationship as close, authentic and intimate. During his presidency, they reportedly displayed frequent affection for one another; one press secretary said, "They never took each other for granted. They never stopped courting."

He often called her "Mommy" and she called him "Ronnie." He once wrote to her, "Whatever I treasure and enjoy... all would be without meaning if I didn't have you."

Nancy Reagan died on March 6, 2016 at the age of 94.

Nevertheless, the reason for Harrison's inclusion in the photo D6 is because of the fact that he is associated with Patti Davis and indeed he looks very much like Olga Sweet's husband, Robert (he is 'A. in photo D6 *)... Robot to his friends... Probably.*

However, before I go any further I should also tell you that the Carter photo is fake. I mean just look at Olga Sweet/Patti Davis' hand in Photo D7 for starters!

PHOTO D7: Anomalies in the photo

Deformed hand and the carpet makes no sense at all.

By Julie Butler on September 30, 2013 in Lead News, News, People · 0 Comments

PHOTO D8: Showing the date that the photo was taken.

PHOTO: D9: Olga and Robot Sweet

PHOTO D10: A reversed section of Robert Sweet overlaid onto photo D9

And that isn't to mention the strange carpet in the background along with the weird shape type thing behind Olga's son's left shoulder and the fact that Olga's dress sleeves do not match!

Moreover, as you can see from photo D8, the picture was supposedly ' taken ' *on or before the 30th of September 2013 – nearly five years ago, whereas Photo D9 was was taken on the 13th of May 2017 … Or to put it another way, Photo D9 was taken around three and a half years after the Carter photo.*

Yet if you look at Photo D10, you will see that by reversing the carter photo and then taking a section of Robot Sweet out of it and overlaying that section onto the photo of him in the photo D9, it matches in perfectly.

This then is a clear indication that the photos of Olga Sweet and her 'family are all faked, given credence to my claim that she is just a made up persona… I mean, what famous artist doesn't have so much as a wikipedia page?

And that is how these fake people are given lives.

Indeed there are very, very few photos of Olga and her ' husband ' *on the interwebb.*

In fact the only other photo that I could find was the one you can see in Photo E1. And you can take that segment of Robot Sweet from the Carter photo and find that lo and behold, it sits perfectly over himself seen in the photo E1.

You can then take a segment of Robot Sweet out of photo E1 and you will see in photo E3 that it fits perfectly over the other photo of Robot.

So, it is now safe to say that " Olga & Robert " *are not a real couple and Jimmy Carter is as bent as the rest of them... And just so as y'know, y'know; no angles were changed on any of those photos other than reversing Robot Sweet from the faked Carter photo.*

Moreover, if you go to Photo E4 you will see that her dress never changed much over the years. Indeed, the two photos were taken at seperate bashes as evidenced by the large plaster on Olga's arm.seen in one but not the other. Course, that is just a trick to fool you into thinking that they were taken on two separate occasions… But they weren't.

They are indeed faked photos evidenced by the fact that you can take a segment of Olga from the first and it will overlay on the second perfectly (see photo E5).

And what's more, you can do the same with just about every photo of Olga (see photos E6 & E7)... Just like her husbands do.

PHOTO E1: Robot & Olga Sweet at a party

PHOTO E2: The segment of Robot Sweet taken from the Carter photo fits over the photo of Sweet in photo E1 perfectly

PHOTO E3: The segment of Robot taken from photo E1 also fits over this photo perfectly

PHOTO E4: Olga's photo taken at two separate parties.

PHOTO E5: Olgas photo overlays the other perfectly.

PHOTO E6: All Olga's photos fit each other.

PHOTO E7: All Olga's photos fit each other.

That will do for now but let me tell you that I can prove that every single photo of Olga's is a fake.

Therefore, the fact that the photos are all fraud straight away adds credence to what I have already shown you and what I am about to show you in Chapter 3.

Chapter 3
Gregory Harrison

Now you are probably wondering what Gregory Harrison has to do with Meghan Markle... And you would be entitled to do so.

And to answer that question, for me to convince you that Meghan Markle is nothing more than a created persona, you need to be aware of the bigger picture in order to see how everything all fits together.

Therefore, all I ask is that you stay alert and read on with an open mind because I am going to bombard you with proof of the fact.

Now, there can be no doubt that Harrison is the splitting image of Robert Sweet, hence his inclusion in the Carter photo D6. However, you do not need to refer back to that and instead just fast forward to Photo E8.

And immediately you will notice that the pair not only look the same, but they share the exact same ears. Now, our ears are unique to only us, or put another way, no one but our 30 billion to one doppelganger's are the same.

Course, the monster-minions are aware of that fact and as such, they usually alter them on photos where an actor is playing a role. Nevertheless, it seems on this occasion that they neglected to do so, possibly because they never dreamed that someone would make the connection between the pair.

But here is where it gets really good. You see Gregory Harrison also played the role of psycho killer, Ted Bundy (Number 1 in the Carter photo D6 *):*

Theodore Robert Bundy (born Theodore Robert Cowell; November 24, 1946 – January 24, 1989) was an American serial

killer, kidnapper, rapist, burglar, thief, and necrophile who assaulted and murdered numerous young women and girls during the 1970s and possibly earlier.

Shortly before his execution and after more than a decade of denials, he confessed to 30 homicides that he committed in seven states between 1974 and 1978. The true victim count will forever be unknown and could be much higher than the number to which Bundy confessed. Source: Wikipedia

And just like the story of John Wayne Gacy, the story of Ted Bundy is fake… Don't believe me? Then take a butchers at Photo E9 and E10.

Indeed, in photo E9 it is very easy to see how Bundy's ears have been changed.

PHOTO E8: Harrison and Sweet comparison.

PHOTO E9: Ted Bundy - Gregory Harrison comparison.

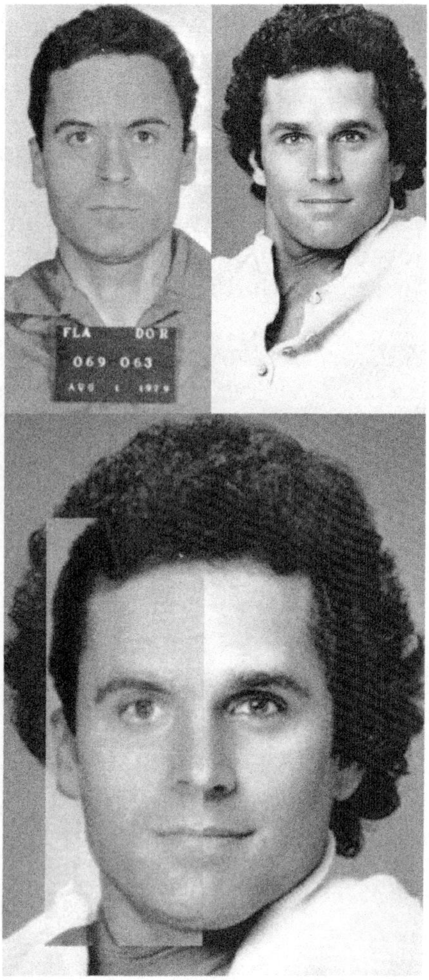

PHOTO E10: Ted Bundy - Gregory Harrison comparison.

Yet what with the Harrison/Bundy comparison and Jeb Bush in comparison to John Hinkley Jr it would appear that the Monster-Minions were even more blasé back in the day about being discovered, than they are today!

Mind you, the masses didn't have the interwebb back then although like the fake Raygun assassination attempt; I am surprised that no one has picked up on the Bundy Bollox since.

Yet all of a sudden, the fact that the Markle's are at the very least Satanically connected to John Wayne Gacy doesn't now seem so far-fetched does it? And I am a long way from being done yet.
So moving swiftly on and as most of you know – because I have fucking told you enough *– these fake personas are always played by at least two actors and in the case of really high-profile fictions such as Princess Diana, there can be half a dozen or more playing the role.*

In fact, I suggest that you go to my website (www.chrisspivey.org) and read my article, ' ***Night Of The Living Dead*** *' for the names of the many actors who played Diana.*

Now, I don't know if people were cottoning on to Bundy being played by Harrison back in the day, or whether the Minions were just being cautious in case they did, but the press at the time all ran stories about Bundy's ever-changing appearance (see photo F1).

And I best point out that photo F1 is actually a screenshot because I wanted to keep the newspapers comment rather than just copy & paste it.

Moreover, you will notice that the " many faces *" are all shown in technicrap so some things never change where the press is concerned.*

But nevertheless, some eagle-eyed members of the public have picked up on the fact that in one of his many guises, Bundy looks very much like George W Bush (see photo F2)... Unfortunately, that is all they have picked up on.

You see, at the very least it is another Satanic connection. And I stress that it is a " Satanic connection *", at the very least.*
Still, in order to do the job properly, we also need to see how Bundy shapes up in comparison to Robert Sweet (see photo F3)

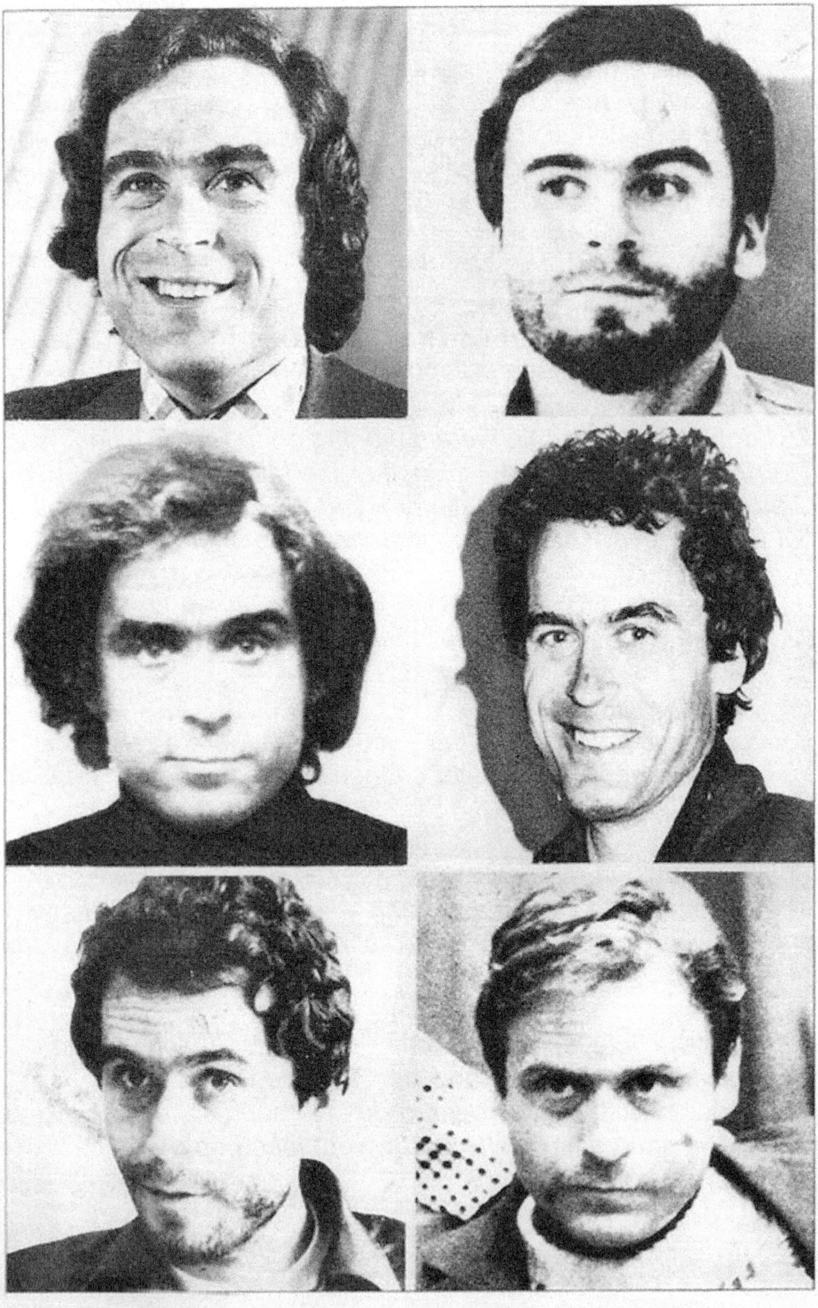

The many faces of a monster . . . this was how Ted Bundy altered his appearance over the years he evaded capture.

PHOTO F1: The many changing faces of Ted Bundy

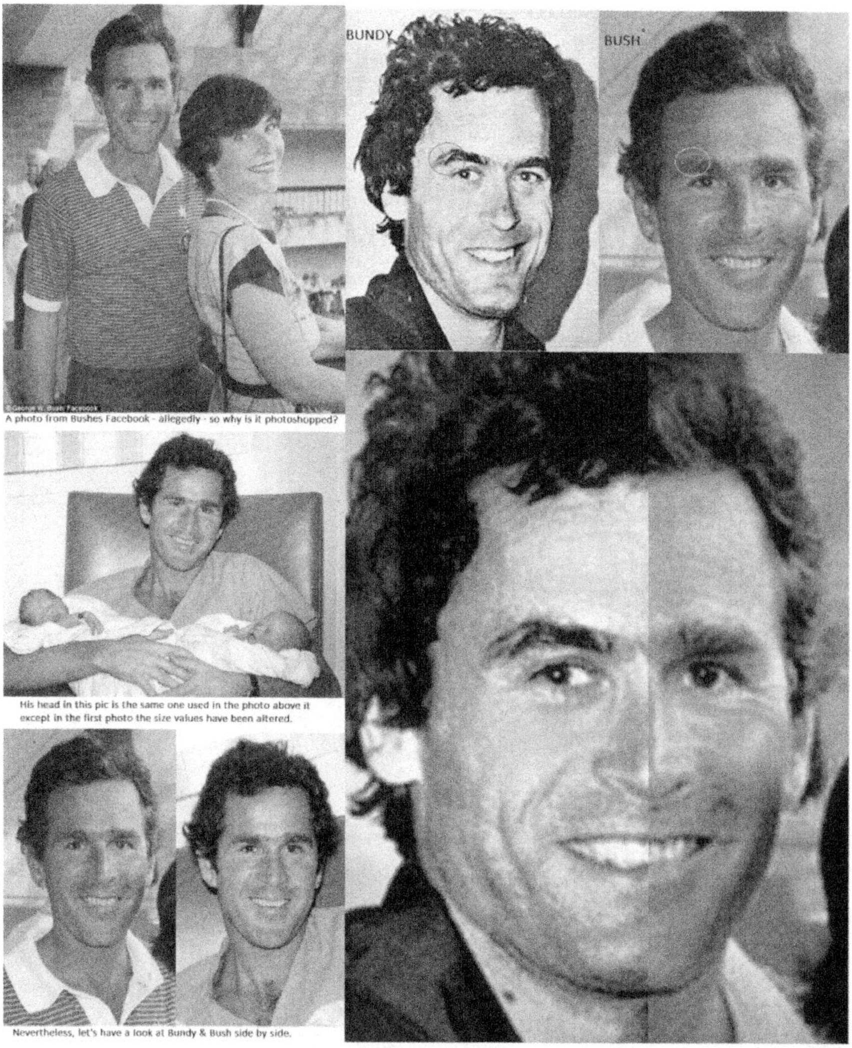

BUNDY
BUSH
A photo from Bushes Facebook - allegedly - so why is it photoshopped?
His head in this pic is the same one used in the photo above it
except in the first photo the size values have been altered.
Nevertheless, let's have a look at Bundy & Bush side by side.

PHOTO F2: Bush/Bundy comparison

PHOTO F3:
Bundy/Sweet
comparison

PHOTO F4: Republished fake Carter photo

And as you can see, they too match perfectly, although I kind of suspect that many of you readers are not yet convinced.

Now at this point, we once again need to refer to the faked Carter photo D6 which - for your convenience I have again republished in that last photo batch as photo F4.

Okay the fella that you now need to look at in the Carter photo is number 2, the actor, Tom Hollander. And as far as I can make out, Tom is the littlest man in the world... Indeed his surname really ought to be Thumb.

The following is taken from Wikipedia:

Thomas Anthony Hollander (born 25 August 1967)] is an English actor. He began his career in theatre, winning the Ian Charleson Award in 1992 for his performance as Witwoud in The Way of the World at the Lyric Hammersmith Theatre.

He is known for his roles in comedic films such as Pirates of the Caribbean and In the Loop and drama films such as Enigma, Pride & Prejudice, Gosford Park, and Hanna. He played the lead role in the sitcom Rev., which won the British Academy Television Award for best sitcom in 2011.

He also played the lead in the ITV 's Doctor Thorne and won] the BAFTA Television Award for Best Supporting Actor for his role as Major Lance "Corky" Corkoran in the BBC series The Night Manager...

However, I am sure that you can see where this is heading – at least in part – *but since Tom was born in 1967 he cannot possibly be either Bundy or Harrison... Although a clone is a real possibility.*

And as for the made-up Robert Sweet; well I really can't say because I don't know how old he is since there is little to no information about him on't thinternet.
However, Tom Thumb-Hollander is in all probability just a Satanic connection, albeit an extremely important one.

Shall we go compare?

Of course we fucking shall, take a look at photo F5, which is pretty conclusive if you ask me.
And what about Bundy? How does he compare to Hollander… Extremely well since you ask (see photo F6).

You really couldn't make it up, I am sure you would agree. However, please try overlaying the photos for yourself if you think that I am using some trickery or other...

That is the Monsters game, not mine. And if you don't know how, I give you a tutorial in my article ***' How The West Was Won ' on my website.***

And as it happens, I also found a Tom Hollander on ' Linkedin *'… You'll like this.*

Now this Tom Hollander is supposedly a Structural Engineer from Iowa in America… A rather shy one at that because his photo was on view for all to display when I first wrote about him on my website.

However, ever since then his Linkedin profile picture has disappeared from the social network site… How very odd, although not a disaster since I had already nicked his profile picture for the piece I wrote on him on my website.

You can find that photo at F7 - study it carefully, because if you do you will see that Tom Hollander is Tom Markle Jr (see photo F8).

What's more, I also found a younger Thomas Hollander living in Iowa who bears an uncanny resemblance to Meghan's mother's bodyguard (see photo F9 and F10).

PHOTO F5: Hollander-Harrison comparison

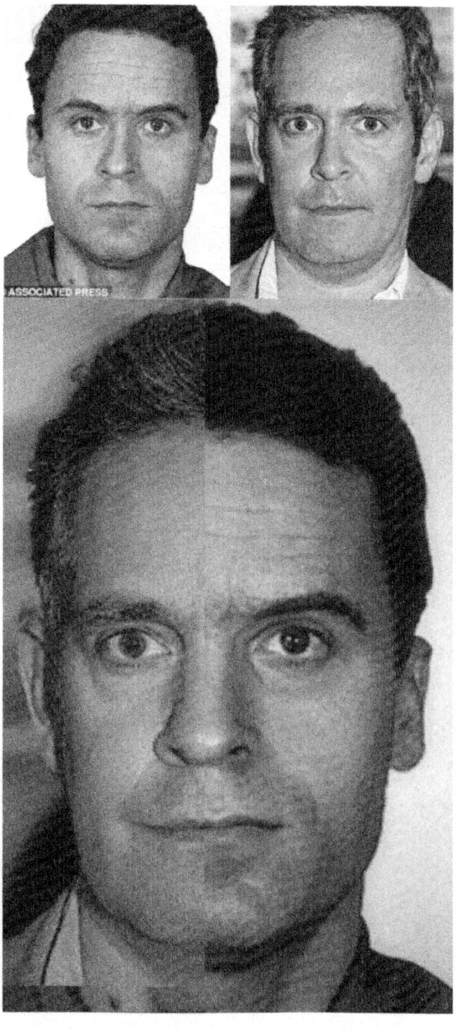

PHOTO F6: Bundy Hollander comparison

Tom Hollander

Structural Engineer

Newton, Iowa | Civil Engineering

Current

PHOTO F7: Tom Hollander from Iowa

Thomas Markle Jr & Darlene Blout, inset: Thomas Hollander
Straight overlay, no angles changed.

PHOTO F8: Tom Hollander/Tom Markle Jr comparison

PHOTO F9: THomas Hollander the younger from Iowa

PHOTO F10: Hollander compared to Meghan's mother's bodyguard.

*Nevertheless, getting back to the actor Tom '*thumb*' Hollander and I can tell you that he is very well socially connected. You see he is very good friends with Camilla Parker Bowles, who is - like Meghan Markle - a member of the Royal Family.*

Indeed, Camilla is married to Prince Charles... At least she is in name. You see, Old Charlie boy is as gay as they come, and has been accused of being a paedophile on many occasions. Indeed, there can be little doubt that neither William or Harry are his biological sons... But I am now going way far off track, so I will leave that there.

Mind you, most of the [not-so] Royal family are actors and not of the "elite" bloodlines. Indeed if I was to theorize I would say that the 'Windsor' bloodline is the weakest of the 12 or 13 bloodline families and is probably on the verge of extinction.

This would be down to a catch 22 scenario caused by inbreeding. You see, the royal bloodline was so polluted by the turn of the 20th century that their females were continually giving birth to mentally retarded, physically handicapped offspring, inflicted with hereditary medical conditions.

And that is where the catch 22 comes in. You see, forget what the press write about them marrying commoners such as Kate Gold-Digger-Smiff (another created persona *) or Meghan Markle, because as far as I can make out, the true-bloodline-families cannot breed outside of those carrying their own genes.*

Therefore, they have no one to breed with.

Nevertheless, as I say, that is just a theory and the actors such as Little Bald Willie (Rothschild *) & Henry of Ginger (* who is possibly of the Windsor bloodline but not the son of Charles *) keep the Millions of Pounds flowing in.*

And just so as you know, Prince Harry of Pubes-Ginger is most definitely not Jimmy Hewitt's son... That is just another conspiracy theory started by the Monsters themselves and allowed to flourish.

Mind you, Camilla Parker Bowles son, Tom, the ever-smug-looking, coke-snorting FOOD-CRITIC did a stint on " Masterchef *" in 2015 and knows Mary Berry very well... Which he would do wouldn't he given as Mary the CHEF, is played by the same actress as his Mother Camilla is (see photo G2 & G3).*

And also let me tell you that I can do comparisons between Berry and Parker Bowles every day of the week and still get 100% match on them.

PHOTO G1: Tom Thumb-Hollander and Camilla Parker Bowles

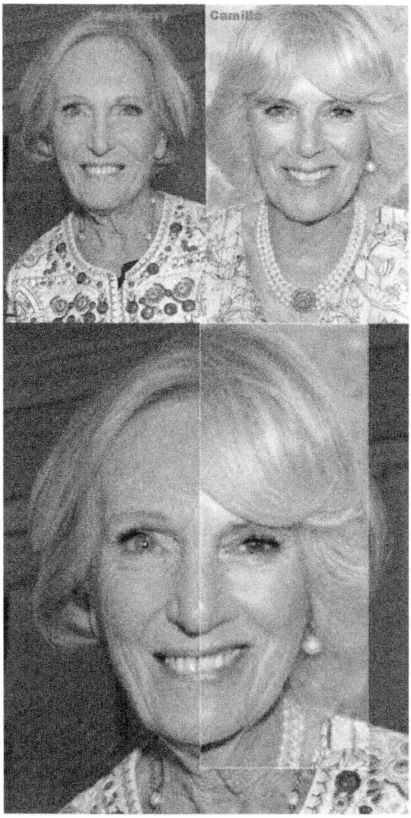

PHOTO G2: Mary Berry/Camilla Parker Bowles comparison

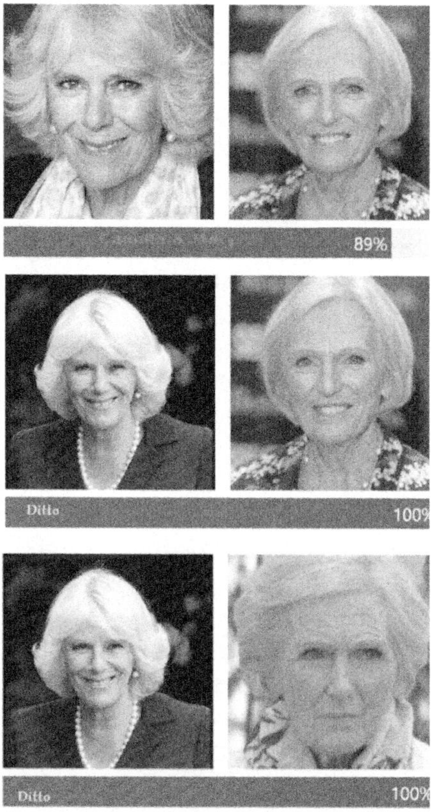

PHOTO G3: Mary Berry/Camilla Parker Bowles comparison using facial
recognition software

PHOTO G4: Tom Parker Bowles and Scary Mary

PHOTO: Berry & Parker-Horseface

Indeed, Camilla recently appeared on the Australian version of 'Master Chef':

The Duchess of Cornwall revealed Prince Charles ' favourite foods, during their joint appearance on MasterChef Australia on Wednesday.

Speaking to MasterChef judge Gary Mehigan, Camilla gushed that her husband was a big fan of local cheeses and home grown produce.

'He's a huge cheese fan, anything to do with cheese he'll love,' she said. *Source: The Daily Mail, July 4th 2018*

Kinda coincidental don't cha think?

Now, for those of you who don't know who Mary Berry is, the following is taken from Wikipedia:

Mary Rosa Alleyne Hunnings CBE (née Berry; born 24 March 1935), known professionally as Mary Berry, is a British food writer and television presenter. After being encouraged in domestic science classes at school, she studied catering and institutional management at college. She then moved to France at the age of 21 to study at Le Cordon Bleu school, before working in a number of cooking-related jobs.

She has published more than 75 cookery books including her bestselling Baking Bible in 2009. Her first book was The Hamlyn All Colour Cookbook in 1970. She hosted several television series for the BBC and Thames Television.

Berry is an occasional contributor to Woman's Hour and Saturday Kitchen.

She was a judge on the BBC One (originally BBC Two) television programme The Great British Bake Off from its launch in 2010 until 2016...

And as for Tom Parker Bowles, Wikipedia has the following to say:

Thomas Henry Charles Parker Bowles (/boʊlz/ ; born 18 December 1974) is a British food writer and food critic. Parker Bowles is the author of five cookbooks and in 2010 won the

Guild of Food Writers 2010 award for his writings on British food.

He is known for his appearances as a judge in numerous television food series and for his reviews of restaurant meals around the UK and overseas for GQ, Esquire, and The Mail on Sunday.

Parker Bowles is the son of Camilla, Duchess of Cornwall, and Andrew Parker Bowles. His stepfather and godfather is Charles, Prince of Wales. He has one younger sister, Laura Lopes...

Indeed that food connection, given Mary Berry's likeness to Tom's mother Camilla is a pretty huge Elephant in the room.

However, the Monster Minions cannot help themselves but give us a clues as to what is going on in the world. Indeed it is said by some that they have to do so because they are obliged to let us know what is what - albeit covertly - in order to gain our consent for their misdeeds... Which apparently somehow makes it all alright.

Course, I have no way of knowing if that is true or not but what I do know is that they most certainly do give us a lot of clues.

Therefore it is no surprise that the Chimp put out an article calling Mary Berry the "The Queen Of cakes" which included the photoshopped image seen at photo G5.

Course on the face of it, the photo is innocent - the Chimp wasn't hiding the fact that the crown is photoshopped onto Berry's head - *until you know all of what I have just told you and then it becomes quite, quite sinister.*

Mind you, the Chimp calling Mary the " Queen of Cakes *" made me titter, although I suppose calling her the much-more-fitting "* Queen of Tarts *" would have been a bit too provocative for some.*

Nevertheless, also in that photo is Mary's son & daughter. And guess what? Her son is also called TOM.

So Camilla has a son Tom who is a food writer and critic and Mary Berry is a top chef who looks just like Camilla and also has a son called Tom… Those coincidence things just keep rolling on don't they? Unless of course you are now coming to realise that everything has to connect with everything in the world of the Satanic elite.

Mind you, it is a good job that TOM Berry looks fuck all like the pint-sized actor, TOM Hollander because if he did it would surely put my case for Satanic Connections beyond doubt wouldn't it?

Oh wait, Tom Berry does look exactly like Tom Hollander (see photo G6)

PHOTO G5: Mary Berry with her 'family' wearing a photoshopped crown

PHOTO G6: Hollander/Berry Comparison

Course, Since Tom Berry looks like Tom Thumb-Hollander he should also look like Greg Harrison shouldn't he?

Of course he should. So best we take a gander at how Harrison compares to Tom Berry (see photo G7).

Have ya looked? Fit together perfectly don't they.

And I can tell you that Berry will also fit together perfectly with Ted Bundy and Robert Sweet.

However, I should also point out that Tom Berry is actually, called Tom March... At least he is according to Wikipedia - although fuck knows why when his 'father' is called, 'Paul John March Hunnings'.

Mary Berry supposedly married Paul John March Hunnings in 1966... Although given that Berry is either the same actress who plays Camilla Parker Horseface or they are clones or a 30 billion to one coincidence, the wedding fact is highly suspect.

Neverthel ess, Hunnings reportedly later worked for Harvey's of Bristol and sold antique books although he is now retired. Hunnings and Berry supposedly had three children: Thomas Alleyne March - the Tom in question - who is supposedly a tree surgeon, and a father of three, and Annabel Mary March (married to Charles William Dan Bosher, a master builder).

Annabel is reported to be a mother of three who went into business with her mother to market salad dressings. However, a second son, named as William John March, died in 1989, in a car accident aged only 19 while a student at Bristol Polytechnic ....
Indeed Bristol Polytechnic is little more than a spy recruitment center for MI5 & MI6.

More telling still is the fact that Tom and William both attended Gordonstoun School - another Spy recruitment center which was also attended by Prince Philip and Prince Charles... The latter being married to Camilla Parker Bowles AKA Mary Berry.

So, surely Tom March-Berry should be a Hunnings too, although surname anomalies are extremely common when all is not above board.

But to get back on track; and not only is the short-arsed Tom Hollander friends with Camilla Parker Bowles, he is also friends with – drumroll please - *Meghan Markle (see photo G8).*

PHOTO G7: Harrison/ Berry comparison

PHOTO G8: Meghan Markle and Tom Thumb Hollander

Now what you have to understand is that when I say that they are " friends *", I don't mean in the normal sense of the word. I am in fact talking about them being "*friends*" in the illusionary world that most people live in and where nothing is real.*

Indeed the photo of Markle & Hollander is a fake – like most photos that are not ordinary peoples snapshots – *and is only in existence to form another Satanic connection with all of the above.*

I mean you cannot form a friendship with someone who does not exist and Meghan most certainly does not as I will PROVE to you before I am done writing this exposé.

However, Tom Thumb is also illusionary-world-friends *with Emilia Wickstead, the* *aherm, aherm, '*dress designer' to the rich & famous - and who's clients includes amongst others, Kate Golddigger-Smiff... Allegedly.*

Chapter 4
Emilia Wickstead

Now Emilia Wickstead is also one of those with a suspiciously, very short Wikipedia page which looks to have been created in a hurry.

Course, that is because she is just another made up persona played by an actress, specifically created to give Meghan Markle credibility.

Indeed, I have reproduced her whole Wikipedia page - or lack of it - below, with comments by myself as we go along:

Emilia Wickstead (born June 1983) is a New Zealand -born fashion designer based in London, England. In 2014 she won the Red Carpet Designer of the Year Award at the Elle Style Awards, and her clients include Samantha Cameron, and the Duchess of Cambridge...

*Indeed Sam Cam isa member of the Satanic Astor family and I strongly suggest that you read my articles: '**Let's Go Play With The Astors**' and '**Cameron's Closet**' which can both be found on my website, **www.chrisspivey.org.***

Wickstead was born in June 1983, in Auckland, New Zealand to Angela Wickstead, a designer with a boutique in Parnell. At the age of 14 she and her mother moved to Milan, Italy. Wickstead studied fashion design and marketing at Central Saint Martins art school in London and interned in New York at Giorgio Armani and Vogue magazine...

And that is the full extent of her "early life" bio... No mention of her father, in fact very lacking in detail altogether.

At the age of 24, Wickstead's boyfriend gave her £5,000 to start her business. She created a small collection of clothes and held showings for family and friends in her living room, taking orders for made-to-measure items. Her work was featured in Tatler and

UK Vogue magazines, and she was able to expand, opening a store in Belgravia, and employing a team of seamstresses. She had her first showing at London Fashion Week in 2012, and holds shows and consultations in New Zealand, New York and Milan.

Wickstead's style has been described as "graceful", "understated elegance" and her choice of colours as "pretty but not saccharine".

In May 2018, Wickstead claimed that the wedding dress of Meghan Markle was "identical" to one of her designs.

And that is her wiki page in its entirety and if you don't find that highly suspect for such a famous dress designer then there is something wrong with you.

However, as I say, Wickstead was created specifically to give Meghan Markle credibility and what better way to do that than to cause controversy at the time of the wedding itself.

The following is taken from a Chimp article published in May 2018:

A British-based designer who claimed Meghan Markle's wedding gown was 'identical' to one of her own creations has had her Twitter account mysteriously suspended.

New Zealander Emilia Wickstead, a favourite of the Duchess of Cambridge, last week commented that the new Duchess of Sussex 's stunning wedding dress was very similar to a £7,000 gown in her own collection - and sparked a backlash on social media.

Meghan's dress was actually created by Givenchy's Clare Wright Keller, costing £200,000, and kept firmly under wraps until the big day.

Ms Wickstead triggered the storm after she reportedly said: 'Her dress is identical to one of our dresses. Apparently a lot of commentators were saying, 'It's an Emilia Wickstead dress." She continued: 'Her dress is identical to one of our dresses. Apparently a lot of commentators were saying, "It's an Emilia Wickstead dress.'"

The designer then went on to have a bit of a dig at Meghan's look. She said: 'If you choose a simple design the fit should be perfect. Her wedding dress was quite loose.'
And she didn't approve of the bride's relaxed hair style: 'I was like, 'Hold the wisps [of her hair] back — it's a Royal Wedding for God's sake.'

The comments have seen Wickstead, who has seen her designs worn frequently by the Duchess of Cambridge, chastised by social media users.

@megananomous wrote: '#EmiliaWickstead has a lot of nerve talking rudely about the #DuchessOfSussex's wedding dress! Emilia actually works as a designer for the royal family!! Highly unprofessional!'

@kmcghee617b added: 'Emilia Wickstead is a very successful designer. She has dressed the Duchess of Cambridge on more than one occasion. It's a shame that she has elected this forum to voice her complaints concerning the dress origin. Why wouldn't she have went straight to Givenchy?'

@MeadhbhMcGrath added: 'Deeply unprofessional comments from Emilia Wickstead on Meghan's Givenchy gown! Will Kate Middleton sever ties with one of her favourite designers over this?'

@pookiesmith2424 added: 'Emilia Wickstead May just have lost her Royal customers!'

So what, you say.

Read on, says I... But do take note of how bitchy the Monkey Kuntz allege Wickstead to have been.

Now, the next day, the Chimp followed that article up with this next one:

Designer Emilia Wickstead has backtracked on her claim that Meghan's £200,000 Givenchy gown looked 'identical' to one of her own designs.

In a statement, the New Zealand -born designer said she does 'not think that her wedding dress was a copy of any of our

designs', adding that she has the 'greatest respect for Clare Waight Keller'.

Emilia, 34, described the Duchess of Sussex as looking 'absolutely beautiful' on her wedding day and said she has the 'utmost admiration and respect for her'.
It comes after she the designer previously suggested to the Mail that Meghan's wedding gown was 'identical to one of our dresses'.

In the statement shared on Instagram, Emilia said: 'I am extremely saddened by commentary that has appeared in the press and on-line over the past few days.

'Her Royal Highness, the Duchess of Sussex looked absolutely beautiful on her wedding day and I have the utmost admiration and respect for her.

Changed her fucking tune a bit but carry on:

'I do not think that her wedding dress was a copy of any of our designs. I have the greatest respect for Clare Waight Keller and the House of Givenchy — a huge source of inspiration to me.'

She added: 'I wish Their Royal Highnesses, the Duke and Duchess of Sussex a wonderful, happy and love filled life together.'

Emilia is one of the Duchess of Cambridge's favourite designers, and was worn by Meghan on Anzac Day in April.

HUH??? What the fuck does that mean?

But following the wedding, she remarked on the similarity between Meghan's stunning Givenchy gown and one of her own off-shoulder designs.
She told the Mail: 'Her dress is identical to one of our dresses. Apparently a lot of commentators were saying, "It's an Emilia Wickstead dress."'

Emilia added: 'If you choose a simple design the fit should be perfect. Her wedding dress was quite loose."

Now, apart from the blatant covert advertising used in the two articles, that was their content in its entirety. And apart from that strangely worded sentence in the latter stages of the second article, there appears to be no connection between Meghan and Wickstead, despite the much repeated claims that the 'dress designer' is a favourite of Kate Gold-Digger-Smiff... Another created persona.

However, we know that not to be true because Tom Thumb-Hollander is a very good friend to them both.

Indeed we have already seen the faked photo of Markle out on the town with Hollander, but he also appears in faked photos with Wickstead (see photo G9).

But what makes me say that they are faked? Well take a look at the next photo along (photo H1).

And indeed you may have noticed that photo H1 and the one where Emelia is posing with Tom look remarkably similar, don't cha think? And that would be because they are (see photo H2& H3). And Wickstead is no different from all the rest (see photo H4 & H5).

PHOTO G9: Wickstead and Tom Thumb Hollander

PHOTO H1: Wickstead & some old sort

PHOTO H2: Hollander fake photos

PHOTO H3: Hollander fake photos

PHOTO H4: PHOTO: Six different photos of Wickstead originating from two
source photos at the most

PHOTO H5: Check out the teeth

PHOTO H6: Olga's children are just a repeat of each other with different coloured hair to fool the public.

PHOTO H7: The two Sweet boys

PHOTO H8: The boys photos are a repeat of their photos from the Carter fake.

Okay, getting back to the fake Carter photo (F4) and Number 5 and Letter 'C 'are supposedly Olga Sweet's children and since she does not exist then it follows that neither do her children and as such, 'C' is just a repeat of '5' (see photo H6).

Moreover, if you look at the two 'brothers in photo H7, you will see that they are just a repeat of themselves from the faked Carter photo (see photo H8).

Same photo sources see, despite the apparent difference in the younger fellows appearance. Yet all that involves is turning the black dots in his eyes and making his hair shorter... Piece of piss really.

As for Number 6 in the Carter photo (alleged Gacy victim, Michael Marino *) and Number 8 (* Thomas Markle the Turd *), well we have* *already seen how alike they are, and with that being the case their likeness to James Sweet (* Letter D *) should come as no surprise to anyone (see photo H9).*

Course, the fact that Marino disappeared in October 1976 when he was 14 years old means that he had around a 35-year head start on James Sweet. Yet that age anomaly crops up time and time again throughout history with these monsters.

However, I am not going to dwell too much on this because I extensively cover the topic in my article " How The West Was Won Part 6 *", which can be found and read for free on my website and I have already shown you earlier on that the Monsters are by and large doppelgangers for someone else.*

And more often than not, they involve criminals. For example John Wilkes Booth who [fake] assassinated President Lincoln and Albert Einstein appear to share the same photo (see photo H10).

Could be a coincidence I suppose... Again.

Wikipedia has this to say about Booth:

John Wilkes Booth (May 10, 1838 – April 26, 1865) was the American actor who assassinated President Abraham Lincoln at Ford's Theatre in Washington, D.C. on April 14, 1865. He was a member of the prominent 19th-century Booth theatrical family from Maryland and a well-known actor in his own right. [1] He was also a Confederate sympathizer, vehement in his denunciation of Lincoln and strongly opposed to the abolition of slavery in the United States. [2]

Booth and a group of co-conspirators originally plotted to kidnap Lincoln but later planned to kill him, Vice President Andrew Johnson, and Secretary of State William H. Seward in a bid to help the Confederacy's cause. [3] Robert E. Lee 's Army of Northern Virginia had surrendered four days earlier, but Booth believed that the American Civil War was not yet over because Confederate General Joseph E. Johnston 's army was still fighting the Union Army.

Only Booth was completely successful in carrying out his part of the plot. He shot Lincoln once in the back of the head, and the

President died the next morning. Seward was severely wounded but recovered, and Vice President Johnson was never attacked.

After the assassination, Booth fled on horseback to southern Maryland and, 12 days later, arrived at a farm in rural northern Virginia where he was tracked down. Booth's companion gave himself up, but Booth refused and was shot by Union soldier Boston Corbett after the barn was set ablaze in which he was hiding. Eight other conspirators were tried and convicted, and four were hanged shortly after...

James has one eye lower than the other - a sure sign of photoshop. Marino's face looks to have been stretched across ways.

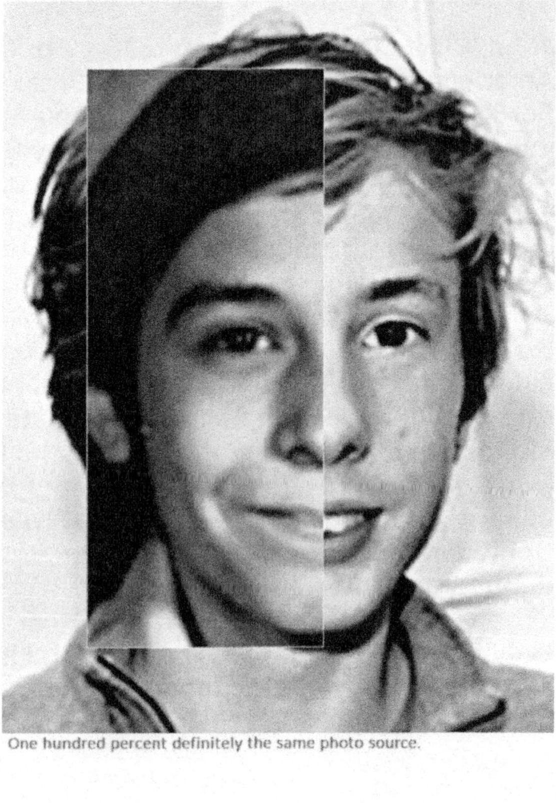

One hundred percent definitely the same photo source.

PHOTO H9: James Sweet & Michael Marino comparison

And when you overlay Booth onto Einstein you find that their heads & faces match perfectly.

Or you can take half of Booth's photo, and half of Uncle Albert's and you don't have to be Einstein to work out that the two halves will join together perfectly

PHOTO H10: John Wilkes Booth and Albert Einstein comparison.

So, Booth was an ACTOR who managed to flee the theatre after shooting Lincoln despite having a broken leg… Hmmm
And on Einstein, the online encyclopedia had this to say:

Albert Einstein (14 March 1879 – 18 April 1955) was a German-born theoretical physicist who developed the theory of relativity, one of the two pillars of modern physics (alongside quantum mechanics). His work is also known for its influence on the philosophy of science. He is best known to the general public for his mass–energy equivalence formula $E = mc^2$, which has been dubbed "the world's most famous equation". He received the 1921 Nobel Prize in Physics "for his services to theoretical physics, and especially for his discovery of the law of the photoelectric effect ", a pivotal step in the development of quantum theory.

Near the beginning of his career, Einstein thought that Newtonian mechanics was no longer enough to reconcile the laws of classical mechanics with the laws of the electromagnetic field. This led him to develop his special theory of relativity during his time at the Swiss Patent Office in Bern (1902–1909), Switzerland. However, he realized that the principle of relativity could also be extended to gravitational fields, and he published a paper on general relativity in 1916 with his theory of gravitation. He continued to deal with problems of statistical mechanics and quantum theory, which led to his explanations of particle theory and the motion of molecules. He also investigated the thermal properties of light which laid the foundation of the photon theory of light. In 1917, he applied the general theory of relativity to model the structure of the universe.

He lived in Switzerland between 1895 and 1914, except for one year in Prague, and he received his academic diploma from the Swiss federal polytechnic school (later the Eidgenössische Technische Hochschule, ETH) in Zürich in 1900. He taught theoretical physics there between 1912 and 1914 before he left for Berlin. He acquired Swiss citizenship in 1901, which he kept for the rest of his life after being stateless for more than five years. In 1905, he was awarded a PhD by the University of Zurich. The same year, he published four groundbreaking papers during his renowned annus mirabilis (miracle year) which brought him to the notice of the academic world at the age of 26...

However, it becomes increasingly hard to make a case for coincidence when you take into account photo I1 of ***Edgar Allen Poe*** *(* born January 19, 1809 and died October 7, 1849 *).*

In 1835, Poe, then 26 did a ' ***Jerry Lee Lewis'*** *by marrying his 13-year-old cousin* ***Virginia Clemm.*** *They were married for eleven years until her early death... So Poe, like most of the Satanic elite was also a paedophile.*

And you can also add Tesla to that mix (see photo I2) of which, like all the rest, none of the photo angles have been changed.

PHOTO I1: Einstein, Booth & Poe comparisons.

PHOTO I2: Poe-Tesla comparison

PHOTO I3: Booth-Teslas comparison

Wikipedia has the following to say about Tesla:

Nikola Tesla (10 July 1856 – 7 January 1943) was a Serbian-American inventor, electrical engineer, mechanical engineer, physicist, and futurist who is best known for his contributions to the design of the modern alternating current (AC) electricity supply system.

Born and raised in the Austrian Empire, Tesla received an advanced education in engineering and physics in the 1870s and gained practical experience in the early 1880s working in telephony and at Continental Edison in the new electric power industry. He emigrated to the United States in 1884, where he would become a naturalized citizen. He worked for a short time at the Edison Machine Works in New York City before he struck out on his own. With the help of partners to finance and market his ideas, Tesla set up laboratories and companies in New York to develop a range of electrical and mechanical devices. His alternating current (AC) induction motor and related polyphase AC patents, licensed by Westinghouse Electric in 1888, earned him a considerable amount of money and became the cornerstone of the polyphase system which that company would eventually market.

Attempting to develop inventions he could patent and market, Tesla conducted a range of experiments with mechanical oscillators/generators, electrical discharge tubes, and early X-ray imaging. He also built a wireless-controlled boat, one of the first ever exhibited. Tesla became well known as an inventor and would demonstrate his achievements to celebrities and wealthy patrons at his lab, and was noted for his showmanship at public lectures.

Throughout the 1890s, Tesla pursued his ideas for wireless lighting and worldwide wireless electric power distribution in his high-voltage, high-frequency power experiments in New York and Colorado Springs. In 1893, he made pronouncements on the possibility of wireless communication with his devices. Tesla tried to put these ideas to practical use in his unfinished Wardenclyffe Tower project, an intercontinental wireless communication and power transmitter, but ran out of funding before he could complete it. [7]

After Wardenclyffe, Tesla went on to try to develop a series of inventions in the 1910s and 1920s with varying degrees of success. Having spent most of his money, he lived in a series of New York hotels, leaving behind unpaid bills.
Tesla died in New York City in January 1943. His work fell into relative obscurity following his death, but in 1960, the General Conference on Weights and Measures named the SI unit of magnetic flux density the tesla in his honor.
There has been a resurgence in popular interest in Tesla since the 1990s...

However, you have to understand that Geometry and facial alignment are also crucial to the workings of the monster-elite. Moreover, ALL of history is a fraud.
*Nevertheless, to understand that fully you again need to refer to my articles: " **How The West Was Won Parts 1-6** ' on my website.*
Now I tell you that because those four famous faces from history are not necessarily just made up personas although I would bet that John Wilkes Booth is.

What it does mean is that their photos have been Satanically manipulated in order that they fit in harmony with each other... Or put another way; they Satanically connect.

Course, if you look at that photo of Tesla that I have used, you may notice that he looks very like Adolf Hitler... Which would be because he is... At least he is in that photo (see photo I4)

PHOTO I4: Hitler and Tesla comparison

PHOTO I5: Jared Polis/ John Key Comparison

Now I can tell you - or bet you if you prefer - that the Tesla & Hitler photos above come from the same source photo... One hundred percent indisputable once you view them together on Zoner Photo-Editor, using varies overlay sections and back-lighting.

Course, Hitler's nose tip has been replaced with a [ridiculous] 'moustache', but there is nothing to stop you investigating the fact that they are one & the same yourselves as I would need to publish a minimum of five different photos to do so and proving it does not warrant the time.

However, as I say, I will bet anyone a minimum £100 that they have the same photo source so if you doubt my claim and you are a lazy fucker with more money than sense, feel free to email me.

So why would Tesla be Hitler - as is Walt Disney (see my articles ' **How The West Was Won** *' on my website)? And my answer to that is: Your guess is as good as mine but what was going on back then is still going on today.*

And by way of example, you need look no further than American politician Jared Polis and former New Zealand Prime Mincer, John Key - an alleged, sexually perverted weirdo.

Jared Schutz Polis (born May 12, 1975) is an American politician, businessman, and philanthropist serving as the U.S. Representative for Colorado's 2nd congressional district since 2009. A Democrat, he is also a former member of the Colorado State Board of Education. He is among the wealthiest members of Congress, with a personal net worth estimated at nearly $400 million.

In June 2017 Polis announced his candidacy for Governor of Colorado in the 2018 election. *Source: Wikipedia*

Sir John Phillip Key (born 9 August 1961) is a New Zealand politician who served as the 38th Prime Minister of New Zealand and Leader of the New Zealand National Party. He was elected leader of the party in November 2006 and appointed Prime Minister in November 2008, resigning from both posts in December 2016.

Born in Auckland before moving to Christchurch when he was a child, Key attended the University of Canterbury and graduated in 1981 with a bachelor of commerce. He began a career in the foreign exchange market in New Zealand before moving overseas to work for Merrill Lynch, in which he became head of global foreign exchange in 1995, a position he would hold for six years. In 1999 he was appointed a member of the Foreign Exchange Committee of the Federal Reserve Bank of New York until leaving in 2001. *Source: Wikipedia*

Surely they have to be clones don't they? Remember that 30 billion to one doppelganger statistic.

Indeed, the Monsters should not be let anywhere near children because the very same excuse that our sick-fuck, psychopath social-workers use to take children from innocent parents i.e a danger of future emotional harm applies exactly to the rich-things.

For instance, let's put the actress Demi Moore under the spotlight.

Chapter 5
Demi Moore & other clones

Demi Moore's story goes that she was born in 1962 although her father - who was a [red flag] airman - supposedly split with Demi's mother before she was born.*
Demi's mother - an alcoholic with a long criminal record, or so the story goes - then married an advertising salesman which meant that the family was constantly on the move... And as such, Demi Moore has no check-able past... That is how easy it is to create a person from thin air.

*There are countless knob-ed celebs whose parents were in the military especially those who were teenagers by the mid 1960's and I will remind you that the 'M' in MI5 & MI6 stands for Military.

So, whilst I can only speculate I would guess that Demi Moore was either born into MK-Ultra captivity or she is a clone.

Project MKUltra, also called the CIA mind control program, is the code name given to a program of experiments on human subjects that were designed and undertaken by the United States Central Intelligence Agency —and which were, at times, illegal. Experiments on humans were intended to identify and develop drugs and procedures to be used in interrogations in order to weaken the
individual and force confessions through mind control. The project was organized through the Office of Scientific Intelligence of the CIA and coordinated with the U.S. Army Biological Warfare Laboratories.

The operation was officially sanctioned in 1953, was reduced in scope in 1964, further curtailed in 1967, and officially halted in 1973. [3] The program engaged in many illegal activities, including the use of U.S. and Canadian citizens as its unwitting test subjects, which led to controversy regarding its legitimacy. MKUltra used numerous methods to manipulate people's mental states and alter brain functions, including the surreptitious administration of drugs
(especially LSD) and other chemicals, hypnosis, sensory deprivation, isolation, verbal and sexual abuse (including the sexual abuse of children), and other forms of torture.

The scope of Project MKUltra was broad with research undertaken at 80 institutions, including colleges and universities, hospitals, prisons, and pharmaceutical companies. The CIA operated through these institutions using front organizations, although sometimes top officials at these institutions were aware of the CIA's involvement.

Project MKUltra was first brought to public attention in 1975 by the Church Committee of the United States Congress and Gerald Ford 's United States President's Commission on CIA activities within the United States.
Investigative efforts were hampered by the fact that CIA Director Richard Helms ordered all MKUltra files to be destroyed in 1973; the Church Committee and Rockefeller Commission investigations relied on the sworn testimony of direct participants and on the relatively small number of documents that survived Helms's destruction order.

In 1977, a Freedom of Information Act request uncovered a cache of 20,000 documents relating to project MKUltra which led to Senate hearings later that year. Some surviving information regarding MKUltra was declassified in July 2001. *Source: Wikipedia*

However, MK Ultra never stopped, it just went further underground. Moreover, our old friend, former US President George H Bush was the Head of the CIA in the 1970's... Just sayin'

Mind you, according to Kevin Hart, everyone who's anyone - including himself - has a clone.
Certainly, if Demi Moore is cloned she came from the same factory as the "Friends" actor, Courtney Cox (see photo J1).

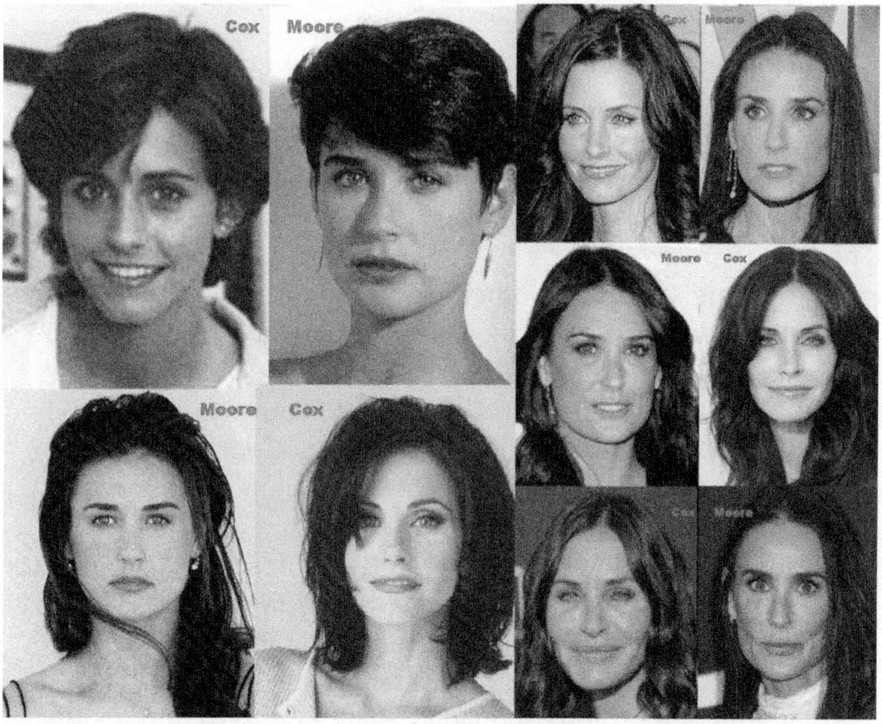

PHOTO J1: Various comparisons of Demi More & Courtney Cox.

Now there is officially 2 years difference between the pair (Cox allegedly being born in 1964 *) and Cox, like Moore has a dubious past.*

Indeed, her story goes that her mother & father (who was a " businessman *" whatever that means), separated when Cox was a child. Her mother -* tellingly *- then went on to Marry "***businessman***", Hunter Copeland - the Uncle of Ian Copeland... At least that is according to Wikipedia.*

And here is where you have to wade through the confusing tentacles of who's who. You see whilst most people of 50 and younger will never have heard of Ian Copeland, many of us will know who Stewart Copeland - the drummer of the band 'Police ' - *is.*

Now Stewart's father/Hunter's brother, was ***Miles Copeland.*** *And according to Wikipedia, Miles Copeland was an American musician, "***businessman***", and most importantly a high ranking CIA officer... Remember Project MK Ultra?*

In fact to quote Wikipedia:

According to Copeland's biographer, there is nothing in Copeland's CIA files to suggest he was ever a "professional musician," but "several relatives and friends have testified to his musical ability.

So he was first and foremost a CIA agent then and Courtney Cox is the [step] 1st cousin of multi-millionaire drummer, Stewart Copeland... Yet to put it that way would have been too easy for Wikipedia.

Now, a lot of you will know that Cox rose to fame in 1984 (apt year *) after being at a Bruce Springsteen concert where she was supposedly chosen at random by the legendary musician, to go up on the stage and dance with with him whilst he sang his big hit "* Dancing In The Dark *". (see photo J2)*

PHOTO J2: Courtney Cox dancing in the dark with Bruce Springsteen

And looking at that photo, Courtney actually appears to have a penis, which would not surprise me and in line with the way that the Monsters like to make mugs of us, would explain her name: Courtney Cox (cocks).

Indeed, many, many of the elite's children and those brought up in the MK Ultra program have been given forced sex changes. However, Cox's rise to fame is just another fairy-tale and as I told you right at the start, fairy-tales do not happen. I mean what would the odds be of Cox - randomly by good fortune & being in the right place at the right time - *finding fame when she is so closely related to Drummer, Stewart Copeland who in 1984 was at the height of his fame... My point being that there are very, very few knob-ed celebs who come from a normal, Joe-Average background.*

Indeed, most come from your Joe 90 type background.
Mind you, they are still using the same formula today as they were in 1984:

The Foo Fighters performed for a crowd of 52,000 at Brisbane 's Suncorp Stadium on Thursday night.
And while fans were thrilled to see the six-piece rock act, there was an unexpected performance that simply stole the show. Mid-way through the night, the band's front man, Dave Grohl, saw fan Joey McLennon holding a placard in the crowd and signalled for him to come up on stage for a jam.

The Foo Fighters fan and 22-year-old amateur guitarist was more than willing to oblige, rocking out for the sold-out stadium with a performance that has now gone viral. Source: *The Daily Mail January 2018*

Yeah, yeah, whatever.

So let's get back to Demi Moore and it is worth noting that she was a doppelganger for Elizabeth Short AKA ' the Black Dahlia *':*

Elizabeth Short (July 29, 1924 – January 14 or 15, 1947), known posthumously as "the Black Dahlia", was an American woman who was found murdered in the Leimert Park neighborhood of Los Angeles, California. Her case became highly publicized due to the graphic nature of the crime, which entailed her corpse having been mutilated and severed at the waist. *Source: Wikipedia*

In fact Short could have been a prototype for Demi's mother what with her cavorting and marrying servicemen (see photo J3).

And Like Demi's mother, Short was also very well known to the police. (see photo J4)

Mind you, I personally think that the story is fake, but Short supposedly ended up like you see in Photos J5.

Indeed, knowing what I do about faces and photos, the fact that you can do what I have done in Photo J6 without changing any angles is highly suspect. In fact the next photo along (photo J7), all but proves the point.

'Marriage' of Slain Girl Told

Beauteous Elizabeth Short, 22, victim of the "werewolf" murder, is shown in this photo with the late Matt Gordon, an army major, who she said was her husband. This picture was found among the contents in the girl's trunk.

PHOTO J3: Newspaper clip about Elizabeth Short.

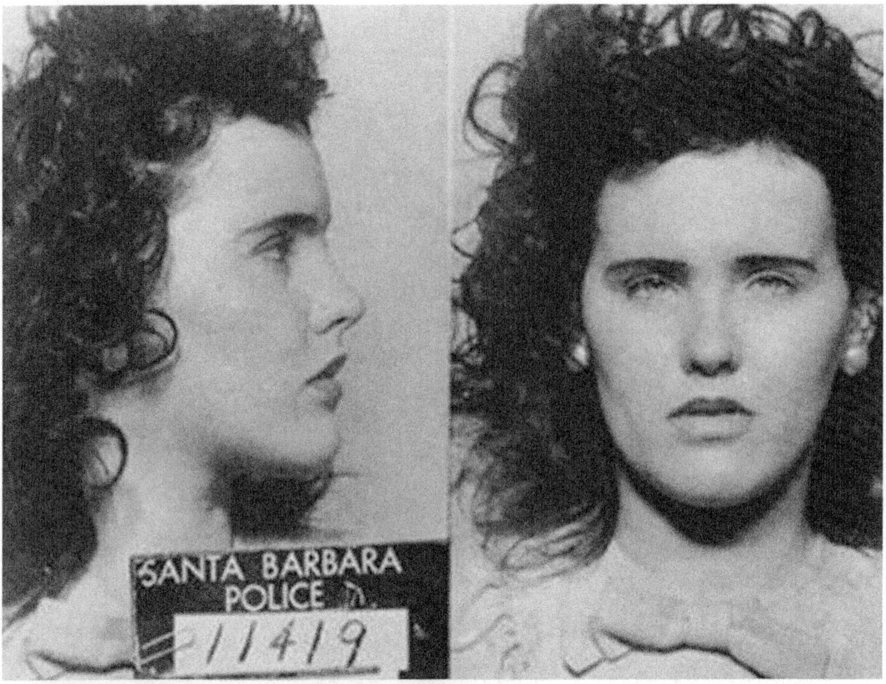

PHOTO J4: Elizabeth Short's mug shot

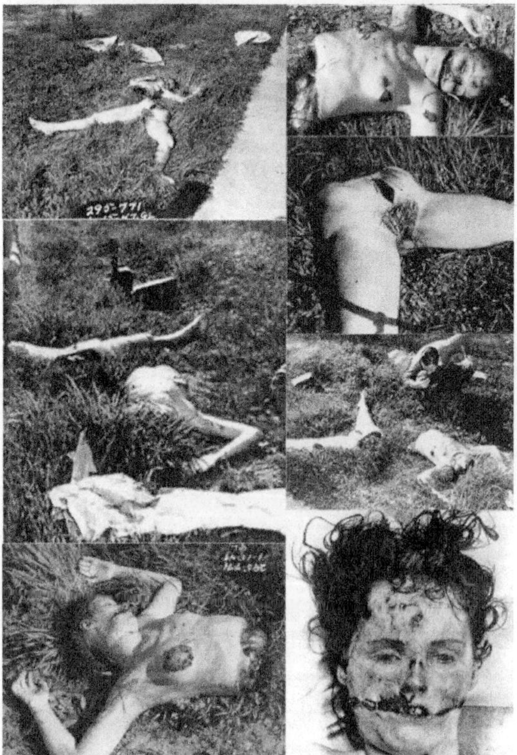
PHOTO J5: Short's crime scene photos

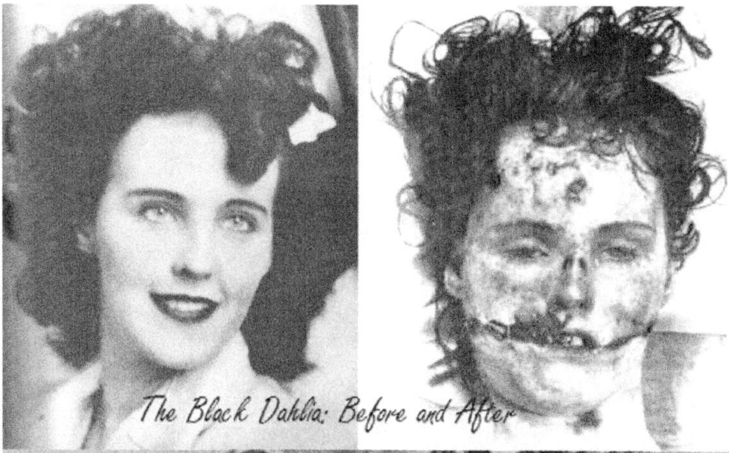

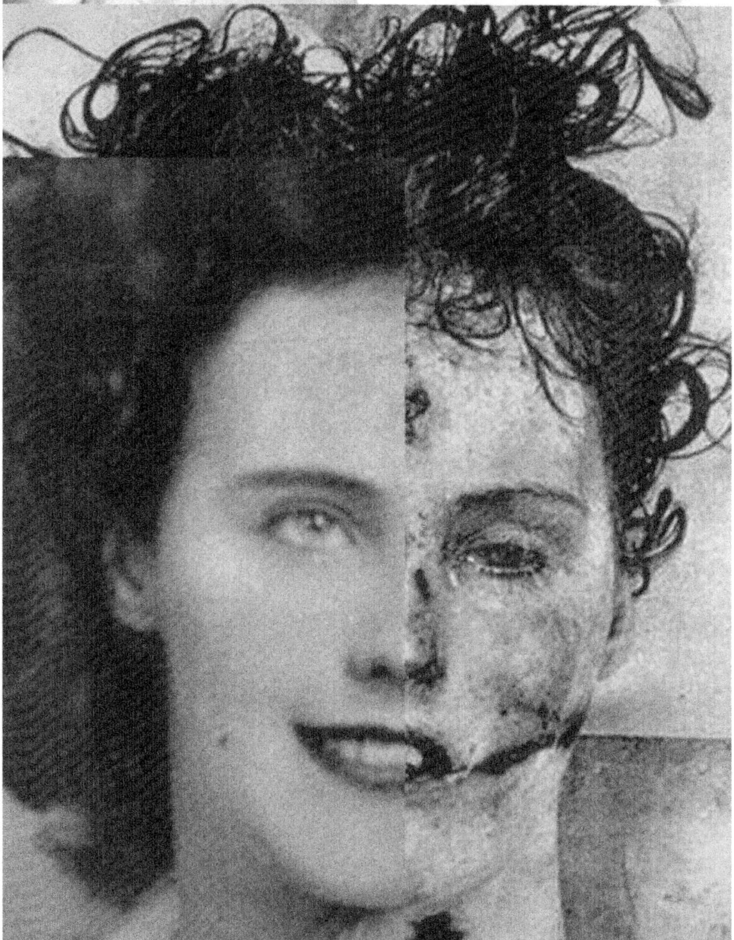

PHOTO J6: Half face comparison of the dead and the living Black Dahlia

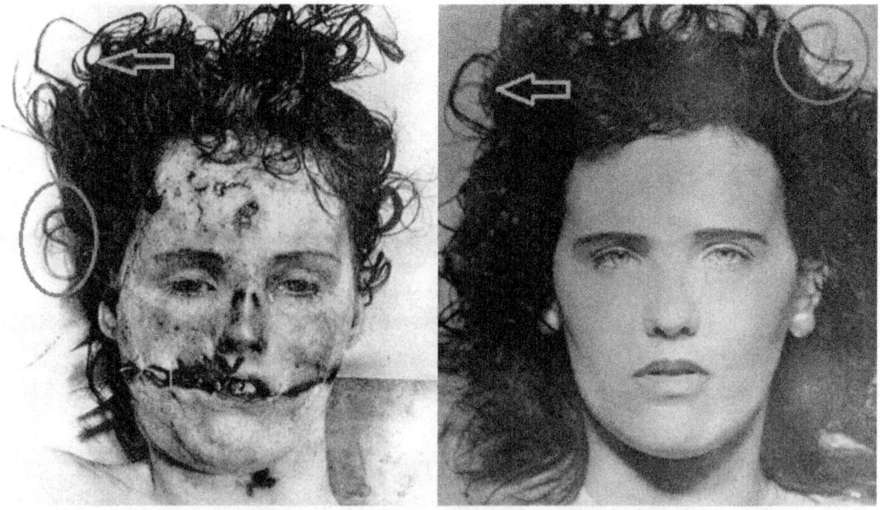

PHOTO J7: Hair anomalies on the living & dead Black Dahlia.

Certainly, the Black Dahlia murder and those connected to Jack the Ripper are at the very least, Satanically connected.

Jack the Ripper is the best-known name for an unidentified serial killer generally believed to have been active in the largely impoverished areas in and around the Whitechapel district of London in 1888. In both the criminal case files and contemporary journalistic accounts, the killer was called the Whitechapel Murderer and Leather Apron.

Attacks ascribed to Jack the Ripper typically involved female prostitutes who lived and worked in the slums of the East End of London whose throats were cut prior to abdominal mutilations.

And there is little doubt that Elizabeth Short is portrayed as having been a prostitute.

The removal of internal organs from at least three of the victims led to proposals that their killer had some anatomical or surgical knowledge. Rumours that the murders were connected intensified in September and October 1888, and letters were received by media outlets and Scotland Yard from a writer or writers purporting to be the murderer. The name "Jack the Ripper" originated in a letter written by someone claiming to be the murderer that was disseminated in the media.

The letter is widely believed to have been a hoax and may have been written by journalists in an attempt to heighten interest in the story and increase their newspapers' circulation.

Just like Journalists today then... Except there are no real Journalists anymore, they are nothing more than copywriters putting their own spin on the script they are given.

The "From Hell" letter received by George Lusk of the Whitechapel Vigilance Committee came with half of a preserved human kidney, purportedly taken from one of the victims. The public came increasingly to believe in a single serial killer known as "Jack the Ripper", mainly because of the extraordinarily brutal nature of the murders, and because of media treatment of the events.

Extensive newspaper coverage bestowed widespread and enduring international notoriety on the Ripper, and the legend solidified. A police investigation into a series of eleven brutal killings in Whitechapel up to 1891 was unable to connect all the killings conclusively to the murders of 1888.

Five victims— Mary Ann Nichols, Annie Chapman, Elizabeth Stride, Catherine Eddowes, and Mary Jane Kelly —are known as the "canonical five" and their murders between 31 August and 9 November 1888 are often considered the most likely to be linked. The murders were never solved, and the legends surrounding them became a combination of genuine historical research, folklore, and pseudohistory. The term "ripperology" was coined to describe the study and analysis of the Ripper cases. There are now over one hundred hypotheses about the Ripper's identity, and the murders have inspired many works of fiction.

And here is the thing; Ripper victim, Elizabeth Stride's name is not that far off the Black Dahlia's name, Elizabeth Short.

Moreover, Elizabeth Strides corpse fits the Black Dahlia's perfectly. (see photo J8). Moreover, all of the photos of the Ripper victims are just manipulated images of each other. For instance, Frances Coles and Alice McKenzie.are the same bird (see photo J9)

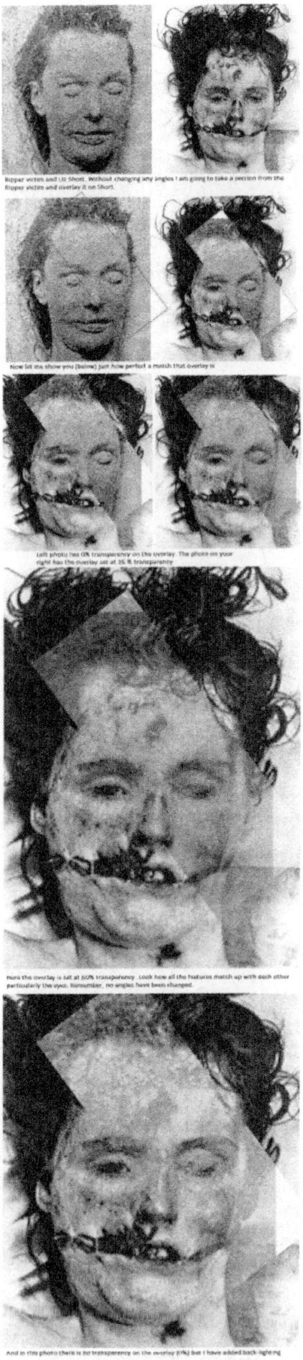

PHOTO J8: Elizabeth Strides corpse fits the Black Dahlia's perfectly.

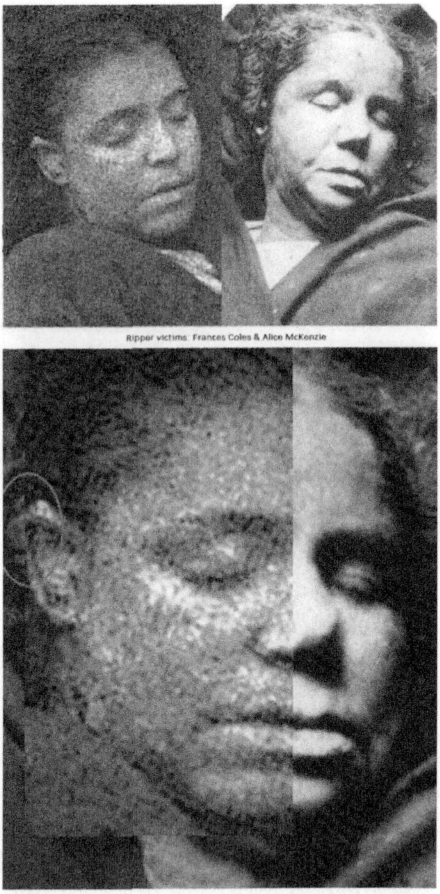

PHOTO J9: Frances Coles and Alice McKenzie comparison

And I can do the same with the rest of the victims too.

So, we now have Jack the Ripper's victims all being duplicated - a practice still used by the Monster Minions today. And since that is another case that I have cracked, tell me again why I am not a millionaire?

But all the same, whether the story be true or fake, Elizabeth Short is most definitely a ringer for Demi Moore.

And what's more is that you really want to pay attention here because I am going to show you how the Monster's Satanic Majik really works. Now in photo K1 are two screenshots that I TOOK, from a video of a youngish Demi Moore giving an interview. However, I wanted one screenshot with her mouth open and another one with her mouth closed so as I could compare her to photos of Courtney Cox.

Therefore, it is important to bear in mind that it was me who decided where to stop the video to take the two random screenshots and indeed that could have been anywhere throughout the course of the video interview.

However, it was shortly after taking the screenshots of Demi that I discovered that she looked exactly like the Black Dahlia and as 'luck' would have it, the photo that I have used of the living Dahlia in photo J6 looked to be the perfect photo to use as a comparison photo with the second screenshot of Demi, giving that interview.

And in fact luckier still, all that I had to do in order to make the comparison was reverse the photo of the living Dahlia... I did not have to change the tilt of their heads or fuck all, which is rare enough in itself if the photos are not from the same source - which of course, with Demi's photo being a screenshot of moving film footage, they could not have possibly been.

Now have a look at the results in photo K2. And whilst that is pretty impressive in itself, it does not convey the true picture of that Satanic Majik - no pun intended.
You see, to get the full impact, you have to add backlighting to Demi's colour photo with the B&W half overlay of the Black Dahlia overlaid on top... And when you do, you get what you see in photo K3

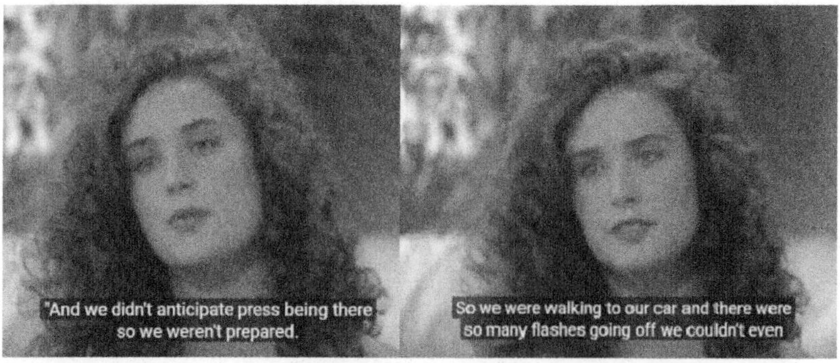

PHOTO K1: Screenshots of Demi taken from a moving video. Or put another way: Taken from where I chose to pause the video.

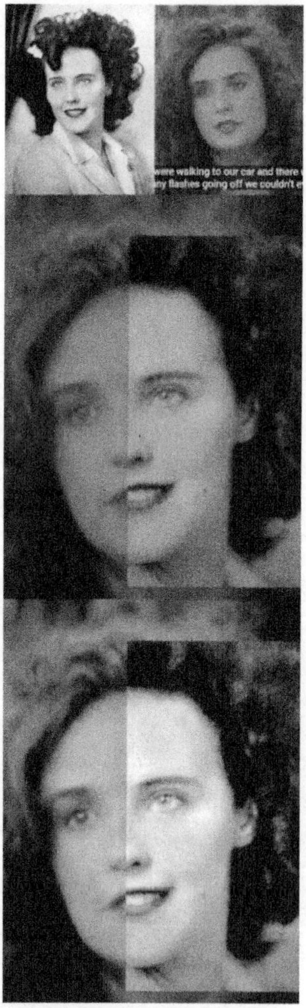

PHOTO K2: Elizabeth Short and Demi Moore comparison

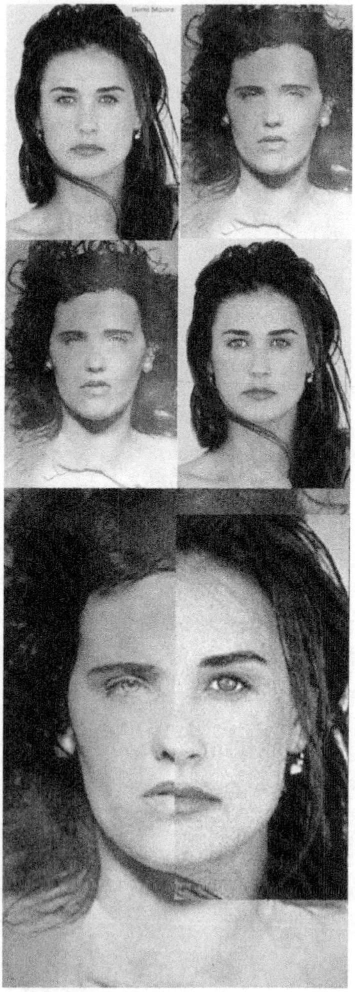

PHOTO K4: Elizabeth Short and Demi Moore comparison

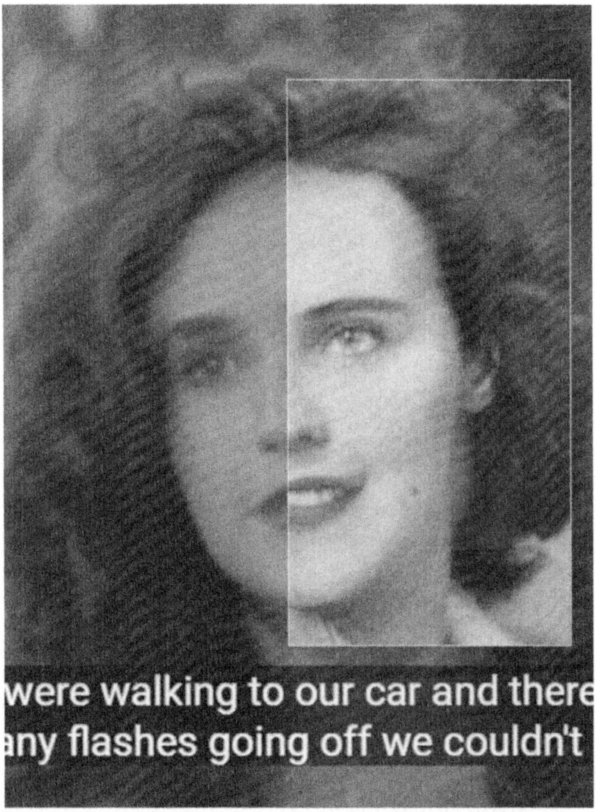

PHOTO K3: Elizabeth Short and Demi Moore comparison with added backlighting.

Now the overlay is set at 0% transparency and as such the transparency that you can see was already in the Dahlia photo itself - meaning that it has been altered.

But that is irrelevant.

What is relevant is that the photo is spot on with Demi's features, right down to where their nostrils sit... And that really is fucking Majik because the odds of all that being coincidence are incalculable.

I mean, I was blown away with the Diana CCTV footage, and if you don't know what I am on about then you will have to read my epic " ***Night Of The Living Dead*** *" found on my website, But the Black Dahlia/Demi Moore overlay sent a very real, very slow, chill down my spine.*

Nevertheless, just to silence the cynics and trolls, photo K4 is another Demi Moore & Liz Short comparison - and once again no angles have been changed.

Yet people still put all this shit down to coincidence and trot out the well worn old mantra: " People do look like each other *"... No they fucking don't, you deluded robots!*
Course, some people do look similar to each other but not so much that you cannot tell them apart.

Nevertheless, Demi then went on to marry, Bruce Willis - who is constantly rumoured to be a deeply perverted homosexual.
Willis is obviously part of the Hollywood elite and no one becomes part of that club without selling their soul:

Walter Bruce Willis (born March 19, 1955) is an American actor, producer, and singer. His career began on the Off-Broadway stage and then in television in the 1980s, most notably as David Addison in Moonlighting (1985–1989). He is known for his role of John McClane in the Die Hard film series (1988–2013).
Willis has appeared in over 60 films, including Death Becomes Her (1992), Pulp Fiction (1994), 12 Monkeys (1995), The Fifth Element (1997), Armageddon (1998), The Sixth Sense (1999), Unbreakable (2000), Sin City (2005), Red (2010), Moonrise Kingdom (2012), The Expendables 2 (2012), and Looper (2012).
Source: Wikipedia

And as a consequence of the union between Bruce & Demi, we are told that they had three children. And those three children, allegedly female: ***Rumer*** *(born August 16, 1988),* ***Scout*** *(born July 20, 1991), and* ***Tallulah*** *(born February 3, 1994) are all fuck-ups.*

However, it would appear that all three were beaten with the ugly stick at birth. Nevertheless, Bruce & Demi split in 1998 and after a series of dalliances Demi Moore took up with, Ashton Kutcher - who was and still is 15-years-younger than her.

So now lets play " Who's The Daddy *". Take a look at Photo K5 and K6.*

PHOTO K5: Bruce, Demi & daughter Tallulah, with Ashton Kutcher inset

PHOTO K6: Ashton Kutcher & Demi Moore with Tallulah & Katie Perry inset

I added Katie Perry because she is surely a clone of Demi.

Nevertheless, who does Tallulah Willis look like; Bruce or Ashton Kutcher?

Course, if Tallulah was the daughter of Kutcher, that would mean the Demi Moore was shagging him when he was 15 years-old... Just sayin'.

Chapter 6
Victims

Now as I have been saying, a large proportion of these carbon copy people are just made up personas and only exist in photos. And obviously photographs are in the main, ageless in that respect.

However, if they are not just photographs or clones then they are Holograms... Yes Holograms are a reality, such as an Elvis hologram dueting with Celine Dion on the X-Factor.

Course, Elvis was a rumoured paedophile and indeed his life story is nothing like we are led to believe.

Moreover, Celine Dion's husband, René Angélil is reported to have been Elvis Presley, and before you dismiss the idea as nonsense let me tell you that I have checked it out and indeed it could very well be true... Although the hard-of-reading-words *should take note that I am not saying the fact is true.*

Celine Dion did of course duet with the Elvis hologram and that could indeed have been another clue given to us by the monster-minions of what is really going on.

Now, in my article " How The West Was Won Part 1 *" I show you how the stories on the Daily Mail's news-feed always connect from top to bottom in order to form a Satanic connection along with the fact that Google-Image does the same.*

And indeed, whilst researching Meghan Markle for this book it became necessary for me to look at photos of [young] Lisa Marie Presley and when I clicked on a [Google image] photo of her sat with her dad (Elvis *) and his bird at the time, Linda Thompson, the "* related images *" also came up with a photo of Celine Dion and her husband Rene.*

Yet I ask you, how can a search for "young Lisa Marie Presley " *overtly connect or relate to Celine Dion and her husband? Course, if these doppelgangers from history are not clones or holograms then the only other explanation is that they are time travelers... And again, I would urge you to keep an open mind on everything because these Monsters do not religiously bow down to Satan if there is fuck all to be had from it.*

After all, the fourth possibility, namely sheer coincidence *just doesn't come into play I'm afraid. Especially so when you take into account the huge number of doppelgangers that there are of current prominent people looking exactly like prominent people from the past... And in particular, those prominent in Nazi Germany and historical Heads of State.*

Nevertheless, to add to the anomalies Thomas the Turd, Michael Marino & James Sweet all look like Ronald Reagan Jr (Number 7 in the faked Carter Photo *) – the son of former US President Ronald Raygun and brother to* ***Patti Davis.*** *(see photos K9 & K10).*

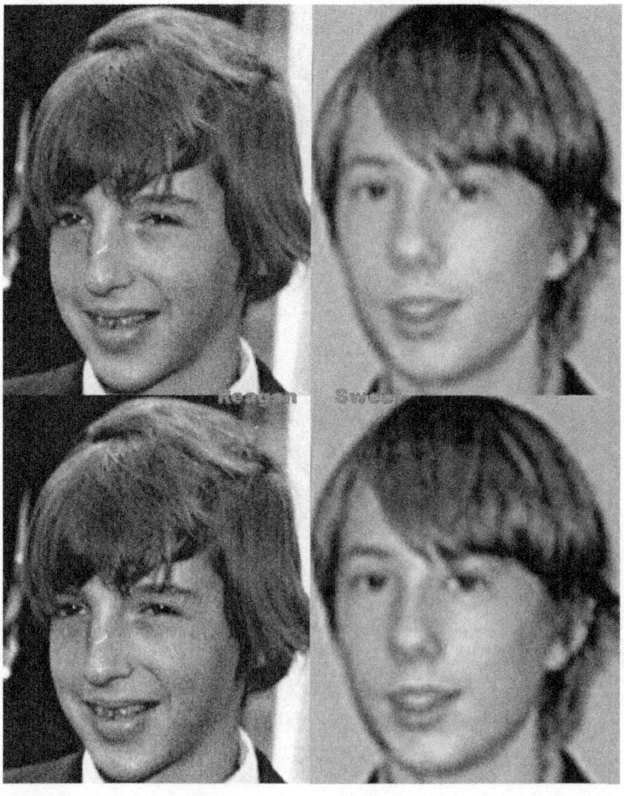

PHOTO K9:
Raygun-Sweet
comparison

PHOTO K10: Raygun-Sweet half faces joined

And that comparison is pretty darn near the mark and at the very least; a Satanic connection... As you are about to find out shortly.

Moreover, you see the orange tint on the top colour photo of James? Well I can tell you that there is a setting on Zoner photo edit (the photo editor that I use *) called "* lighting *" and what it does is turn black & white photos into colour when you overlay them on a coloured background.*

However, in doing so you tend to get orange patches - EXACTLY like Sweet has on his hair - *on the B&W overlaid section.*

Nevertheless, those orange patches are a piece of piss to match in. Therefore, it is blatantly obvious to me that a B&W photo has been used as an overlay on the original colour photo... Just sayin'

Moreover, just like his sister - Patti Davis - Ronald Reagan Jr is also a deeply flawed character and rumoured to be homosexual. Now to my mind, the Social Services would serve a far better purpose investigating these monsters than stealing the children off vulnerable single mothers.

In fact the evidence is overwhelming that the so called elite abuse their children. Nevertheless, despite the rumours about Reagan Jr's sexuality, he married his wife, Doria Palmieri (who was 7 years older than him) when he was only 22 years old.

The wedding came shortly after his father's inauguration but sadly, Doria died in March 2014 of a progressive neuromuscular disease. *They had no children. Course, what is especially interesting about that fact is that Meghan Markle's mother is also called Doria - a far from common name. And as such, we can add that to the already long list of Satanic connections.*

Moreover and rather interesting is the fact that one of John Wayne Gacy's victims had the surname BUNDY and another was only identified by his first name; GREGORY.

And I am sure that I do not need to remind you that the actor GREGORY Harrison played the part of Ted BUNDY… Coincidence? Or another Satanic connection?

Now, it isn't just Ronald Reagan Jr's looks in relation to the trio of Sweet, Marino & Markle the Turd that implicates him in the fraud. You see you now need to look at photo L1: I mean ignore the fact that the image is photoshopped to fuck, it is the barber that you want to be looking at because he looks to me, very much like John Wayne Gacy (see photos L2).

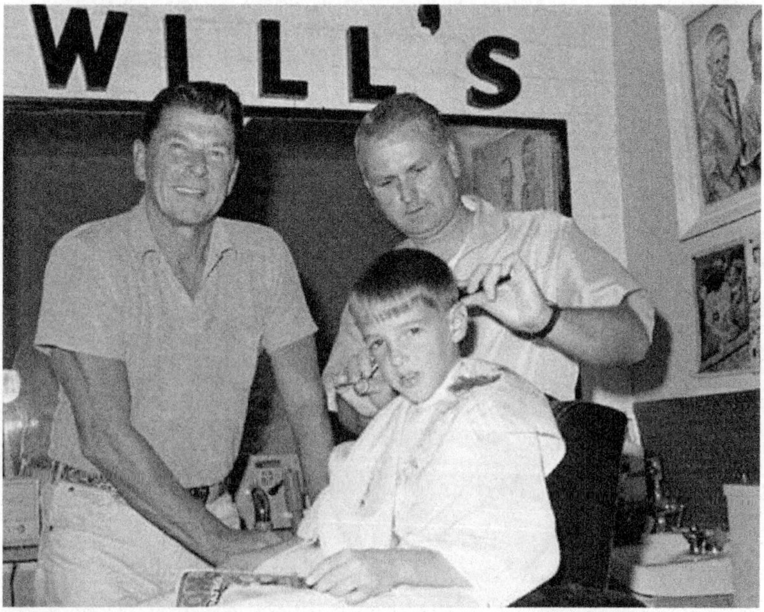

PHOTO L1: Raygun Jr has a haircut as dad Ronnie looks on

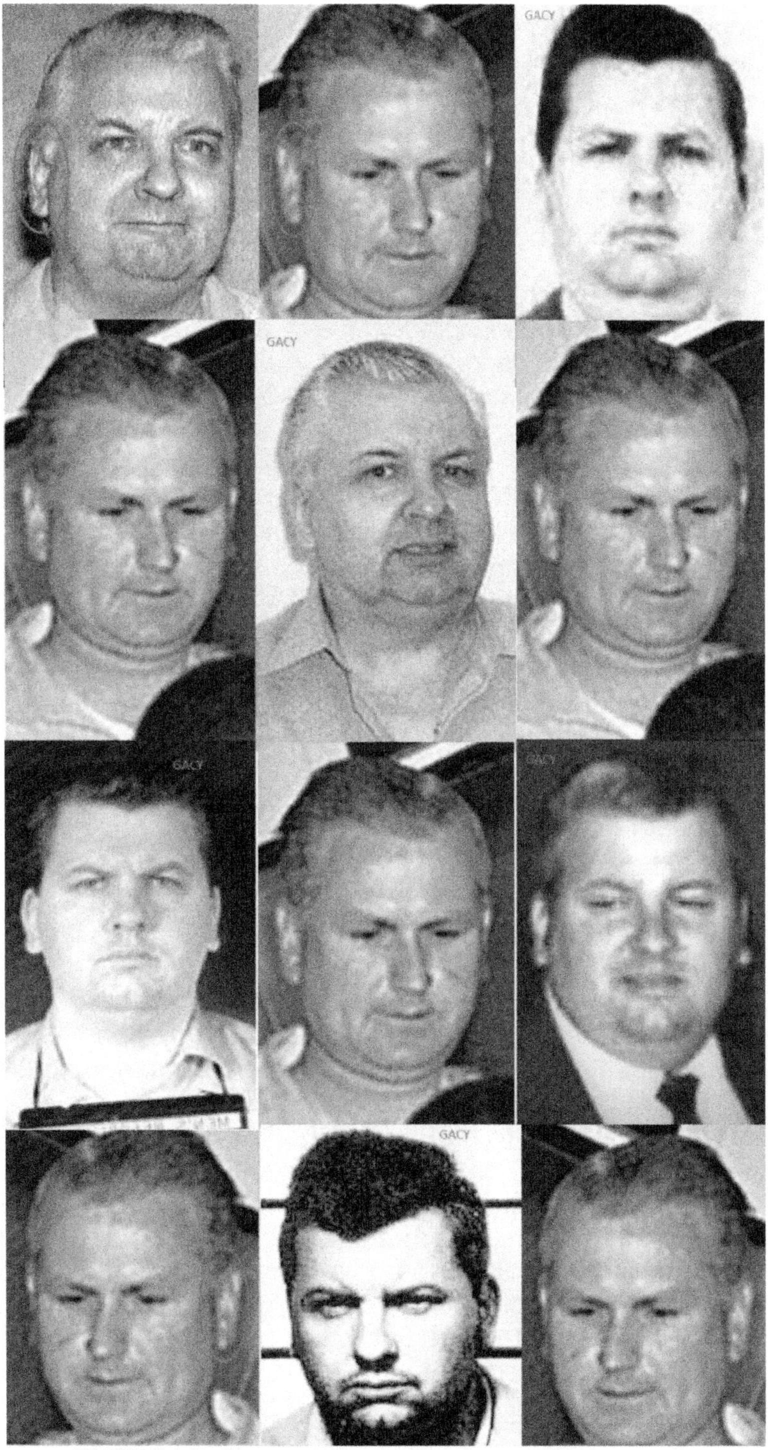

PHOTO L2: Gacy and the barber comparison.

Course, Ronald Reagan Jr was born in 1958 which would mean that the photo – if it was genuine *– would have been taken in the mid to late 1960's... Or in other words, before Gacy started his killing spree.*

However, the image isn't genuine because it is most certainly a photoshop and as such, just another example of the Monsters taking the right fucking piss.

Yet that is not even half of it where Ron-Son-Of-Ron *is concerned... And I am not even talking about the fact that he used to be a professional ballet dancer. You see, Reagan Jr is also the splitting image of Robert Piest – one of John Wayne Gacy's alleged victims. (see photo L3).*

On the afternoon of December 11, 1978, Gacy visited a Des Plaines pharmacy to discuss a potential remodeling deal with the owner of the store, Phil Torf.
While Gacy was within earshot of a 15-year-old part-time employee named Robert Jerome Piest, he mentioned that his firm hired teenage boys at a starting wage of $5 per hour—almost double the pay Piest earned at the pharmacy.

After Gacy left the store, Piest told his mother that "some contractor wants to talk to me about a job". Piest left the store, promising to return shortly. [189] When Piest failed to return, his family filed a missing person report on their son with the Des Plaines police. The owner of the pharmacy named Gacy as the contractor Piest had most likely left the store to talk with about a job.

Gacy denied talking to Piest when Des Plaines police visited his home the following evening, indicating he had seen two youths working at the pharmacy and that he had asked one of them—whom he believed to be Piest—whether any remodeling materials were present in the rear of the store. He was adamant, however, that he had not offered Piest a job and promised to come to the station later that evening to make a statement confirming this, indicating he was unable to do so at that moment as his uncle had just died. At 3:20 a.m., Gacy, covered in mud, arrived at the police station, claiming he had been involved in a car accident.

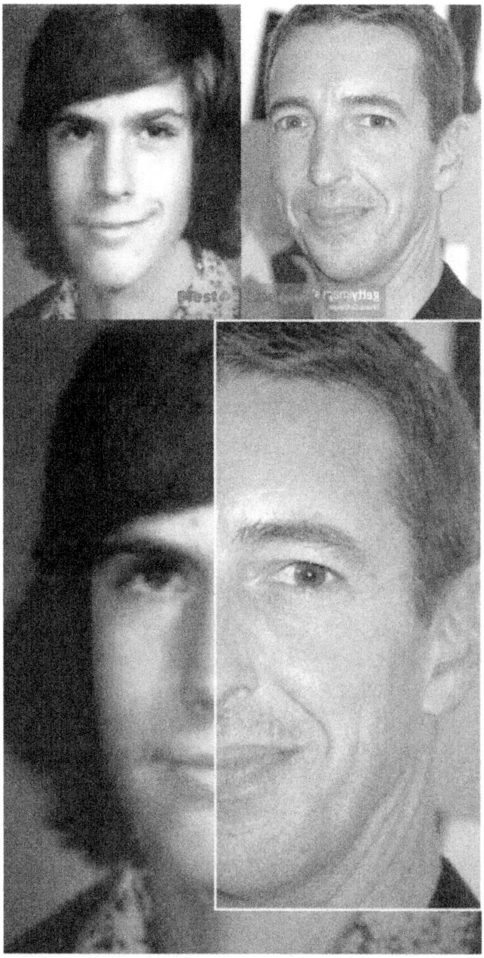

PHOTO L3: Reagan Jr and Robert Piest comparison

PHOTO L4: Reagan Jr and Robert Sweet comparison

Upon returning to the police station later that day, Gacy denied any involvement in the disappearance of Robert Piest and repeated that he had not offered the youth a job. When asked why he had returned to the pharmacy at 8 p.m. on December 11, Gacy claimed he had done so in response to a phone call from Phil Torf informing him he had left his appointment book at the store.

Detectives had already spoken with Torf, who had stated he had placed no such call to Gacy. At the request of detectives, Gacy prepared a written statement that detailed his movements on December 11.

Des Plaines police were convinced Gacy was behind Piest's disappearance and checked Gacy's record, discovering that he had an outstanding battery charge against him in Chicago and had served a prison sentence in Iowa for the sodomy of a 15-year-old boy. *Source: Wikipedia*

Now bizarrely - or not as the case well now may be - Reagan's face photos also join perfectly with those of Robert Sweet.
So, if we are to believe that the comparison between Reagan Jr and Robert Sweet is just a coincidence then we would have to also believe that the two youngest children of the 40th President of the United States (Ron Raygun Jr & Patti Davis *) look exactly the same as the husband & wife (* Robert & Olga Sweet *) seen meeting the 39th President of the United States, Jimmy Carter in the faked photo seen earlier on.... Not to mention everything else that I have shown you.*

And remember, although they fit together like two things that fit together, that could just be for the purposes of a Satanic connection, made possible with a lot of photo manipulation on the part of the monster-minions.

However, as I have already said, half face photos do not just randomly join up so perfectly but if you do not believe me then there is nothing to stop you trying it yourself.

Moreover, I can tell you that Reagan Jr's face also matches with half face photos of both Gregory Harrison and Ted Bundy.

However, it gets better. Here have a gander at this next batch of photos (photo batch L5) starting with President Carter, his wife and his three sons... And take note of those that I have arrowed because it is obvious that the James Sweet that we see in the well referenced faked Carter photo is actually made up from one of Carter's sons.

Also take note that the Carter son in question is to the far right of the photo as is James Sweet.

PHOTO L5: Sweet overlaid on one of Carter's sons

PHOTO L6: A screenshot of the Twitter profile of a fella called Michael Marino

Indeed, it just gets harder and harder for the paedo-trolls to pour scorn on it let alone debunk it... Short-arsed, no-nothing, creepy-crawley, sewer-dwelling, kiddie-fiddlers, that they are.

Mind you, I am glad that I now know what those strange lines behind James Sweet's shoulder are now because it is little things like that which keep me awake at night.
Okay, now, let's once again play " What's-In-A-Name *" by taking a pee at photo L6... Which is actually a screenshot, but let's not split whatsits.*

And of course you will recall that Michael Marino is also the name of the Gacy victim that has cropped up time and again in this report... Although as it happens, it turns out that Moreno isn't a Gacy victim after all:

A mother from Chicago has been waiting nearly 40 years for answers about her son.

Michael Marino is listed as one of the 33 victims of John Wayne Gacy, but his mother, Sherry Marino, always had her doubts.

She had his body exhumed for DNA tests.

The DNA test came back and showed the body is not that of her son Michael, which means there may be another unidentified Gacy victim.

Michael was 14 when he disappeared in October of 1976.

His mom always doubted he was in Gacy's crawlspace, or buried underneath the tombstone bearing her son's name.

However there was a possibility that Marino's body had been switched with another Gacy victim, Kenneth Parker, who was a friend of Michael's.

Attorney Steve Becker wants the Cook County Sheriff's Department to respond. They will enter Michael's name in a missing person's database, and will contact Sheriff Dart to let him know that after 40 years, there may be another unidentified victim of John Wayne Gacy. *Source: wgntv.com*

But that is what they do you see? The Minions are constantly keeping these high-profile serial killers in the news with stories that are mostly very far fetched – for example the story of how the Yorkshire ripper and Soham child-killer Ian Huntley play chess together in prison.

In fact one of those high-profile prisoners that the press like to keep in the news is the recently deceased, Charles Manson, although when you see some of the later-in-life photos of the midget hippie guru looking tanned and hair transplanted it becomes obvious that he hasn't been in prison at all.

Moreover, Manson's face - like Gacy & Bundy's – was used for other people and in Charlie's case one of those people was death-row prisoner Randy Kraft.

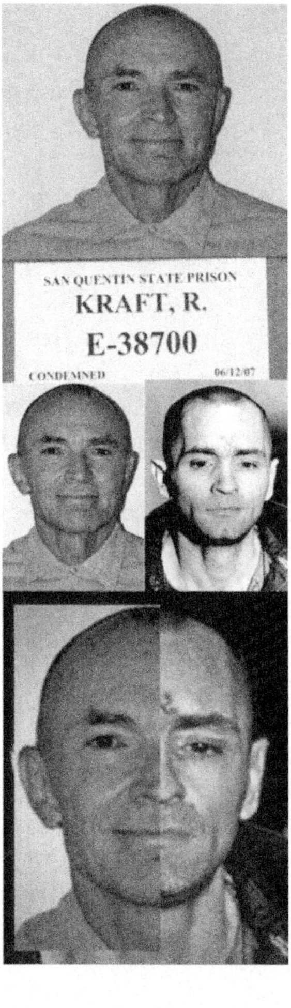

PHOTO L7: Kraft/Manson comparison

For nearly 30 years Randy Kraft has sat on California's death row attempting to clear his name. A gay man given the nicknames "the Scorecard Killer" and "the Freeway Killer," Kraft has been described as one of the "deadliest and most depraved serial killers" in the state's history.

In May 1989 a jury convicted him of killing 16 men over the course of 11 years in southern California and, that November, recommended the death penalty.
Prosecutors had also tied him to the deaths of eight additional men in Oregon and Michigan.

In the summer of 2000, with Kraft's appeals of his verdict in state court exhausted, the California Supreme Court upheld his conviction and death sentence. Kraft then turned to the federal courts to seek a new trial of his case.
He has been mired in the federal appeals system ever since, and on numerous occasions, he has petitioned to have a new federal public defender assigned to represent him.

To this day Kraft has never confessed to the murders he was found guilty of committing. And other than an interview with a Los Angeles Times reporter six months after his arrest in 1983, Kraft has not spoken publicly about his case other than through copious court filings over the years.

During his jury trial, Kraft did not testify on his behalf. After the trial court judge refused to grant his request to testify about only one of the murder charges he was facing, he opted, based on the advice of his attorneys, not to take the stand to defend himself.

Kraft, 71, contacted the The Pride Los Angeles last fall about his desire to publicly discuss his case before he dies.

"This has been bottled up so long," a graying Kraft, dressed in dark blue pants and a light blue shirt, said during an interview in March over a lunch of a microwaved southern fried chicken sandwich and a cheese and bean burrito.
"I am getting older. I am going to die here. And I am frustrated my attorneys aren't saying these things. If I don't say something it will never be said." *Source thepridela.com*

So, either Kraft is another coincidental thirty billion to one doppelganger for Charles Manson, or the story is as fake as Mansons is. Indeed I suggest that you do a bit of research on Manson but stay away from the Mainstream Media to do so. Nevertheless, I really am now straying off topic so let's get back to that fella called Michael Marino. Did you clock who he looks like? (see photo L8)

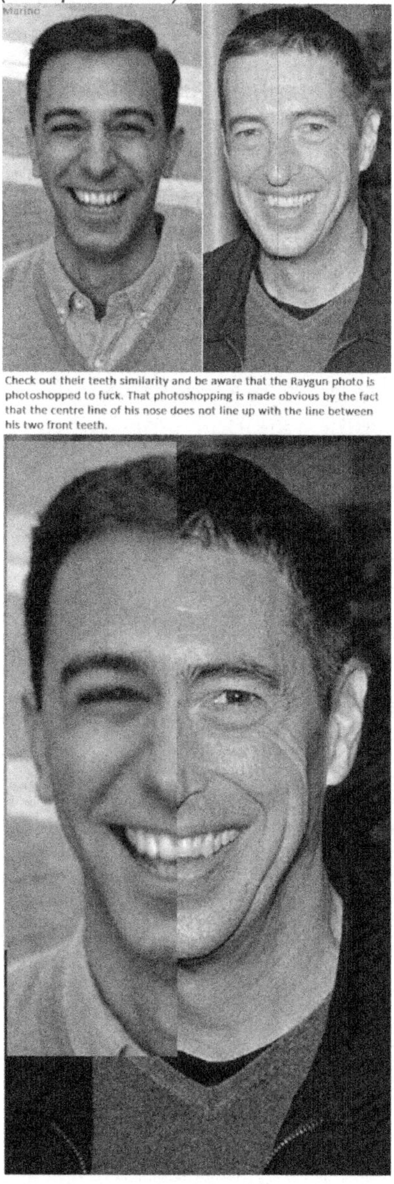

Marino
Check out their teeth similarity and be aware that the Raygun photo is photoshopped to fuck. That photoshopping is made obvious by the fact that the centre line of his nose does not line up with the line between his two front teeth.

PHOTO L8: Michael Moreno/ Ronald Reagan Jr comparison

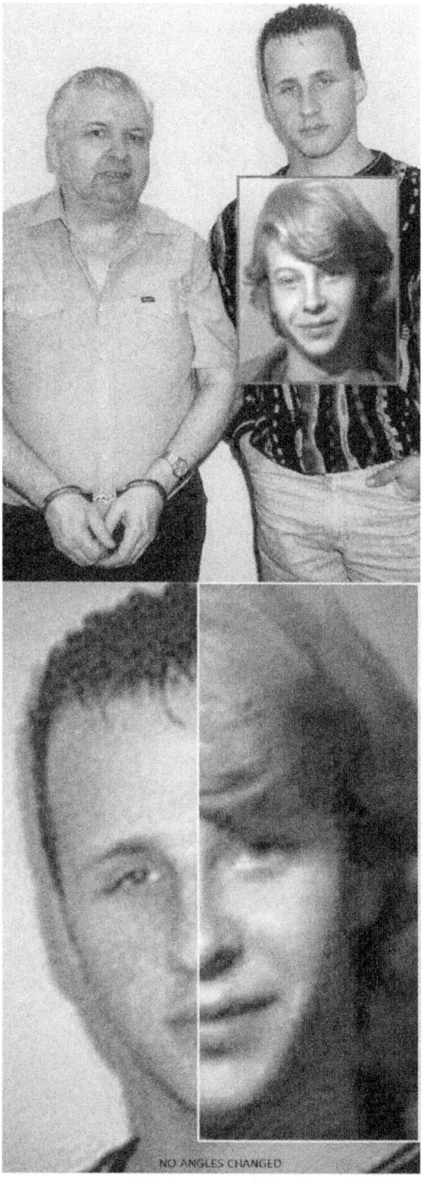

PHOTO L9: Gacy gets visited by his dead victim Darrell Sampson

And as I pointed out earlier; like all serial killers that get an overkill of articles in the press (because they are all fake *), their victims are a mix & match of each other as well as photoshops of famous people all presented in photos taken in Techni-Shite Deluxe...*
And Bundy's & Gacy's are no exception.

I mean some of Gacy's victims even went to visit him on death row after he had already killed them, for fucks sake. (see Photo L9)

That victim was called Darrell Sampson and according to Wikipedia:

The majority of Gacy's murders were committed between 1976 and 1978, which he later referred to as his "cruising years" now that he had his house to himself. One month after his divorce was finalized, Gacy abducted and murdered an 18-year-old youth named Darrell Sampson. Sampson was last seen alive in Chicago on April 6, 1976.

Five weeks later, on the afternoon of May 14, a 15-year-old named Randall Reffett disappeared while walking home from Senn High School ; the youth was gagged with a cloth, causing him to die of asphyxiation. Hours after Reffett had been abducted, a 14-year-old named Samuel Stapleton vanished as he walked to his home from his sister's apartment.

Sampson was found buried beneath Gacy's dining room floor. Godzik was buried in the crawl space. *Source: Wikipedia*

Or so the official version goes. And as for the victims being repeated? Well take a look at photo M1.

PHOTO M1: Greg Godzik/Robert Piest comparison... Proof that the murder 'victims' are repeated

PHOTO M2: Greg Godzik/ Greg Harrison comparison.

*And of course you can cross-reference the victims because Gacy victim, **GREG** Godzik is the Ted Bundy actor **GREG** Harrison. (see photo M2).*

The following information about Greg Godzik is taken from Wikipedia:

In December 1976, another PDM employee, 17-year-old Gregory Godzik, disappeared: he was last seen by his girlfriend outside her house having driven her home following a date.

Godzik had worked for PDM for only three weeks before he disappeared. In the time he had worked for Gacy, he had

informed his family Gacy had had him "dig trenches for some kind of (drain) tiles" in his crawl space.

Godzik's car was later found abandoned in Niles. His parents and older sister, Eugenia, contacted Gacy about Greg's disappearance. Gacy claimed to the family that Greg had run away from home, having indicated to Gacy before his disappearance that he wished to do so.

Gacy also claimed to have received a recorded answering machine message from Godzik shortly after the youth had disappeared. When asked if he could play back the message to Godzik's parents, Gacy stated that he had erased it.

Moreover, when you look at Ted Bundy's victims you quickly realise that they are constructs in the same way that Gacy's victims are.

For example if you look at Bundy's victim, Lynda Healy you quickly realise that she is Ronald Raygun's daughter, Patti Davis. (see photo M3)

Indeed, it is also worth mentioning that Healy is also the original surname of Kate McCann… Mother to Madeleine McCann and as such, another example of Satanic connecting.

PHOTO M4: Gacy and his Attorney

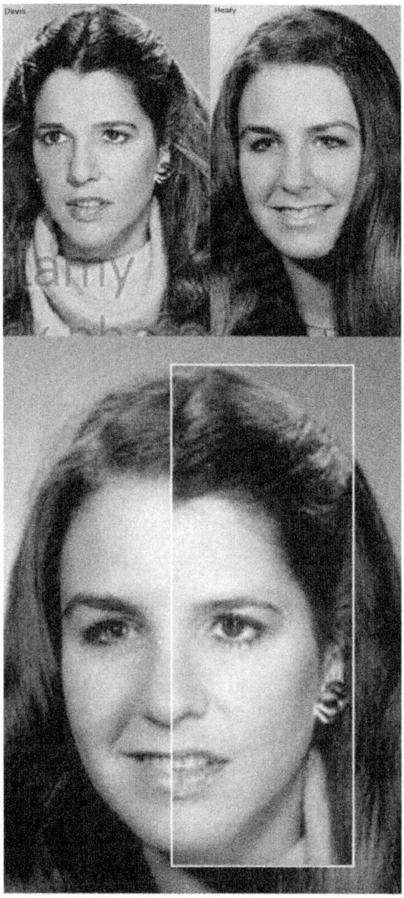

PHOTO M3: Davis/ Healy comparison

And while I'm at it, we will just have a very quick peep at another Gacy photo. (see photo M4)

Now the bird with Gacy is supposedly one of his Attorney's, named Karen Conti... And it would seem that Conti is just about everyone.Including Linda Thompson.

Chapter 7
Linda Thompson & friends

Now if you have been paying attention, you will know that Linda Thompson was mentioned in the last chapter in connection to the young Lisa Marie Presley. And rightly so since Thompson plays a major part in the [fake] story of Elvis Presley's life.

Linda Diane Thompson (born May 23, 1950) is an American songwriter/lyricist, former actress and beauty pageant winner. Thompson was born and raised in Memphis, Tennessee, the daughter of Margie (née White) and Sanford Abel Thompson. Her older brother, Sam, was one of Elvis Presley 's bodyguards.

In 1977, Thompson became a regular on the television series Hee Haw. She later had small one-episode roles in such television series as CHiPs, Starsky & Hutch, Vega$, Fantasy Island, The Fall Guy and Beverly Hills, 90210.

She began her career as a lyricist with the Kenny Rogers single "Our Perfect Song" from his album The Heart of the Matter (1985). Thompson collaborated with composer Richard Marx on Josh Groban 's first hit record, " To Where You Are ", with composer Steve Dorff on the Celine Dion hit " Miracle ", with Andreas Carlsson for " Drowning " by the Backstreet Boys, and composer David Foster on several compositions, including "No Explanation" for the film Pretty Woman (1990), and " I Have Nothing " for the film The Bodyguard (1992), for which they were nominated both for the Academy Award for Best Song in 1993 and the Grammy Award for Best Song Written Specifically for a Motion Picture or for Television in 1994, and " Grown-Up Christmas List ".

In 1999, Linda Thompson, Clint Eastwood and Carole Bayer Sager wrote " Why Should I Care " for the film True Crime. In

2001, she wrote " Drowning " for the American boyband Backstreet Boys. In 2011, Thompson, Foster and Jackie Evancho collaborated on the title track for Evancho's album Dream With Me.

On July 6, 1972, Thompson attended a private movie screening hosted by Elvis Presley at the Memphian Theater in Memphis. She and Elvis hit it off and subsequently dated for 4½ years before breaking up around Christmas 1976.
They broke up because, like Elvis' ex-wife Priscilla, she wanted a "normal" life which was not possible with Elvis. However, they broke up on good terms and remained good friends until Elvis' death. *Source: Wikipedia*

Now that reference to Thompson's collaboration on the Celine Dion hit record, "Miracle" is massively important for reasons that will become clear shortly. You also need to bear in mind the connection that we have already read about between Elvis and Celine Dion in Chapter 6.

However, before I elaborate further, you need to look at the comparison picture (photo M5) of Linda Thompson and John Wayne Gacy's attorney, Karen Conti.

PHOTO M5: Karen Conti/ Linda Thompson comparison

PHOTO M6: Thompson & Elvis

Fuck me, Elvis is looking well in that photo isn't he?

Mind you, according to some researchers, that is actually Elvis's twin brother Jesse Aron who supposedly died at birth. It is therefore important that you read the article by Miles Mathis on my website entitled: ***Elvis Aron Presley – Intelligence Project***

But here's a thing; Thompson is loosely related to the Satanic Kardashians, having married Bruce Jenner in 1981 - long before Bruce pretended to be a Transylvanian... Or whatever it is that he is mincing about as these days.

The marriage between Bruce Jenner and Linda Thompson produced two children, Brandon & Brody Jenner - both boys, thus making them half-brothers to Kendall & Kylie Jenner and step-brothers of Kim Kardashian and her Satanic siblings.

Linda Thompson then went on to marry Peter Foster, who is step-father to the top-models Gigi & Bella Hadid - a pair of wrong-uns without a doubt… But my, my, isn't she a busy woman?

Mind you, on the other hand what would you expect. These things are filth... Scum. And in fact Gigi and Bella's alleged old-man, Mohamed Hadid was recently accused of rape.

Bella and Gigi Hadid 's architect father has strenuously denied allegations made by another model that he date raped her.

Mohamed Hadid, 69, said that he met Miranda Vee, 23, several years ago because she claimed to be a fan, but at no point did anything untoward happen.

'When we met it was not a date and not once did I touch her,' he was quoted by Tmz.com as saying.

Mr Hadid, who has been engaged to Shiva Safai since 2014, described Vee's claims - made in a lengthy Instagram post - as 'totally untrue'.

He said that if she wanted to make such serious accusations against him she should have gone to the police instead of using social media.

Mr Hadid said that he is in contact with his attorney with the intention of filing a defamation suit against Vee. *Source: The Daily Mail, February 2018.*

Now, interestingly enough Brucella Jenner also has another daughter named, Cassandra - his 2nd oldest child - *who calls herself Casey. Casey was the product of Brucella's first marriage to Chrystie Crownover... Crownover? Interesting surname, don't cha think?.*

However, Brucella's 1st wife, Chrystie Crownover looks exactly like his 2nd wife Linda Thompson. (see photo M7 on the next page)

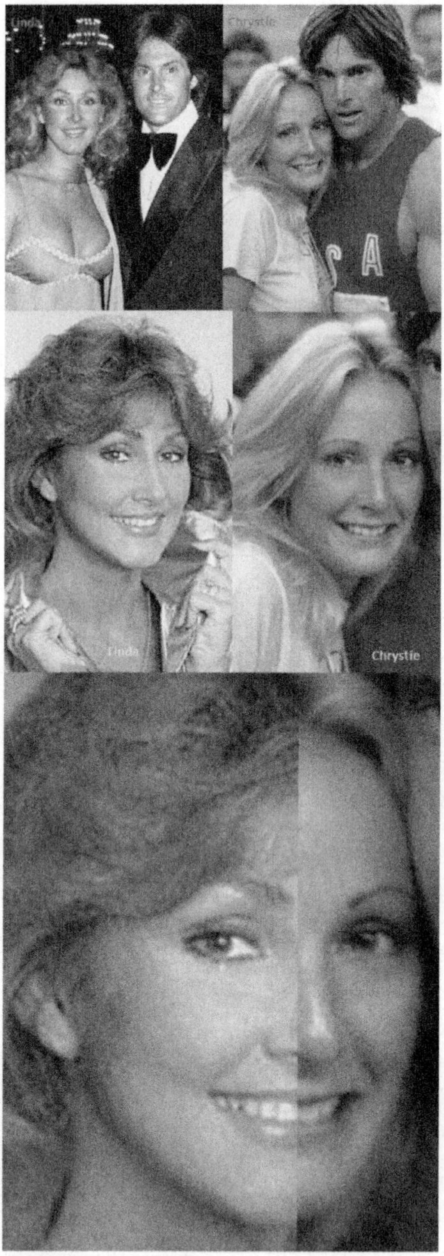

PHOTO M7: Linda Thompson/ Chrystie Crownover comparison

PHOTO M8: Chrystie Crownover/Karen Conti comparison

And in turn, Crownover looks exactly like John Wayne Gacy's lawyer, Karen Conti (see photo M8)... Big yawn, it all gets too easy.

Predictably Crownover is an actress and is help pushing the myth that ex-husband Brucella is now a woman:

Bruce Jenner 's first wife Chrystie Crownover admitted that she was absolutely "shocked" when her ex-husband revealed to her in their first year of marriage that he was struggling with gender identity issues.

(At this time, Bruce Jenner has not chosen to publicly identify as a woman and so E! News will continue to refer to him as Bruce and use male pronouns, until he indicates otherwise.)

Jenner and Crownover were married from 1972 to 1981, but he confided in her early on. Although she was very surprised, she kept his secret because she knew that it took a lot of respect and trust to confess something like that. "I can't remember the exact words because it was such a shock to me, but he opened up his heart and confessed, and he had to share this deep, dark secret," she told Good Morning America's George Stephanopoulos Monday.
"He told me he wanted to be a woman, and understandably, I didn't know what to say," she added. *Source Eon News*

Okay, now it may appear that I am drifting off topic again but trust me; all of this is important because you have to be able to understand the elaborate network of far reaching tentacles built on deceit involved, that have allowed Meghan Markle to be created. So getting back to Cassandra/Casey 'Jenner'; and her and her husband made Brucella a Grandmapa for the 3rd time in October 2016:

However, you will never guess what Cassandra's surname is? You see she actually uses her married name which in itself is a rarity for the monsteress's, although that could be to do with the fact that she is married to MICHAEL MARINO... Now how the fuck is that for a big shit-pie coincidence?

The following is taken from In Touch and was published on October 21st 2016:

Congratulations are in order for Caitlyn Jenner's daughter Cassandra Marino! The 36-year-old — who is also known as Casey Jenner — and her husband, Mike Marino, welcomed their third baby together, and it's a boy.

Casey confirmed her son's arrival on her private Instagram account.

"He made it! One day before his due date and on Mike's dad's birthday," she wrote. "I am elated and exhausted but a super happy non-pregnant mama."

According to Us Weekly, they named the child Luke.
Casey and Mike are also parents to two daughters, Isabella and Francesca. It was first revealed in April that they were expecting a new addition. We are so happy for them!

Crawl arse bastards! Nevertheless, that marriage too is fake and the name Michael Marino was doubtlessly allocated to Casey's 'husband' as a Satanic connection.

You see, hubby Michael Marino is really just Brody Jenner - Cassandra Marino's half brother - playing the role. (see photo M9) They really could make it up... As they do on a daily basis. And unsurprisingly the pair (Michael/Brody *) look very much like Tom March – the Son of Mary Berry. (see photo M10)*

PHOTO M9: Brody Jenner/Michael Marino comparison

PHOTO M10: Marino/March comparison

Now you will notice that the ears are different in that Marino/March comparison but as I say, the Monster-Minions more often than not alter the ears of an actor playing real life roles to avoid detection since every person's ears are unique to themselves.

Yet even the hair matches in on the photo despite March being balder than Marino, which suggests to me that both photos originated from the same source.

However, before we go any further we need to bring Kim Kardashian into the mix… Kim Kardashian obviously being Brucella Jenner's step daughter and Casey Marino's step sister.

So what follows is Kim's official bio according to Wikipedia:

Kimberly Kardashian West (born October 21, 1980) is an American reality television personality and socialite. Kardashian first gained media attention as a friend and stylist of Paris Hilton, but received wider notice after a 2003 sex tape with her former boyfriend Ray J was leaked in 2007.

Later that year, she and her family began to appear in the E! reality television series Keeping Up with the Kardashians. Its success soon led to the creation of spin-offs including Kourtney and Kim Take New York and Kourtney and Khloé Take Miami. Kardashian's personal life soon became subject to widespread media attention.

In recent years, Kardashian has grown an influential online and social media presence, including tens of millions of followers on Twitter and Instagram. She has released a variety of products tied to her name, including the successful 2014 mobile game Kim Kardashian: Hollywood, a variety of clothing and products, and the 2015 photo book Selfish.

Her relationship with rapper Kanye West has also received significant media coverage; the couple married in 2014 and they have three children together.

Time magazine included Kardashian on their list of 2015's 100 most influential people, while Vogue described her in 2016 as a "pop culture phenomenon."

Critics and admirers have described her as exemplifying the notion of being famous for being famous. She was reported to be the highest-paid reality television personality of 2015, with her total earnings exceeding US$53 million...

And Kim - like Patti Davis-Raygun - also did a nude photoshoot for Playboy.

"So what", you say?

To which I would answer that the two photoshoots are linked. (see photo N1) And of course I am not saying that Patti Raygun is Kim Karcrashion, but that naked photoshoot was certainly no accident... And neither was that duet between the hologram Elvis and Celine Dion that I mentioned earlier. (see photo N2)

PHOTO N1: Davis/Kardashian Playboy shoot comparison

PHOTO N2: Celine Dion & Elvis the hologram Presley duet

You see, there is much more to the Canadian singer, Céline Marie Claudette Dion than first meets the eye. However, her official story is that she was born in Charlemagne, Quebec on the 30 March 1968 making her 50 years old.

French speaking Dion first came to prominence in the 1980s after winning both the 1982 Yamaha World Popular Song Festival and the 1988 Eurovision Song Contest where for some reason or other she represented Switzerland.

However, following the release of a series of albums recorded in French she signed a recording contract with Epic Records in the United States who released her debut album, **Unison** - recorded in English.

During the 1990s, with the help of her future husband Rene Angélil - the man some researchers believe to be Elvis Presley - she achieved worldwide fame with a series of international number-one hits, including "The Power of Love", "Think Twice", "Because You Loved Me", "It's All Coming Back to Me Now ", "My Heart Will Go On", and "I'm Your Angel".

Now interestingly enough, Elvis was reportedly a paedophile and it is a matter of record that Angélil signed Dion when she was just 12 years-old.

Course, whether or not their relationship was a sexual one at that stage is a much debated topic of conversation.

Nevertheless, in 1999 at the height of her success, Dion decided to take a break from recording in order to " start a family and spend time with her husband ", who had by then been diagnosed with cancer.

Dion eventually made her come-back in 2002 after agreeing to appear on a nightly basis in the show **"A New Day"**, at the Colosseum, Caesars Palace, on the Las Vegas Strip in Paradise, Nevada - doing so up until 2007.

In 2011, Dion once again signed a contract until 2019 to reprise her role in the show making her the highest paid resident performer ever, reputedly earning $500,000 per show. She performed her record breaking 1000th show on 8 October 2016.

Indeed,.Dion remains the best-selling Canadian artist of all time with record sales of over 220 million copies worldwide.

And guess what? Celine Dion is the double of Elvis' ex-bird, Linda Thompson – mother to the two Jenner boys, Brody & Brogan. (see photos N3 & N4)

PHOTO N3: Dion/Thompson comparison

PHOTO N4: And again with no angles changed

Chapter 8
Calling Elvis

Course, Celine Dion is far too young to be Thompson - Thompson being 18 years Dion's senior - but nonetheless she ties in with the conspiracy theory about Dion's husband, the probable paedophile, Rene Angelil and the known paedophile Elvis.

The following is taken from Wikipedia:

René Angélil, (January 16, 1942 – January 14, 2016) was a Canadian musical producer, talent manager and singer. He was the manager (1981–2014) and husband (1994–2016; his death) of singer Celine Dion.

So, straight away we learn that Rene was a singer - like Elvis. Elvis was born in January 1935 making a 7 year discrepancy in their ages... Which in the world of showbiz is fuck all.

Angélil was born in Montreal, Québec, Canada, of a father of Syrian descent and a Canadian mother of Lebanese origin. His father, Joseph Angélil, was born in Montreal to parents from Damascus, Syria, and his mother, Alice Sara, was born in Montreal to Lebanese parents. Both of his parents were members of the Melkite Greek Catholic Church. Angélil studied at College Saint-Viateur (high school), in Outremont and at College André-Grasset (post secondary), in Montreal.

In 1966, Angélil married his first wife, Denyse Duquette.

And that wedding took place two years before Celine Dion was even born... Meaning that Angélil is twenty six years older than her.

Course, that is fuck all until you take into account that Rene became her manager when he was 38 and Dion was just 12 years old... How long after that before they started a relationship is - as I already said - a matter of speculation.

They had a son, Patrick (born 1968), and divorced in 1972. In 1974, he married singer, Anne Renée — the couple had two children, Jean-Pierre (born 1974) and Anne-Marie Angélil (born 1977), they divorced in 1988.

Angélil, a well-known former singer-turned-manager, was sent a tape of then 12-year-old singer, Céline Dion, and invited her to audition in Quebec.

Now that last sentence could indeed be clever wording - in particular the part that states: "a well-known former singer-turned-manager".

I mean, as we have already seen, the Monster's like to give us a clue as to what they are up to. Moreover, whilst not wishing to blow my own trumpet - because it kills my back, trying to do so - I pride myself on having extensive knowledge of music dating between 1960 and 1990. Yet I have never heard of Rene Angelil in his capacity of a singer.

Therefore, could the " well known former singer *" refer to Angelil's time as Elvis? Just a thought - carry on Wikipedia:*

He began managing her career, taking the teen and her mother on tour in Canada, Japan and Europe. He mortgaged his house to finance her first album in 1981. Angélil and Dion began a personal relationship in 1988 when she was 20 years old and he was 46. They married on December 17, 1994, in a lavish wedding ceremony at Montreal's Notre-Dame Basilica, which was broadcast live on Canadian television.

Remember, this is the official bio, and not necessarily the truth. I mean Wikipedia are highly unlikely to state that Angélil and Dion began a personal relationship in 1982 now, are they?

The couple had difficulty conceiving, resorting to in vitro fertilization. Their efforts were extensively publicized. Their son, René-Charles Angélil was born on January 25, 2001. Dion suffered a miscarriage in 2009, then gave birth to twin boys on October 23, 2010. The boys were named Eddy after Eddy Marnay, who produced Dion's first five albums, and Nelson Angélil after former South African president, Nelson Mandela

And of course, that last sentence sounds like total bollox to me. Nevertheless, I am not going to go to deeply into whether or not Elvis is Angelil because I am not altogether convinced that he is myself let alone trying to convince you lot. However, I am more than convinced that they are Satanically connected. Moreover, in defiance of the thirty billion to one odds, they do have exactly the same face... And ears. (see photo N5)

PHOTO N5: Elvis/Angelil comparison

PHOTO N6: Elvis & his 14-year-old-bird and Rene & his 12 year old protoge.

Course, there are other comparisons in their lives such as Elvis shacking up with 14-year-old Priscilla and Rene shacking up with the 12-year-old Celine Dion. (see photo N6).

Mind you, that photo of Elvis and Priscilla is very photoshopped for some reason. I mean just look at Elvis' left eye, along with Priscilla's ear shadow. And then there is Elvis' hand particularly the area between his finger and thumb. Now why would they do that if everything was above board?

Moreover, therein is an example of how far the Monsters are ahead of us since such alterations to photographs wouldn't have been dreamed possible back then.

Nevertheless, it looks almost as if Elvis and Celine Dion had the same mother (see photo N7).
The researcher, Miles Mathis had the following to say about Gladys Presley and her son, Elvis:

We are told that Gladys' great-grandmother may have been a Cherokee, but that is misdirection. The truth is, Gladys' great-grandmother was Jewish.

Gladys herself was Jewish, though she apparently did not practice due to disapproval by her husband. However, Elvis knew she was Jewish and considered himself to be Jewish as well (knowing the descent was matrilineal).
There is a Star of David on Gladys' original tombstone, though it has been replaced.

Elvis was a life member of the Jewish Community Center in Memphis. He always wore a Chai pendant.
Chai means "life" in Hebrew, and indicates the lowest emanation of God.

Growing up, Elvis had been head of the Memphis Mafia, a group of boys known for their swagger. Other members included George Klein*, Marty Lacker, Larry Geller and Alan Fortas — all Jewish...

Elvis was chosen from the cradle, first because he was a prominent local Jew, and second because he was a twin. It helped later that he became good looking and an expressive performer. Some are chosen, very few succeed like this.

As a teen, Elvis worked summers and weekends as an usher at Loew's State Theater. Of course this was a string of theaters owned by Marcus Loew, a billionaire Jewish tycoon. He also formed MGM, Metro-Goldwyn-Mayer.

Loew was a business partner with Adolph Zukor, another Jewish tycoon who founded Paramount Pictures. Note the name Adolph, which you wouldn't think belonged to a Jew.

We are told that at age 18, Elvis suddenly walked into Sun Records and asked to record. It doesn't work that way. Sun Records wasn't open to the public in late 1953.

Phillips had opened Memphis Recording Service almost four years earlier, and by late 1953 he was working with dozens of name acts. You didn't just walk in off the street and pay for studio time in the hopes you would be discovered.
This story is told to make you think Elvis chose Sun Records, rather than the reverse.

As we have seen, Elvis had been groomed from an early age, from the time he was in Tupelo up to this moment in Memphis.
And he didn't just accidentally run into Sam Phillips, owner of Sun Records.
The bio and genealogy of Samuel Cornelius Phillips has been scrubbed.
According to mainstream sources, his father and mother are not known, much less older relatives.
This is a red flag. *Source: Elvis Aron Presley - Intelligence project published December 2015.*

In fact the more you look at Presley's life the more unreal it becomes. I mean for a start he wasn't drafted into the army until he was 23-years-old.
Furthermore, he looked far too much like the actor, Rock Hudson when he was young for my liking (see photos N8 & N9)

PHOTO N7: Dion/Gladys comparison

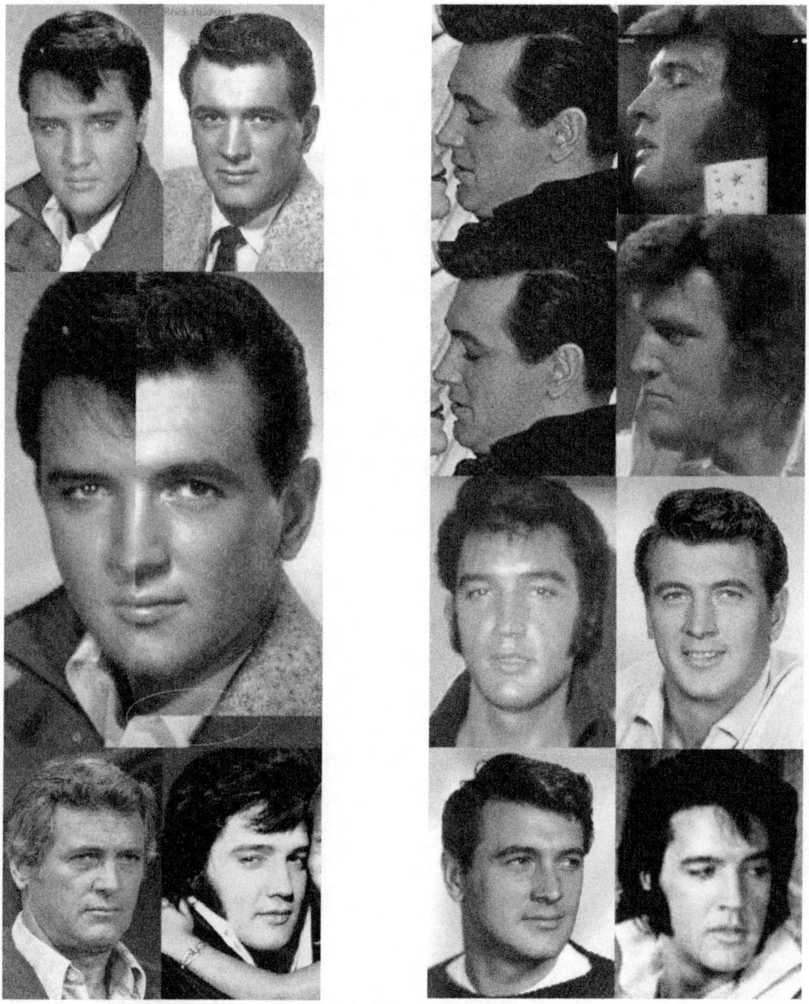

PHOTO N8 & N9: Elvis/Rock Hudson comparison

Rock Hudson supposedly died of AIDS sparking a classic joke at the time:

Fella 1: That AIDS epidemic is getting serious isn't it?

Fella 2: Yes it has reached Rocks bottom.

Not that you would be able to retell it nowadays of course.

Rock Hudson had been born as Roy Harold Scherer, Jr on; November 17, 1925 and later died of AIDS on October 2, 1985 - he was gay.although he tried his best to hide the fact.

And once again, according to Wikipedia:

Hudson was generally known for his turns as a leading man during the 1950s and 1960s. Viewed as a prominent "heartthrob" of the Hollywood Golden Age, he achieved stardom with roles in films such as Magnificent Obsession (1954), All That Heaven Allows (1955) and Giant (1956), and found continued success with a string of romantic comedies co-starring Doris Day in Pillow Talk (1959), Lover Come Back (1961) and Send Me No Flowers (1964).

After appearing in films including Seconds (1966), Tobruk (1967) and Ice Station Zebra (1968) during the late 1960s, Hudson began a second career in television through the 1970s and 1980s, starring in the popular mystery series McMillan & Wife and the primetime ABC soap opera Dynasty.

Following Hudson's death, Marc Christian, Hudson's former lover, sued his estate on grounds of "intentional infliction of emotional distress".

Christian claimed Hudson continued having sex with him until February 1985, more than eight months after Hudson knew that he had HIV. Although he repeatedly tested negative for HIV, Christian claimed that he suffered from "severe emotional distress" after learning from a newscast that Hudson had died of AIDS. Christian also sued Hudson's personal secretary, Mark Miller, for $10 million because Miller allegedly lied to him about Hudson's illness. In 1989, a jury awarded Christian $21.75 million in damages, later reduced to $5.5 million. Christian later defended Hudson's reputation in not telling him he was infected: "You can't dismiss a man's whole life with a single act. This thing about AIDS was totally out of character for him", he stated in an interview.

And indeed, just like the Google image search for Lisa Marie Presley came up with a 'related' photo of Celine Dion and her old man, a Google Image search for Rock Hudson brought up a 'related' photo of Elvis. (see photo N10)

You therefore once again have to ask yourself; why on earth a Google-Image search for Rock Hudson would bring up a link to Elvis?

Nevertheless, the reason that I was searching for Lisa Marie Presley in the first place was because of the photo N11 of Ronnie Raygun and a very young Patti Davis:

PHOTO N10: Google Image search Result for Rock Hudson

PHOTO N11: Young Patti Davis with her 'mom & dad' and Lisa Marie Presley (inset)

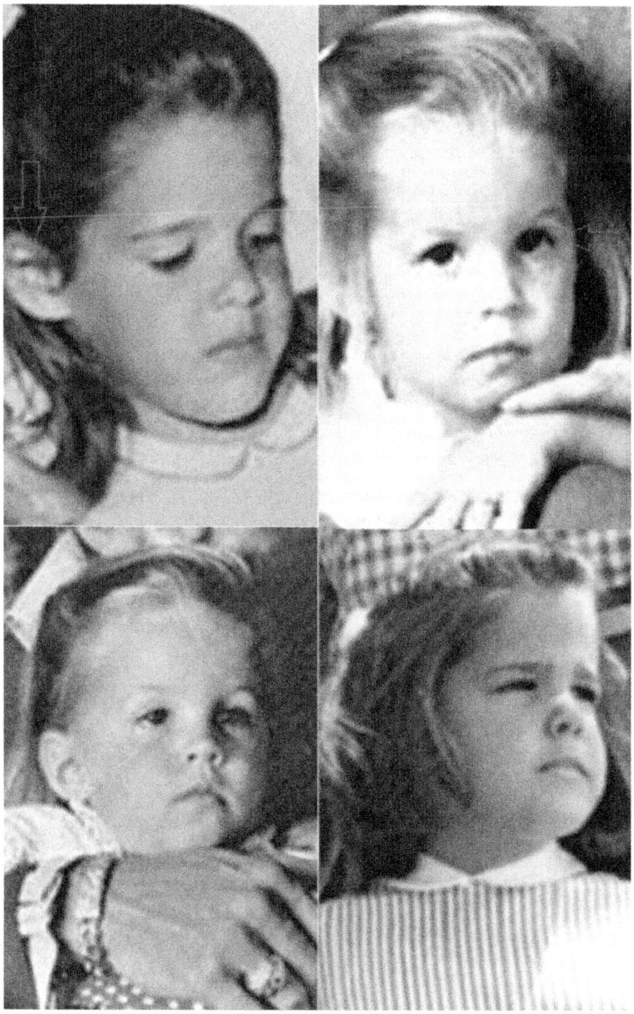

Photo N12

And although – as you can see in Photo N12 – the search turned out to be a dead end, both girls do have abnormally high foreheads..

Least I am fairly sure that they are not each other.

Moreover, the last bird that Elvis was with before he died was called Ginger Alden.

Ginger Alden is an American model and actress who was born in Memphis, Tennessee on November the 13th 1956.

However, she is best known as the woman who found Elvis dead on the toilet, in his bathroom at 'Graceland' on the 16th of

August 1977… She was 20 years old at the time while Elvis was 42.

Alden had supposedly met Elvis as a child in 1961, through her father who was Elvis' superior officer during his army years… The story goes that her family was invited to join Elvis at the fairgrounds, to spend an evening of fun.

Alden was then supposedly reintroduced to Elvis as a 20 year old along with her older sister Terry (then Miss Tennessee) and their other sister Rosemary at one of his concerts held on January 26, 1977.

The story then has it that on that Presley asked Alden to marry him in front of the audience during a concert broadcast by CBS in the same year.

On the day that Elvis died, he and Ginger had allegedly played racquetball although given the physical shape that Elvis was in, I find that a bit far fetched… Either that or it was a very short game.

Later that night the singer went for a crap and took a book to read, indicating to Alden that it could be a long jobby. Ginger fell asleep and didn't wake up until the early afternoon only to discover her 'boyfriend's lifeless body laying on the bathroom floor.
After his death, Alden began her career in film, radio and televisio n where she apparently worked on numerous commercials, appeared in various television shows and in 1986 became part of the cast of the soap opera, "Capitol" alongside Teri Hatcher.

In 1991 she married Ronald Leyser with whom she had a son named Hunter.

And whatsmore, Alden bears an uncanny likeness to Priscilla Presley (see Photo O1)

Yet there is still more. You see the other woman associated with having an affair with Elvis was the actress, Ann Margaret. And she too looks very much like Priscilla. (see photo O2 & O3)

PHOTO O1: Ginger/Priscilla comparison

PHOTO O2: Priscilla/Ann Margaret comparison

PHOTO O3: Priscilla/Ann Margaret comparison. Both photos were taken in 1963.

And Ann Margaret's bio reads thus:

Ann-Margret Olsson (born April 28, 1941), known professionally simply as Ann-Margret, is a Swedish-American actress, singer, and dancer.

As an actress, Ann-Margret is best known for her roles in Bye Bye Birdie (1963), Viva Las Vegas (1964), The Cincinnati Kid (1965), Carnal Knowledge (1971), Tommy (1975), Grumpy Old Men (1993), and Grumpier Old Men (1995).
She has won five Golden Globe Awards and been nominated for two Academy Awards, two Grammy Awards, a Screen Actors Guild Award, and six Emmy Awards.

In 2010, Ann-Margret won her first Emmy Award for her guest appearance on Law & Order: Special Victims Unit. Her singing and acting careers span five decades, starting in 1961; initially,

she was billed as a female version of Elvis Presley. She has a sultry vibrant contralto voice She had a minor hit in 1961 and a charting album in 1964, and scored a disco hit in 1979. In 2001, she recorded a critically acclaimed gospel album, and an album of Christmas songs from 2004 continues to be available.

Ann-Margret has no children, but she was stepmother to the three children of husband Roger Smith, an actor who later became her manager. She and Smith were married from May 8, 1967 until his death on June 4, 2017. Prior to this, she was romantically linked to Elvis Presley during the filming of Viva Las Vegas. *Source: Wikipedia*

Chapter 9
Wacko Jacko

Now as most of you will know, Elvis Presley's daughter, Lisa Marie was famously married to the nonce, Michael Jackson who had three supposedly surrogate kids of his own – the youngest of who was named 'Blanket'.

And indeed those old enough to remember will recall that Michael Jackson caused outrage by dangling Blanket over his hotel balcony in front of 1000's of his fans.

The following is from a BBC news report published in November 2002:

Pop star Michael Jackson has admitted he made a "terrible mistake" in dangling a baby over a hotel balcony as he greeted fans.

The singer caused a stir when he appeared with the child in Berlin, precariously clutching the infant out of a third floor window, and draping a towel over the baby's head.

"I got caught up in the excitement of the moment. I would never intentionally endanger the lives of my children," Jackson said. A spokesman for the Bambi entertainment award ceremony, where Jackson is due to receive a lifetime achievement award, told the Associated Press news agency the child was Jackson's youngest son Prince Michael II.

Rumours have been circulating for months that Jackson has a third child, but it is not yet known if the child is adopted or is his biological offspring.

About 200 fans gathered at the entrance to the Adlon Hotel, near the Brandenburg Gate, as Jackson's motorcade arrived on Tuesday.

The reclusive performer had to fight his way through the crowd of fans to get into the hotel, in a scrum that injured one person.

Later, Jackson dangled the baby out of the window of his room on the third floor, holding it with one arm under its shoulders. Many onlookers feared the 44-year-old would drop the infant, although he brought the child back inside safely.
As fans cheered for him to appear again, Jackson came out onto the balcony covering his face and threw a towel down to the crowd below.

Jackson has two other children, Prince Michael, who is five, and Paris, who is four.

The singer's close friend, psychic Uri Geller, condemned Jackson's actions but did not believe he was capable of harming a child.

"I just would not put any child over a railing at such a height," he said.
"I think it was a silly thing to do. He probably did it because he was overwhelmed emotionally by the fans."
But he had suspected the baby was a fake, saying he was "too protective" of his children to do something like this.

But as I say, in my opinion these so-called elites should never, ever be allowed anywhere near children.
However, I wouldn't be surprised if Blanket is actually a girl. (see Photo O4) Indeed that would fit right in with the Monster's transgender agenda. Nevertheless, the point of bringing Blanket up is the fact that he looks so much like Celine Dion's son, Rene Charles. (see photo O5)

PHOTO O4: A very feminine looking Blanket

PHOTO O5: Celine Dion with her son Charles-Rene. Inset: Blanket Jackson.

Rene Charles - who has now followed his 'mother' into the music business - won widespread praise in the press for the eulogy he gave at his 'father's' funeral:

Although he is only days shy of his 15th birthday, Celine Dion's son has captured the heart of Canada with a moving eulogy to his late father.

René Charles Angelil has been a pillar of strength for his devastated mother, and during his father René Angélil's funeral on Friday at the Notre-Dame Basilica he was even for a moment able to make her smile.

'Fifteen years is not a long time to get to know your father,' René Charles began.

'He had a busy life but we were getting to know each other through golf, poker, smoked meat and other wonderful food.'

It was at the line about smoked meat that René Charles got a few knowing laughs from the audience, a smile spreading to both his and his mother's faces.

'Bonding more and more as time went by,' he continued.

'You left me now with enough good memories of you to share with my younger brothers. As they grow older without you being around, I'll make sure to pass on what I've learned from you.'

'You are a tough act to follow, but with your help everything is going to be fine.'

'Dad, I promise you there that we are all going to live up to your standards.'

René Charles' eulogy was widely praised on Twitter, where he was lauded for his poise and strength. *Source: The Daily Mail*

Mind you, as the boy got older he also became a ringer for Wacko-Jacko's first born, Prince Jackson (see photo O6).

Prince Jackson was was born on February 13, 1997 to a surrogate mother named Debbie Rowe. It is still not known for sure whether or not Wacko-Jacko was the sperm donor, but can you imagine how quick the Social Services would have removed the children from some ordinary Joe with the same form as the singer?

Indeed, the likes of Jackson and Elton John is exactly where Social Workers should be looking.

However, I am drifting off topic again, so to get back on track I will tell you that Celine Dion is also a ringer for John Wayne Gacy's lawyer, Karen Conti. (see photo O7)

Furthermore, Dion is identical to the singer, Louise Dorsey - the daughter of Englebert Humperdink.

Engelbert Humperdinck (born Arnold George Dorsey; 2 May 1936) is an English pop singer. Humperdinck has been described as "one of the finest middle-of-the-road balladeers around."

His singles "Release Me" and "The Last Waltz" both topped the UK music charts in 1967, and sold more than a million copies each.In North America, he also had chart successes with "After the Lovin' " (1976) and "This Moment in Time" (1979). He has sold more than 150 million records worldwide.

In 1964, Humperdinck married Patricia Healey.

PHOTO O6: *Prince Michael Jackson compared to Charles Rene Angelil*

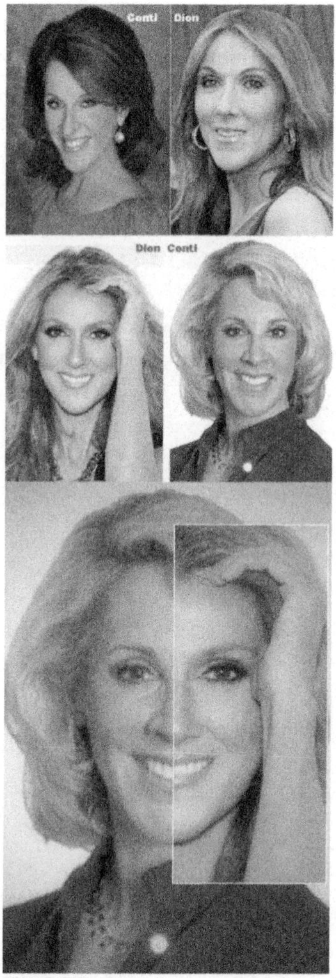

PHOTO O7: *Celine Dion compared to Karen Conti*

And there we see that surname Healy again, which I am sure I do not need to remind you is the maiden name of Kate McCann - the mother of missing child, Madeleine McCann.

They have four children. Through the years, Humperdinck has maintained a strong family life, even as the family alternated between homes in Britain and in southern California. He is a practising Roman Catholic. His daughter-in-law, Jo Dorsey, has remarked that the singer "tries to visit a cathedral in every town or city he tours globally." In 2017, the singer revealed that his wife has been suffering from Alzheimer's disease for 10 years.

Humperdinck retains firm ties with Leicestershire, where he spent much of his youth, and is a keen fan of Leicester City.

BINGO!

The McCann's also live in Leicestershire... Allegedly... Those coincidences just keep right on coming.

In August 2005, he auctioned one of his Harley-Davidson motorbikes on eBay to raise money for the County Air Ambulance in Leicestershire. In 2006, the University of Leicester awarded Humperdinck with an Honorary Doctorate of Music.

On 25 February 2009, Leicester City Council announced that Humperdinck would be given the Honorary Freedom of Leicester alongside author Sue Townsend and former professional footballer Alan Birchenall.

In 2010, Humperdinck was one of the first nine people to be honoured with a plaque on the Leicester Walk of Fame. *Source: Wikipedia*

Hmmm! Moreover, Englebert's father was a career MILITARY man, as was the father of his Manager, Gordon Mills - who also managed Tom Jones.

And I can guarantee that there will be much scandal surfacing on old Tom when he kicks the bucket... But I will keep what I know about him to myself for now.

Still, as far a Louise Dorsey goes, the proof is in the Pudding so take a look at the next photo batch.

Louise - as far as I can ascertain - was born in 1965; three years before Celine Dion.
Indeed there is very little information available about Louise - not even a Wikipedia page - which is very strange given her thirst for stardom.

Indeed Louise Sarah Dorsey is the only legitimate daughter of the world famous singer. However, like most of of these knob ed celeb's - all of whom have extremely loose morals - Englebert also has an illegitimate daughter, Jennifer who was born in 1977.

PHOTO O8: Louise Dorsey & Englebert Humperdink

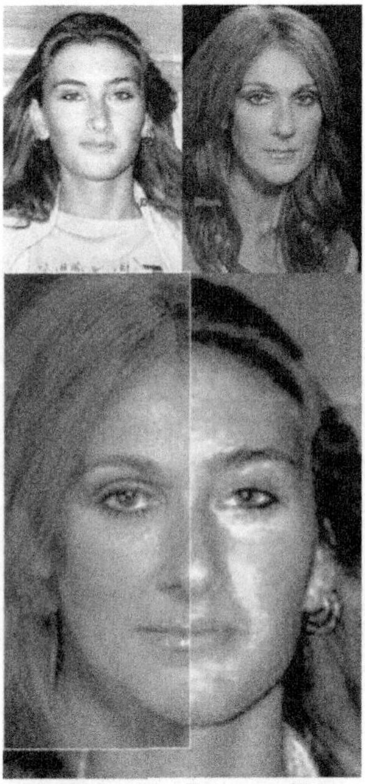

PHOTO O9: Dorsey/Dion comparison

PHOTO O10: A young Dorsey/Dion comparison

PHOTO O11: A young Dorsey/Dion comparison

Louise originally pursued a career in acting during the 1980's, but didn't get far as she was shite at it. Indeed, she is best known for providing the voice of Jetta on the popular 1980s cartoon series,'Jem'... I have never heard of it although I tend not to watch too many children's programs.

So, having failed to crack it as an actor, Louise teamed up with her brother Scott Dorsey in a bid to become the next best thing since **The Carpenters** *... Yet they got nowhere.*

In 1995 Louise went solo and released two singles... Which were shite.Presently, she lives in Nashville and works as a PR-consultant for her father - whom she sometimes sings on stage with.

But guess what? Two of her aunts - Englebert's sister's *- are also called Celine and Olga, which you can put down to coincidence if ya like.*

And of course Louise matches all the other suspects - Linda Thompson for example (see photo P1), although Thompson is obviously too old to be Louise.

However, if you want proof that Louise matches all of the others then you will just have to do them for yourselves, but what is already very, very clear is that there is a Satanic connection here at the very least... Which I am now going to build on considerably.

So let's start with Louise's mother, Patricia Healy. The following is taken from a Daily Express article published in November 2017:

SINGER Engelbert Humperdinck has revealed there is a "glimmer of hope" that his wife, who is battling Alzheimer's, will one day get better.

Patricia Healey, married to the star for 54 years, has lived with the incurable brain condition for seven years and is receiving pioneering treatment in Los Angeles.

Twice a week she sees a doctor who turns skin cells into stem cells and an acupuncturist then transfers them into the brain. Engelbert, 81, and still touring, maintains the experimental therapy has made a difference, saying: "She is talking again and saying 'Hello' and she's making sense with what she is saying.

"This is very inspiring and very rewarding. She's making progress which I'm thrilled about. It's not possible after seven or eight years for anybody to talk again but she's beginning to talk again...

And as you can see in photo P2, she too slots nicely into the doppelganger gang.

PHOTO P1: Louise Dorsey/Linda Thompson comparison

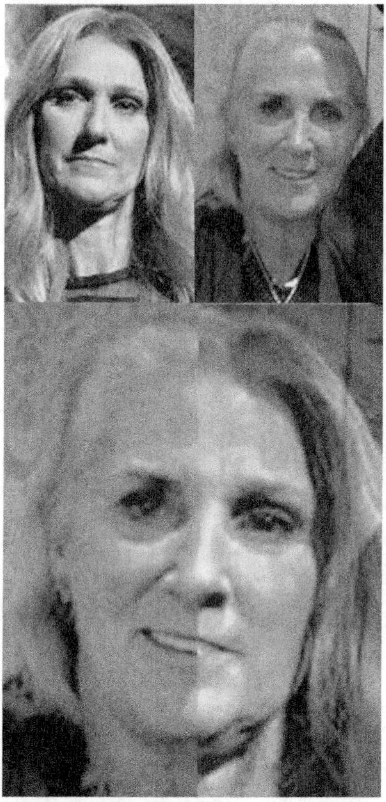

PHOTO P2: Patricia Healy/Celine Dion comparison

PHOTO P3: Elvis & Engle had parallel lives

PHOTO P4: Angelil/ Humperdink/ Presley comparisons

Now I shouldn't have to keep saying it, but I do because some factions for some reason are more intent in proving me wrong rather than being greatly disturbed by what I am showing you.

So, for the benefit of those of you who are silly as arseholes, I am not saying that Celine Dion is Patricia Healy, but they most definitely have a connection of the Satanic kind... As do Patricia's husband and the fella some claim to be Celine's old-man. (see photo P3)

Moreover, there are indeed similarities between Englebert Humperdink & Rene Angelil. (see photo P4)

Indeed, only a closed minded fool would dismiss the possibility out of hand.

And then there is Vernon Presley - Father to Elvis. You see, Vernon is a ringer for the Raygun barber and at least one of his photos almost certainly originated from the same source photo. (see photos P5 & P6)

What follows is Vernons official bio although it is bollox:

Vernon Elvis Presley was born on April 10, 1916 in Fulton, Mississippi to Jesse (1896-1973) and Minnie Mae Hood, 'Grandma Dodger' Presley (1890-1980).

Elvis' Mother Gladys Love Smith was born on April 25, 1912, Pontotoc County, Mississippi to Bob (1873-1931) and Doll Smith (1876-1935).

Vernon was but seventeen when he married Gladys Love Smith, four years his elder, in 1933. Like his relatives before him, Vernon worked at any odd job that came along.

For a while, he and Vester, his older brother, farmed together, raising cotton, com, soybeans and a few hogs. Later, he took a job with the WPA, a federal government make - work program during the Depression.

Next, he drove a delivery truck for McCarty's, a Tupelo wholesale grocer, delivering grocery items to stores throughout northeast Mississippi. These, then, were the Presley genes, passed along from generation to generation, some of which undoubtedly were inherited by the infant born in that two-room house in the hills of East Tupelo. *Source: biography.elvis.com.au*

PHOTO P5: Vernon Presley/Barber comparison

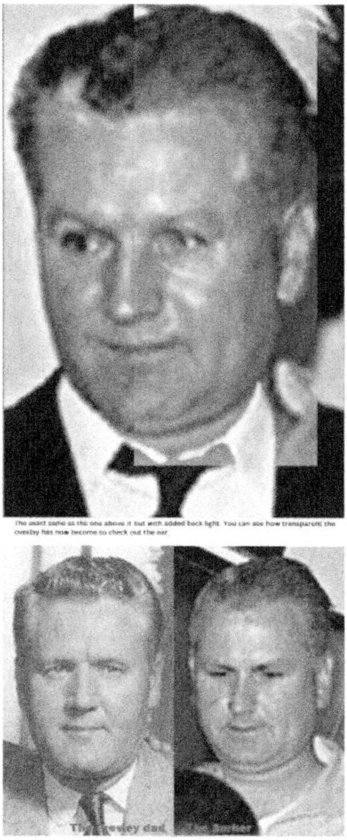

PHOTO P6: Vernon Presley/Barber comparison

PHOTO P7: The Presley family album

This of course also ties in with Celine Dion's mother looking exactly like Gladys Presley... They are all Satanically connected to each other. Indeed we are told that when Elvis was born his parents were dirt-poor, yet they have more photographs of themselves than most parents of that era. (see photo P7)

And that makes me very suspicious because poor 'white-trash' certainly didn't have the money to waste on what at the time was a very expensive hobby.

Furthermore, the fact that Rene Angelil's death was deserved of so many international headlines makes me suspicious.

I mean he was hardly a household name and he already had cancer when I first heard about him - which must have been around 20 years ago... Neither did Celine & the boys look crushed, when you consider that she called him the "love of her life" when he died in 2016. Yet a year later Dion had got herself a toyboy named Pepe Munoz - allegedly one of her back-up dancers.

Yet crucially Munoz is a doppelganger for BRODY JENNER (see photo P8) - see how it all falls into place.

Yet more disturbingly still is the fact that Munoz also looks like Dion's son Charles-Rene (see photo P9)... Which I gotta tell'ya; I find rather disturbing.

PHOTO P8: Brody Jenner & Pepe Munoz comparison

PHOTO P9: Munoz/ Charles Rene comparisons

Chapter 10
The Murdoch connection

Now I could easily write a whole book about the media mogul Rupert Murdoch on his own. Indeed I can state without fear of contradiction that he is a fully paid up member of the Monster's club... Much higher up the ladder than a Monster -Minion.

Keith Rupert Murdoch, (born 11 March 1931) is an Australian-born American media mogul.

Murdoch's father, Sir Keith Murdoch, was a reporter and editor who became a senior executive of The Herald and Weekly Times publishing company, covering all Australian states except New South Wales. After his father's death in 1952, Murdoch declined to join his late father's registered public company and created his own private company, News Limited.

In the 1950s and 1960s, Murdoch acquired a number of newspapers in Australia and New Zealand before expanding into the United Kingdom in 1969, taking over the News of the World, followed closely by The Sun. In 1974, Murdoch moved to New York City, to expand into the U.S. market; however, he retained interests in Australia and Britain. In 1981, Murdoch bought The Times, his first British broadsheet and, in 1985, became a naturalized U.S. citizen, giving up his Australian citizenship, to satisfy the legal requirement for U.S. television ownership.

In 1986, keen to adopt newer electronic publishing technologies, Murdoch consolidated his UK printing operations in Wapping, causing bitter industrial disputes. His holding company News Corporation acquired Twentieth Century Fox (1985), HarperCollins (1989), and The Wall Street Journal (2007). Murdoch formed the British broadcaster BSkyB in 1990 and, during the 1990s, expanded into Asian networks and South American television. By 2000, Murdoch's News Corporation owned over 800 companies in more than 50 countries, with a net worth of over $5 billion.
In July 2011, Murdoch faced allegations that his companies, including the News of the World, owned by News Corporation, had been regularly hacking the phones of celebrities, royalty, and public citizens. Murdoch faced police and government

investigations into bribery and corruption by the British government and FBI investigations in the U.S.

On 21 July 2012, Murdoch resigned as a director of News International. On 1 July 2015, Murdoch left his post as CEO of 21st Century Fox. However, Murdoch and his family continue to own both 21st Century Fox and News Corp through the Murdoch Family Trust.

In July 2016, after the resignation of Roger Ailes due to accusations of sexual harassment, Murdoch was named the acting CEO of Fox News *Source: Wikipedia*

Now at this juncture we need to go back to Cassandra Marino. You see, she is in fact a ringer for Sarah Murdoch, daughter-in-law of the media mogul, Rupert the bear *Murdoch (see photo Q1)... Which makes sense since none of this deception would be possible without the full cooperation of the worlds media – which is more or less controlled by 6 families.*

PHOTO Q1: Cassandra Jenner/ Sarah Murdoch comparison

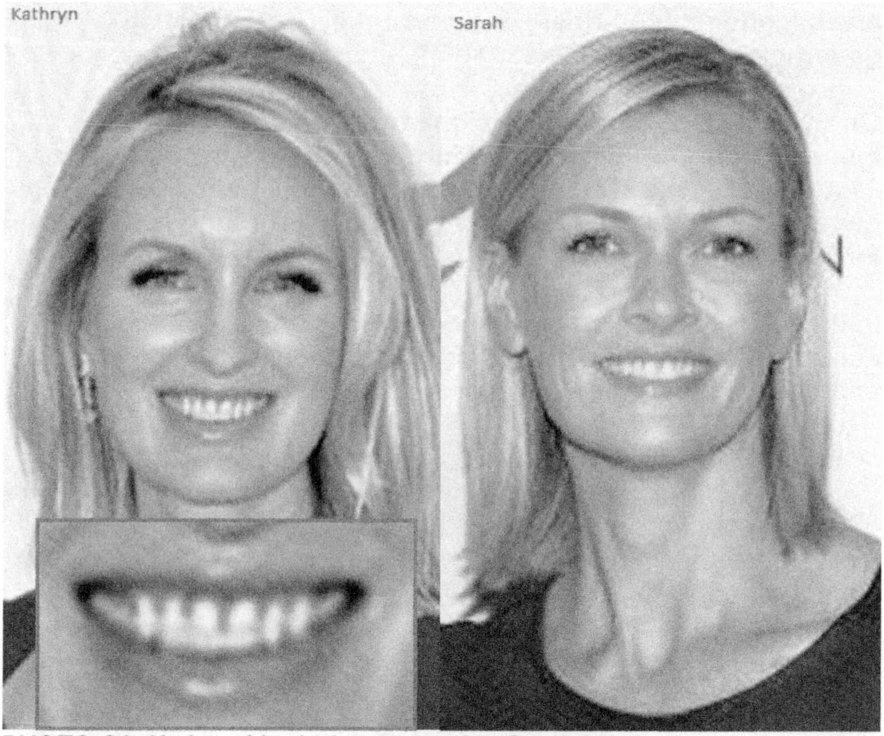

PHOTO Q2: Kathryn Murdoch compared to Sarah Murdoch

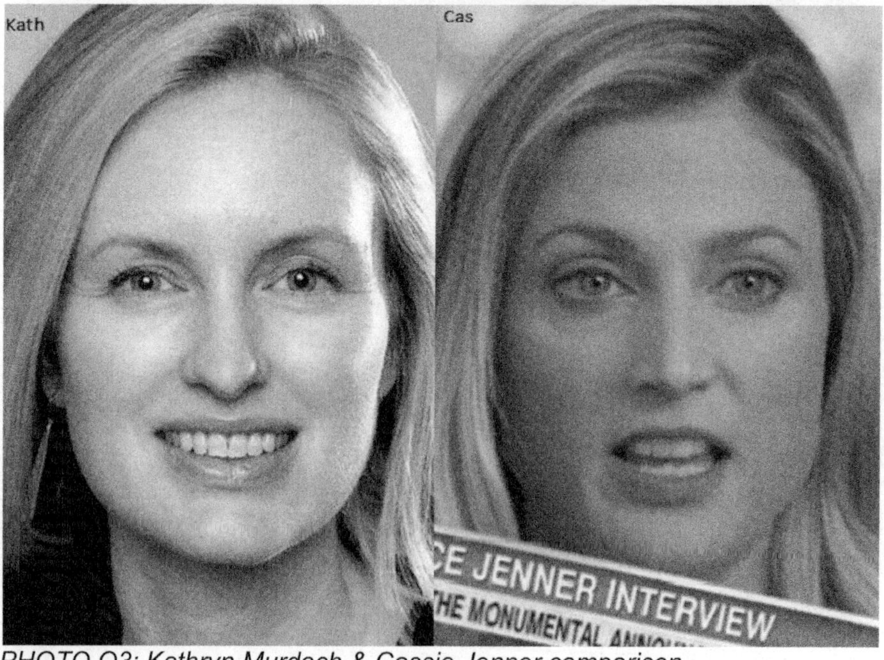

PHOTO Q3: Kathryn Murdoch & Cassie Jenner comparison

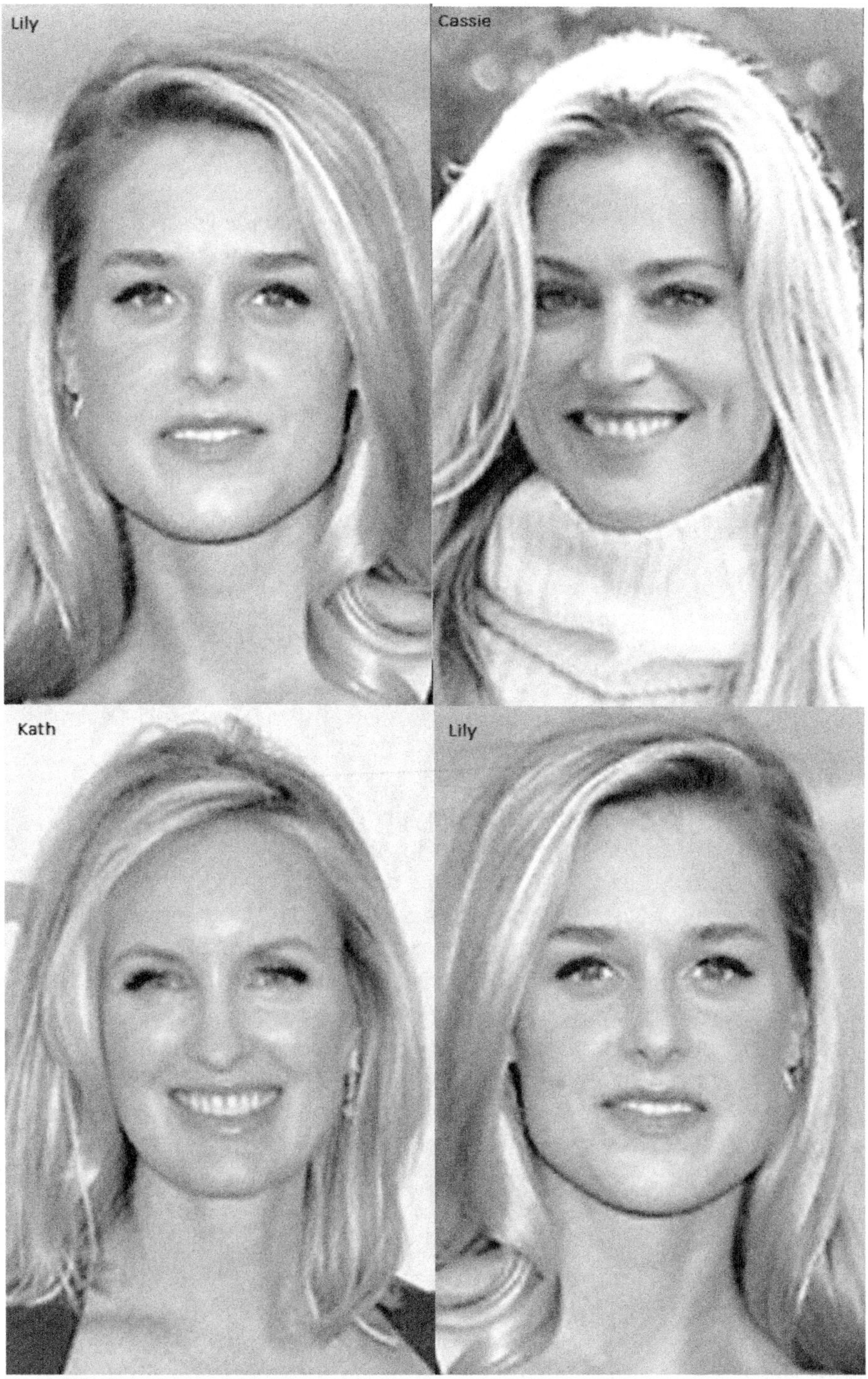

PHOTO Q4: *Jenner-Murdoch-Harrison comparison*

And indeed Cassandra's teeth are every bit as weird as Sarah's ears! Just sayin'.
Course, Sarah is married to Lachlan Murdoch and looks very, very similar to her brother-in-law, James Murdoch's wife, Kathryn (see photo Q2).

And doesn't Kathryn also have a set of very strange teeth?
Course, whilst it isn't uncommon for brothers to share the same taste in things, having such similar looking wives is just plain fucking weird. Mind you, that weirdness should mean that Kathryn also looks like Cassie Marino/Jenner shouldn't it?

Of course it fucking should (see photo Q3).

And it is also worth mentioning that the Jenner-Murdochs look a lot like Greg Harrison's daughter, Lily Harrison (see photo Q4).

Predictably of course, Brucella Jenner pushes the Transsexual Agenda for all its worth.

Caitlyn Marie Jenner (born William Bruce Jenner on October 28, 1949) is an American television personality and retired Olympic gold medal -winning decathlete.

Jenner was a college football player for the Graceland Yellowjackets before incurring a knee injury that required surgery. Coach L. D. Weldon, who had coached Olympic decathlete Jack Parker, convinced Jenner to try the decathlon. After intense training, Jenner won the 1976 Olympics decathlon event at the Montreal Olympic Games, gaining fame as "an all-American hero".
Jenner set a third successive world record while winning the Olympics. The winner of the Olympic decathlon is traditionally given the unofficial title of "world's greatest athlete". With that stature, Jenner subsequently established a career in television, film, writing, auto racing, business and as a Playgirl cover model.

Jenner has six children with three successive wives: Chrystie Crownover, Linda Thompson, and Kris Jenner. Since 2007, Jenner has appeared on the reality television series Keeping Up with the Kardashians with Kris, their daughters Kendall and Kylie Jenner, and step-children Kourtney, Kim, Khloé, and Rob Kardashian.

Previously identifying publicly as male, Jenner revealed her identity as a trans woman in April 2015, publicly announcing her name change from Bruce to Caitlyn in a July 2015 Vanity Fair cover story.
Her name and gender change became official on September 25, 2015. She has been called the most famous openly transgender woman in the world.
From 2015 to 2016, Jenner starred in the reality television series I Am Cait, which focused on her gender transition. *Source: Wikipedia*

Indeed in photo Q5 which shows Brucella with the transgender model, Andreja Pejic it looks more like a case of father (in drag) & daughter to me, but isn't it amazing how pretty these transgender birds are.

I mean not so long ago - and still very much the norm today - transgender people looked like men dressed as women… Yet to me the he-she, Pejic looks like all the usual suspects. (see photo Q6)

PHOTO Q5: Brucella and Andreja

PHOTO Q6: Cassie Marino/ Andreja Pejic comparison

In fact I strongly suggest that you read my article ***"A Political Transformation Shrouded In Evil*** *" on my website* ***www.chrisspivey.com.***

Nevertheless, I am now proper starting to drift away from what this exposé is about so to get back on track let's put Meghan Markle's mum, Doria Raggan-Boneman – or whatever the made up persona's name isn't - under the spotlight.

Chapter 11
Doria Ragland

Doria Ragland's official bio states that she was born in to an African-American family in Cleveland, Ohio, in September 1956 and is the daughter of Nurse Jeanette Arnold and her second husband Alvin Ragland - an antique dealer.

She has two older maternal half-siblings, Joseph Jr. and Saundra Johnson, and a younger paternal half-brother, Joffrey Ragland.

Indeed Doria would have been very aware of the black segregation that was in force back then since her maternal grandparents, James and Netty Arnold, worked as a bellhop and an elevator operator, respectively, at the whites-only Hotel St. Regis on Euclid Avenue in Cleveland and they were descended from African Americans enslaved in Georgia.... At least they did and are according to Wikipedia.

However, when Ragland was a baby, her parents moved to Los Angeles where she supposedly attended Fairfax High School. After high school, Ragland worked as a makeup artist and later met her husband to be Thomas Markle while employed at a TV studio whilst working on the set of the popular show **General Hospital.**
Doria married lighting director Thomas Markle, at Paramahansa Yogananda 's Self-Realization Fellowship Temple in Hollywood by Brother Bhaktananda on December 23, 1979 after which she worked as a travel agent.

However Doria then went on to attain a Bachelor of Arts in psychology and in 2015 she became a Licensed Clinical Social Worker after having received a Master of Social Work from the University of Southern California. She has also worked as a yoga instructor.

Doria was the only member of Meghan's family to attend her wedding to Harry... So let's see if we can make mincemeat of that too.

I mean if Meghan isn't a real person and neither are her dad, brothers and Nephews then it follows that Doria – daft name – *isn't real either.*

Course, that would explain the need for faked photos (see photo Q7).

Moreover, the Doria seen in the photo Q7 should really be called

Doria II since she clearly isn't the first actress to play the role (see photo Q8).

So, best we compare Mk I & Mk 2 don't cha think?

Of course you fucking do, so go to Photo Q9

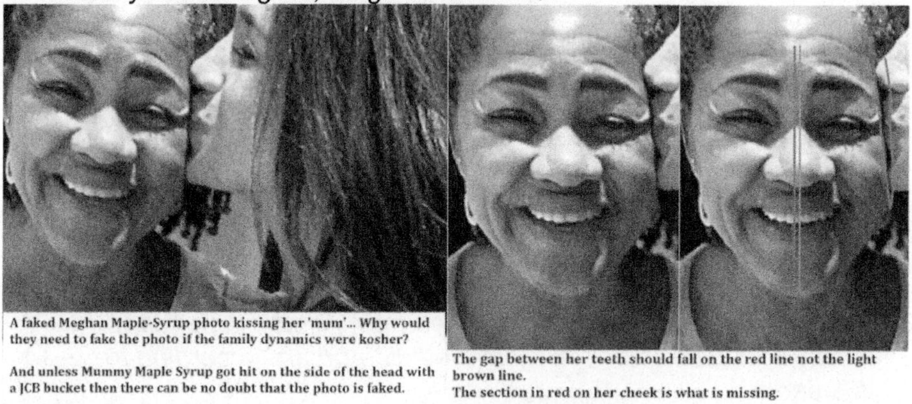

A faked Meghan Maple-Syrup photo kissing her 'mum'... Why would they need to fake the photo if the family dynamics were kosher?
And unless Mummy Maple Syrup got hit on the side of the head with a JCB bucket then there can be no doubt that the photo is faked.
The gap between her teeth should fall on the red line not the light brown line.
The section in red on her cheek is what is missing.

PHOTO Q7: A clearly faked photo of 'mum & daughter'

PHOTO Q8: Meghan & her mum, Doria the 1st

PHOTO Q9: Doria compared to Doria
Close call... Not!

In fact Meghan looks more like her ex-sister-in-law, Tracey Dooley MK2 in photo Q8 than Rag-tag looks like herself in the comparison photo Q9 (see photo Q10)...
Despite Meghan & Tracey not being related by blood.

PHOTO Q10: Meghan compared to Tracey Dooley

However, Doria II does look quite like the feminist activist, Dorothy Pitman-Hughes to me.

Over to you Wikipedia:

Dorothy Pitman Hughes (born 1938) is a feminist, child-welfare advocate, African-American activist, public speaker, author, pioneering African-American small business owner, and mother of three daughters.

She was a co-founder of Ms. Magazine in 1972. She organized the first shelter for battered women in New York City and co-founded the New York City Agency for Child Development (now the New York City Administration for Children's Services).

Hughes also co-founded with Gloria Steinem and others the Women's Action Alliance in 1971. The two women toured together speaking about gender, class and race throughout the 1970s.

Hughes owned and operated three early child-care centers helping establish the modern convention in the 1960s. She also owned an office supply business in Harlem from 1997 to 2007 and wrote about her experiences in Wake Up and Smell the Dollars! (2011) and I'm Just Saying... It Looks Like Ethnic Cleansing (The Gentrification of Harlem) (2012), advocating small business ownership to other African Americans as a form of empowerment, as well as advising how to avoid potential pitfalls specific to African Americans.

The National Portrait Gallery selected for its collection a photograph of Hughes and Steinem sharing a large skirt, each with a raised fist salute to demonstrate feminist solidarity. The photograph was shot by photographer Dan Wynn for Esquire Magazine in 1971. Ms. Pitman Hughes commissioned photographer Dan Bagan to create an homage portrait of the two friends together again in a similar pose for Ms. Steinem's 80th birthday.

Oprah Winfrey honored Hughes as one of America's "Great Moms".
Hughes is the aunt of actress Gabourey Sidibe.

Hughes has focused her activism in the Northside community of Jacksonville, Florida, growing food within the neighborhoods to combat poverty. She owns the Gateway Bookstore in Jacksonville.

Dorothy Pitman Hughes was born 1938 in Lumpkin, Georgia. Her father was beaten when she was ten years old and left for dead on the family's doorstep; the family believes it to be a crime committed by Ku Klux Klan members.
Pitman Hughes moved from Georgia to New York City in 1957 where she worked in entertainment as a singer through the 1960s.

So, straight away we see that Dotty's father was beaten in a racist attack in GEORGIA... The same place that Ragland's slave ancestors came from.

Or put another way; another Satanic connection - everything has to connect to everything. Moreover, Dotty had a foot in showbiz... Or put another way, a performer just like everyone else mentioned in this book.

Therefore, I best show you a comparison of Pitman-Hughes & Ragland.

PHOTO R1: Ragland & Pitman comparison

PHOTO R2: Young Rag-Tag & Pitman

Now admittedly they are not a great match although to be fair Ragland is photoshopped to fuck and is probably a mixture of people. I should also tell you not to take any notice of the fact that Ragland has a much lighter skin-tone than Pitman because clever cameramen can make that look so depending on the lens they use and the lighting.

However, the two old buzzards did look a lot more similar to each other when they were younger (see photo R2).

I should also point out that no angles were changed in photo R2... And I am actually pleasantly surprised that the two halves matched so well.

However, there is still more to my suspicion that Rag-Tag is also the Pits-Man. You see, the Pits-Man has that large Mole on her upper cheek which is kinda like the mole that Ellen Johnson Sirleaf has (see photo R3)... Sirleaf being the 24th President of Liberia up until January 2018.

Ellen Johnson Sirleaf was born in Monrovia to a Gola father and Kru -German mother. She was educated at the College of West Africa before moving to the United States, where she studied at Madison Business College and Harvard University. She returned to Liberia to work in William Tolbert 's government as Deputy Minister of Finance from 1971 to 1974 and later went to work for the World in the Caribbean and Latin America. Mrs. Sirleaf returned to work for the late president Tolbert's government again as deputy minister of Finance before being promoted to the post of Minister of Finance from 1979 to 1980. After Samuel Doe seized power in a coup d'état and executed Tolbert, Sirleaf fled to the United States. She worked for Citibank and then the Equator Bank before returning to Liberia to contest a senatorial seat for Montserrado county in the disputed 1985 elections.

After returning to Liberia, Sirleaf ran for office, and finished in second place at the 1997 presidential election won by Charles Taylor. She won the 2005 presidential election and took office on 16th January 2006. She was re-elected in 2011. In June 2016, she was elected as the Chair of the Economic Community of West African States, making her the first woman to hold the position since it was created.

In 2011, Sirleaf was jointly awarded the Nobel Peace Prize with Leymah Gbowee of Liberia and Tawakkol Karman of Yemen. The three women were recognized "for their non-violent struggle for the safety of women and for women's rights to full participation in peace-building work."
Sirleaf was conferred the Indira Gandhi Prize by Indian President Pranab Mukherjee on 12th September 2013. In 2016, she was listed as the 83rd-most powerful woman in the world by Forbes magazine. *Source: Wikipedia*

Sean Gallup/Getty Images

Ellen Johnson Sirleaf, President of Liberia In 2011, Sirleaf was jointly awarded the Nobel Peace Prize with Leymah Gbowee of Liberia and Tawakkol Karman of Yemen for their "non-violent struggle for the safety of women and for women's rights to full participation in peace-building work." She is the first woman to be elected as a head of state in Africa and the chair of the Economic Community of West African States. Sirleaf also happens to be the aunt of actress and comedian Retta, who portrayed Donna on "Parks and Recreation."

PHOTO R3: Ellen Johnson Sirleaf with Pitman-Hughes inset.

PHOTO R4: Pitman & Sirleaf comparison

PHOTO R5: Ragland & Sirleaf comparison

PHOTO R6: Ragland/Sirleaf comparison

They do like to dish out those Knob-Hell-Piss-Prizes *to the bad guys don't they... And of course we now see another President involved in the Markle manipulation.*

Nevertheless, best we check that we are not barking up the wrong tree before we go any further, so take a butchers at photo R4. It's certainly going well isn't it?

So, while we are on a roll we best compare Raggady Ann Doria with Shirtlift or whatever it is the criminal calls herself (see photo R5): And the comparison looks good to me although I suppose that I best do another just to appease the Doubting-Thomasisisisisis... Don't cha just hate those words/names that you can never end! (see photo R6)

Now funnily enough, not too long ago Sirtealeaf was replaced as the President of Liberia by the former footballer George Weah... Proof positive then that you don't need brains to be a President.

Mind you, the timing couldn't have been better as no longer being the President would free up another couple of hours per week to allow Harvard educated Sirleaf to play the part of Doria Ragbag.

However, I also feel the need to tell you that Sirleaf has a [camera shy] step-son who no one in the press appears to know how to spell his first name; so, I am not sure if it is Fombah or Fumba or a variation of.

However, that fact is rather strange given that he was apparently the head of the Liberian secret service, as well as the stepson of the President and he is implicated in a major multi-million (some say a billion) pound fraud.

Nevertheless, I cannot help but think that Chumba-Fumba looks very much like Meghan Markle's cousin Joffrey (couldn't be Jeffrey obviously) Ragland (see photo R7)

And make sure that you take a close look at the ears! The ears – which are unique to each individual person – *are the same... And the intel services do like to keep it in the family, don't cha know.*

Moreover, if you have read my " **How The West Was Won** *" series of articles on my website www.chrisspivey.org you will know that these High Profile, with Low Profile people usually have a historical blast from the past and in Doria Raganbone's case I would image that her doppelganger is Patrice Clarke – the first female air captain for an international airline (see photo R8).*

Patrice Francise Clarke was born on 11 September 1961 in Nassau, The Bahamas to Peggy Ann and Nathaniel Clarke.

From the age of five, when she took her first flight, Clarke was interested in aviation. Raised by a single, divorced mother, along with her two sisters, Clarke learned responsibility at a young age.

During her high schooling in Nassau she participated in career week activities hoping to become a stewardess, by the time she graduated, she had dreams of becoming a pilot.

PHOTO R7: Joffrey & Fombah comparison

PHOTO R8: Patrice Clarke compared to Doria Ragland

In 1979, intent on her goal, Clarke enrolled in the Embry–Riddle Aeronautical University of Daytona Beach, Florida, despite the fact that she was the only black student and spoke only Bahamian Creole.

In April 1982, Clarke graduated as the first black woman in the school's history with a BS in aeronautical science and her commercial pilot's certification Soon after her graduation, Clarke began working at a charter company, Trans Island Airways, in the Bahamas, as a pilot. She continued her studies

and was able to earn her qualifications to fly Boeing 737 and Boeing 747-8 aircraft over the next few years.

In 1984, Clarke became the first woman pilot of Bahamasair, when she was hired as a First Officer by the air service. Though often facing discrimination Clark persevered and in 1988, she was hired by United Parcel Service (UPS) as a flight engineer.

Her three-person crew flew routes from Louisville, Kentucky to Anchorage, Alaska, as well as to Australia and Cologne, Germany. In 1990, Washington was promoted to First Officer with UPS.

In 1994, Clarke married Ray Washington, a pilot for American Airlines. In December 1994, she was promoted to captain by UPS, becoming the first black female, and one of only eleven female captains, to command planes for a major U.S. airline.

In 1995, Washington and other female pilots founded the Bessie Coleman Foundation with the purpose of preserving Coleman 's legacy, promoting the aviation profession among African American men and women, and providing a network for mentoring women in the airline sector.

In 2000, Washington was presented with the Trumpet Award from Turner Broadcasting for her pioneering work in aviation on behalf of women. *Source: Wikipedia*

So best we have another comparison (see photo R9)

PHOTO R9: Patrice Clarke compared to Doria Ragland

PHOTO R10: Pitman-Hughes & Steinem's iconic 1972 photograph

PHOTO R11: Shirtlift doing her tubthumping thing and looking very much like Doria Ragland in the process

PHOTO R12: The 2014 version

Okay, returning now to the feminist Dotty-Doria Pitman-Hughes and here is a thing: Pitman is known for her iconic photograph taken with the Feminist, Gloria Steinem in 1972 and seen in photo R10.

Mind you, Shirtlift is also all for a bit of air-thumping too (see photo R11).

And indeed the pair of rug-munchers - Pitman & Steinem *-posed for a recreation of that air-thumping photo in 2014.*
Somehow, photo R12 just doesn't have the same impact as the original does it?
Although the pair have milked the pose for all its worth.
Nevertheless, best we have a bit of background on Gloria Steinem, don't cha think?

Steinem was born on March 25, 1934, in Toledo, Ohio, the daughter of Ruth (née Nuneviller) and Leo Steinem. Her mother was a Presbyterian of mostly German (including Prussian), and some Scottish, descent.

Her father was Jewish, the son of emigrants from Württemberg, Germany and Radziejów, Poland.

Her paternal grandmother, Pauline Perlmutter Steinem, was chairwoman of the educational committee of the National Woman Suffrage Association, a delegate to the 1908 International Council of Women, and the first woman to be elected to the Toledo Board of Education, as well as a leader in the movement for vocational education.

Pauline also rescued many members of her family from the Holocaust.

The Steinems lived and traveled about in the trailer from which Leo carried out his trade as a traveling antiques dealer. Before Steinem was born, her mother Ruth, then aged 34, had a "nervous breakdown" which left her an invalid, trapped in delusional fantasies that occasionally turned violent.

She changed "from an energetic, fun-loving, book-loving" woman into "someone who was afraid to be alone, who could not hang on to reality long enough to hold a job, and who could rarely concentrate enough to read a book."

Ruth spent long periods in and out of sanatoriums for the mentally ill. Steinem was ten years old when her parents finally separated in 1944. Her father went to California to find work, while she and her mother continued to live together in Toledo.

While her parents divorced as a result of her mother's illness, Steinem did not attribute it to a result of chauvinism on the father's part, and she claims to have "understood and never blamed him for the breakup."

PHOTO S1: Steinem & Pitman-Hughes milking their moment of glory

PHOTO S2: A Fella in the same t-shirt as Steinem & Pitman-Hughes are wearing

Nevertheless, the impact of these events had a formative effect on her personality: while her father, a traveling salesman, had never provided much financial stability to the family, his exit aggravated their situation. Steinem concluded that her mother's inability to hold on to a job was evidence of general hostility towards working women.

She also concluded that the general apathy of doctors towards her mother emerged from a similar anti-woman animus. Years later, Steinem described her mother's experiences as having

been pivotal to her understanding of social injustices. These perspectives convinced Steinem that women lacked social and political equality. *Source: Wikipedia*

Now the thing is, that " Equal Rights Now *" t-shirt of theirs (seen in photo S1) proved to be very revealing to me. You see, on my internet travels - unconnected to the two activists - I came across a photo of a fella wearing the exact same one (see photo S2).*

*And apparently the mush in that photo is the quite well known American actor, Rainn Wilson – strangely spelled name again. Wilson is supposedly most famous for his role in the American tv version of "*The Office*".*

Rainn Dietrich Wilson (born January 20, 1966) is an American actor, comedian, writer, director, businessman, and producer. He is best known for his role as Dwight Schrute on the American version of the television comedy The Office, for which he earned three consecutive Emmy Award nominations for Outstanding Supporting Actor in a Comedy Series.

A native of Seattle, Washington, Wilson began acting in college at the University of Washington, and later worked in theatre in New York City after graduating in 1986. Wilson made his film debut in Galaxy Quest (1999), followed by supporting parts in Almost Famous (2000), Steven Soderbergh 's Full Frontal (2002), and House of 1000 Corpses (2003). He also had a recurring part as Arthur Martin in the HBO series Six Feet Under from 2003 to 2005.

Wilson was cast as Dwight Schrute in The Office in 2005, a role which he would play until the show's conclusion in 2013. Other film credits include lead roles in the comedies The Rocker (2008) and Super (2010), and supporting roles in the horror films Cooties (2014) and The Boy (2015).

In addition to acting, Wilson published an autobiography, The Bassoon King, in November 2015, and also co-founded the digital media company SoulPancake in 2008. *Source: Wikipedia*

Mind you, I have to say that the above photo looks to be a fake with the two women superimposed on his shirt. Moreover, his shoulder appears all wrong and he also looks too wide on that side.

In fact I would imagine that the photo was knocked up specifically in order to form a Satanic connection.

Why?
Good question, let me show you. Now Wilson does in fact look exactly like Scott Rasmussen in some photos (see photo S3). " But who the fuck is Rasmussen ", *I don't hear you yell.*

Nevertheless, I will tell you that Scott Rasmussen is the created persona of Meghan Markle's ex-brother-in-law, who was created in order to give her a past life.

Rasmussen is also without doubt his ex-brother-in-law, Thomas Markle Jr (see photo S4)

I have touched in the background because what with the hat and what not it was all quite distracting. I have not however, touched the face at all

PHOTO S3: Scott & Rainn comparison

PHOTO S4: Rasmussen/Markle comparison

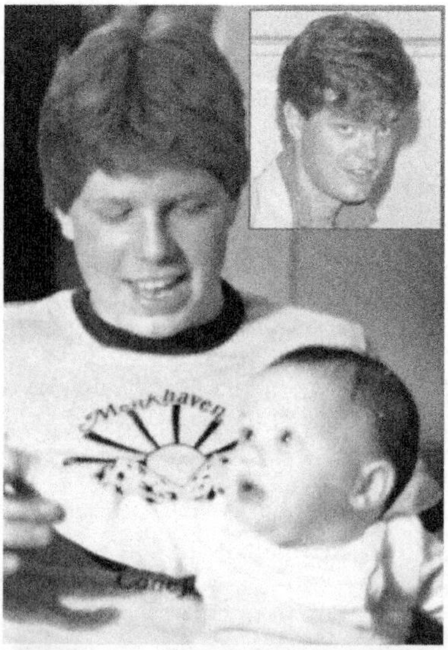

PHOTO S5: Thomas Markle Jr & Meghan with Rainnnn Wilson inset

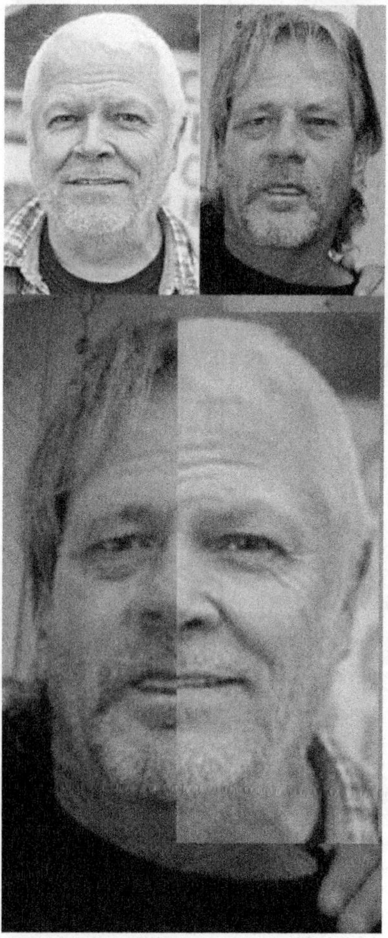

PHOTO S6: Rasmussen & Harold Lovell comparison

Indeed you only need look at the ear to see that the photos are from the same source.

Young Thomas Markle Jr also looks a lot like young Rainnnnnn Wilson (see photo S5). Moreover, I believe that Rasmussen-Markle-Rainn are a fella named Harold Lovell, seen in the comparison photo S6.

So who is Lovell?

Well it would seem that Harold ***WAYNE*** *Lovell was originally thought to be a 1977 victim of John* ***WAYNE*** *Gacy until he turned up alive and well in 2011:*

CHICAGO - Siblings who feared that their brother was one of serial killer John Wayne Gacy's eight unidentified victims were amazed and overjoyed to learn that he's been living in Florida for decades.

Tim Lovell and Theresa Hasselberg hadn't seen their brother, Harold Wayne Lovell, since he left their family's Chicago home in May 1977 in search of construction work. At the time, Gacy was trolling for young men and boys in the area. He was a contractor, and he lured many of the 33 young men and boys he killed by offering them work.

Cook County Sheriff's detectives reviewing unidentified remains cases discovered that eight of the 33 people Gacy was convicted of murdering were never identified, and they obtained exhumation orders over the past few months to test the remains for DNA, hoping relatives of young men who went missing in the area in the 1970s might submit to genetic testing.

Lovell's siblings, who now live in Alabama, were planning to do just that when they discovered a recent online police booking photo of their brother taken in Florida. They reached their brother, who goes by his middle name, by phone

and bought him a bus ticket, and the family was reunited Tuesday for the first time in 34 years.

"It was awesome, awesome, a shock, disbelief," Wayne Lovell, now 53, told CBS News station WBBM-TV of Chicago. "I'm still pinching myself. I mean, 34 years is a long time."

He said he left for Florida all those years ago because he wasn't getting along with his mother and stepfather. Over the years, he's worked various manual labor jobs and has had occasional brushes with the law.

"I've gone from having nothing to having all this," Lovell said. "I'm still pinching myself."

Cook County Sheriff Tom Dart has said that dozens of families of men who disappeared during the 1970s have come forward for DNA testing.

Investigators searching Gacy's home following his 1978 arrest found most of his victims buried in a basement crawl space, although detectives said Gacy dumped four victims in a nearby river after he ran out of room at his house.
Gacy confessed to the slayings after his arrest and was executed in 1994. *Source: CBS News, October 26, 2011*

You couldn't make it up y'know!

And again it is also worth playing ' What's-In-A-Name *' since I found a photo of a fella called Butch Rasmussen whose image most certainly provided (* or came from *) a source photo for Thomas WAYNE Markle Snr (see photo S7).*

However, because the two comparison photos are so crap I have set the overlay at 40% transparency so as you can see just how EXACTLY they match up.

And then there is the Scott Rasmussen seen in photo S8… Scott Rassmussen being the same name as Meghan's ex-brother-in-law.

PHOTO S8: Scott Rasmussen

PHOTO S7: Markle-Rasmussen comparison

Nevertheless, the Scott Rasmussen in photo S8 is a n American political analyst and digital media entrepreneur who was born on Eglin Air Force Base near Valparaiso, Florida to Lois Ann and Bill Rasmussen on the March 30, 1956… And once again we have somebody with military and political connections.

Moreover, according to Wikipedia:

Rasmussen is best known as the founder of Rasmussen Reports, where he served as pollster and president until leaving the company in 2013. Earlier in his professional life, Rasmussen co-founded the sports network ESPN. After leaving Rasmussen Reports, Rasmussen founded Rasmussen Media Group, working as a political analyst, author, public speaker and columnist. He is also a Senior Fellow at The King's College in

New York City, where he is responsible for development at the Institute for Community Driven Solutions.

Rasmussen is a New York Times bestselling author and speaker, and his political commentary is distributed through a nationally syndicated weekly newspaper column.

However, what I found especially intriguing about this Ragamuffin-Rasmussen is the fact that he looks like Aleister Crowley & Victor Rothschild - who you will know if you have read my article "How The West Was Won", are probably the same person.
So best we do some comparisons. (see photos S9 & S10)

PHOTO S9: Rasmussen/Rothschild Comparison

PHOTO S10: Ramussen/Crowley comparison

And for those of you who don't know, Aleister Crowley was an English occultist, ceremonial magician, poet, painter, novelist, and mountaineer. Mind you, he was also a predatory paedophile, junkie and one of the most evil bastards to ever walk the earth... And as such, the Monsters and their minions absolutely worship him. Crowley was born into a wealthy Plymouth Brethren family in Royal Leamington Spa, Warwickshire, attended Cambridge University and wrote a load of books about Satan, black magic and other shit like that.

But like I say, in reality he was in all probability a Rothschild... Most likely MI5 spy, Victor.

Nathaniel Mayer Victor Rothschild, 3rd Baron Rothschild, Bt, GBE, GM, FRS (31 October 1910 – 20 March 1990), was a senior executive with Royal Dutch Shell and N M Rothschild & Sons, an advisor to the Edward Heath and Margaret Thatcher governments of the UK, as well as a member of the prominent Rothschild family.

Rothschild was the only son of Charles Rothschild and Rozsika Rothschild (née Edle von Wertheimstein). The family home was Tring Park Mansion. He had three sisters. Rothschild suffered from the suicide of his father when he was 13 years old. He was educated at Harrow School.

At Trinity College, Cambridge, he read physiology, French, and English. He played first-class cricket for the University and Northamptonshire. At Cambridge he was known for his playboy lifestyle, driving a Bugatti and collecting art and rare books.

Rothschild joined the Cambridge Apostles, a secret society, which at that time was predominantly Marxist, though he stated himself that he "was mildly left-wing but never a Marxist". He became friends with Guy Burgess, Anthony Blunt and Kim Philby ; members of the Cambridge Spy Ring.

In 1933, Rothschild gave Blunt £ 100 to purchase "Eliezer and Rebecca" by Nicolas Poussin. The painting was sold by Blunt's executors in 1985 for £100,000 and is now in the Fitzwilliam Museum.

His flat in London was shared with Burgess and Blunt. This later aroused suspicion that he was the so-called Fifth Man in the Cambridge Spy Ring.

Rothschild inherited his title at the age of 26 following the death of his uncle Walter Rothschild, 2nd Baron Rothschild on 27 August 1937. He sat as a Labour Party peer in the House of Lords, but spoke only twice there during his life (both speeches were in 1946, one about the pasteurization of milk, and another about the situation in Palestine. *Source Wikipedia*

However, another thing that connects this TV pundit, Rasmussen to the Meghan Markle deception is the photo T1.

You see, the fella on the right hand side of the photo is Michael Reagan... The adopted son of former US President, Ronald. And as coincidence would have it, Michael Reagan looks very much like the fella in the photo T2.

PHOTO T1: Rasmussen in a TV debate with Michael Reagan

PHOTO T2: (main) Celine Dion, Rene Angelil & Mystery man (inset) Michael Raygun

The nose certainly looks right... Just sayin'.

Likewise I believe that there is a Satanic connection between the Markles et al and

the fake Las Vegas shooting... Although obviously there would be since everything has to connect.

Mind you, I am pleased to say that only the really, really daft are buying into that hoax.

Chapter 12
The Las Vegas Shooting

Now the official version of the Las Vegas shooting goes thus:

The 2017 Las Vegas shooting occurred on the night of Sunday, October 1, 2017 when a gunman opened fire on a crowd of concert goers at the Route 91 Harvest music festival on the Las Vegas Strip in Nevada, leaving 58 people dead and 851 injured. Between 10:05 and 10:15 p.m. PDT, 64-year-old Stephen Paddock of Mesquite, Nevada, fired more than 1,100 rounds from his suite on the 32nd floor of the nearby Mandalay Bay hotel. About an hour after he fired his last shot into the crowd, he was found dead in his room from a self-inflicted gunshot wound. His motive remains unknown.

The incident is the deadliest mass shooting committed by an individual in the United States. It reignited the debate about gun laws in the U.S., with attention focused on bump fire stocks, which Paddock used to fire semi-automatic rifles at a rate similar to that of a fully automatic weapon.

The Las Vegas Strip is a stretch of Las Vegas Boulevard immediately south of the city of Las Vegas in Clark County, Nevada. The Strip is known for its concentration of casinos and resort hotels, including the 43-story Mandalay Bay southwest of its intersection with Mandalay Bay Road, in the unincorporated town of Paradise.
Las Vegas Village, a 15-acre (6.1-hectare) lot used for outdoor performances, is located diagonally across the intersection to the northeast. From 2014 onward, the venue hosted the annual Route 91 Harvest country music festival. The 2017 festival ran from September 29 to October 1, with over 22,000 attendees on the final day.

Stephen Paddock was a 64-year-old former auditor and real estate businessman who had been living 80 miles (130 km) northeast of Las Vegas in a retirement community in Mesquite,

Nevada. Paddock was twice divorced, had a long-term girlfriend, and had no known children. He was a son of Benjamin Paddock, a bank robber who was on the FBI 's most-wanted list between 1969 and 1977. Paddock's only recorded interactions with law enforcement were traffic citations.

Paddock was a high-stakes gambler who placed bets at a high enough level to earn valuable comps —free benefits such as rooms and meals. He was a familiar figure to casino hosts in Las Vegas, but was not well known among other high-stakes gamblers because he mostly played video poker. He reportedly kept to himself and was a heavy drinker. Paddock had lost a significant amount of his wealth over the previous two years, but had paid off all gambling debts before the shooting...
Source: Wikipedia

But that is of course, just pie in the sky. Nevertheless, let's get the comparisons between the fake shooter, Stephen Paddock and his lookalikes out of the way first - starting with Thomas Markle Jr (see photo T3)... And pay close attention to how their t-shirts matchup and the likeness of their ears.

PHOTO T3: Paddock & Thomas Markle Jr comparison

PHOTO T4: Paddock & Rainn comparison

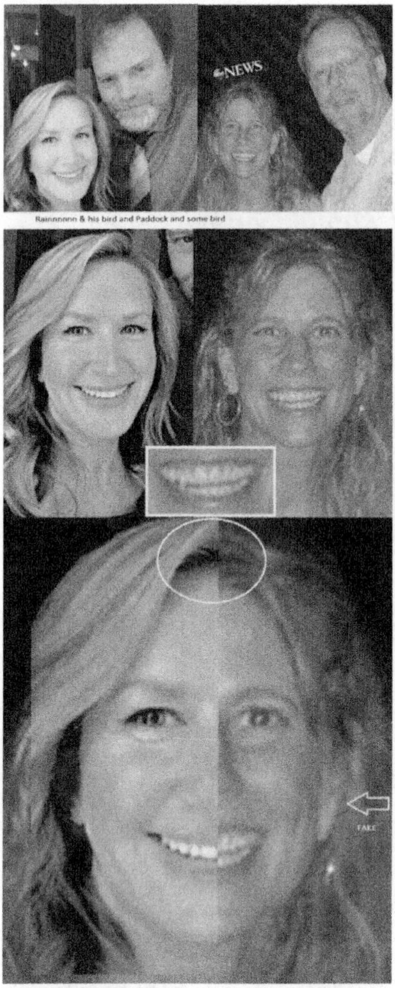

PHOTO T5: Rainn & his bird and Paddock & his bird

PHOTO T6: Paddock's bird compared to Mrs Markle the 1st

And like Markle Jr, Rainnnnnn Wilson also fits the bill well (See photo T4). But there is more... A lot more. You see, Rainn's bird also looks like Paddock's bird (see photo T5).

Now the nose doesn't fit but then again it wouldn't would it given the larger smile of Paddock's bird and the different head angles... Not to mention the photoshopping that has been done.
Furthermore there is the matter of tho bird seen with Paddock in photo T6. Indeed, to me she does in fact look a lot like Thomas Wayne Markle's alleged first wife.

And I'm not even done yet. You see the Vegas hoax like most hoaxes had the usual police officer killed. Her name was allegedly Rachael Parker and it has to be said that she traveled an awful long way for a 2 bit country-music festival since she supposedly worked at Manhattan Beach in California.

A police department employee from California was among those shot and killed during the Route 91 Harvest country music festival on Sunday.
Manhattan Beach Police Department records technician Rachael Parker, 33, died at a Las Vegas hospital, department spokeswoman Kristie Colombo wrote in an email. She was employed with the department for 10 years.

Another department employee, an unidentified police officer, was shot and suffered minor injuries, Colombo wrote.
Parker is not the only government employee from Manhattan Beach fatally wounded during the music festival. Special education teacher Sandra Casey also died. *Source: Las Vegas Review Journal, October 2017*

However, she does look an awful lot like Ted Bundy victim, Lynda Healy, with a touch of face altering software applied. (See photos T8 & T9)

She looks a bit demented doesn't she?
Nevertheless, this is what the monster-minions ALWAYS do… They use photos of previous 'victims' to create new 'victims'.

PHOTO T8: Rachael Parker

PHOTO T9: Parker compared to Bundy victim Lynda Healy

Mind you, you would have to be demented to take that country-music festival seriously. I mean the festival is meant to be an annual, 3 day event - think about that fact - *that started in 2014 (* plenty of time for planning the fake shooting then *) with the headline acts, according to Wikipedia being as follows:*

The following country music artists were the major acts in the respective years:

• 2014: The inaugural festival featured Jason Aldean, Blake Shelton and Miranda Lambert

• 2015: Florida Georgia Line, Thomas Rhett, Gary Allan, Lady Antebellum, Tim McGraw and Brett Eldredge

• 2016: Headliners included Luke Bryan, Toby Keith, Brad Paisley, Little Big Town and Chris Young

• 2017: Major acts were Eric Church, Sam Hunt, Jason Aldean, Jake Owen and Lee Brice

So, for instance if we take the first festival I would imagine on day 1 you had Jason Aldean. On day 2 you had Blake Shelton headlining and on day 3 Miranda ' who the fuck are you *' Lambert being the star of the show... Now I know that the Americans are big on country-music, but none of them are household names so who were the support acts?*

The Eagles of Death Metal probably. Indeed if you research those headliners some of them do not even appear in the US top 100 country music acts!.

Moreover, it is also interesting that Jason Aldean (by far the biggest name amongst that motley crew*) was the headline act for the FIRST ever show and was on stage for the LAST show to date when the shooting allegedly began.*

Therefore, it would be prudent to take a closer look at Aldean, would it not?

Of course it fucking would.

Aldean was born in Macon, Georgia. His parents separated when he was three. He was raised by his mother in Macon, and

during the summer he would spend time with his father in Homestead, Florida.
Before his father went to work he would map out guitar chords on notebook paper to show Jason where to place his fingers to play the chords, and the boy would sit and practice all day while his dad was at work. When his dad got home, he got out his own guitar and they played together.

Soon he could play a song after hearing it only a few times. His early favorites included George Strait 's "The Cowboy Rides Away", Hank Williams Jr. 's "The Blues Man", and Alabama 's "My Home's in Alabama".

Both of his parents encouraged young Aldean as he progressed musically.
From age 14, after watching the country-music awards on television, he wanted to perform on stage.

With his mother's help, he performed at the local VFW hall in Macon. He sang John Anderson 's song " Seminole Wind " and Tracy Lawrence 's "Sticks and Stones".

He then began performing at area talent contests and local fairs. At 15, he joined the "house band" at Georgia nightspot Nashville S.

In order to stand out, Aldean changed the spelling of his middle name, Aldine, to come up with the name Aldean.

Now personally, I think that Aldean is either Garth Brookes or a clone of him (see photo U1)

PHOTO U1: Aldean/Brookes comparison

PHOTO U2: Casey Marino AKA Cassandra Jenner & Brittany Kerr comparison

Course, that is as I say, just my opinion and relatively unimportant. However, Aldean's bird, Brittany Kerr does look very much like Casey Marino (see photo U2).

Indeed, Aldean & Kerr caused a bit of a scandal, ramped up by the worlds press when they first got together:
He has apologised for 'screwing up' after he was caught on camera kissing a former American Idol contestant.

Photos taken at a Hollywood bar show country star Jason Aldean, who is married with two children, getting very cosy with Brittany Kerr.

The 35-year-old appears to be all over the cheerleader, placing his arms around her waist and nuzzling her neck.

After flirting for a while Aldean can be seen leaning in for a kiss with the pretty blonde, who places her hands on his shoulders and recipro. Meanwhile 24-year-old Kerr, whose first time singing in front of people was at her American Idol audition, wore a tight white tank top and jeans.

While Aldean has utilised Twitter to publicly declare his regret, it seems the backlash became too much for Kerr.

The Bobcats dancer has deleted her own account on the social networking website after fans of Aldean labelled her a 'homewrecker', sent profanities and accused her of 'taking advantage' of the married country star.

The pair were pictured last Wednesday night in the patio area of The Den, a popular hangout for locals and tourists along L.A.'s Sunset Boulevard.

Aldean, 35, was wearing a checkered shirt, silver hoops in his ears and bracelets, but must have left his trademark cowboy hat at home. *Source: Daily Mail. October 2nd 2012*

And to close this Vegas Chapter it is worth looking at Stephen Paddocks high school photo (see photo U3).

You see, they too are a motley crew and there are a couple of three or four things to point out about Paddocks yearbook photo - such as his classmate, Susan Pack looks far too much like Ted Bundy's 'victim', Kim Leach (interesting surname) to be a coincidence (see photo U4)... And there were no angles changed in compiling that comparison photo.

Moreover, classmate, Kevin Page looks very much like Stephen Paddock himself (see photo U5). And again, no angles were changed. Or put another way, I simply took the half face Paddock photo and laid it on top of the Page photo... Yet the two half faces fit together better than if you had taken another random photo of Page and laid half of his face over his class photo.

And here is the thing. You can then take that photo of Kevin Page, cut it in half, and without changing any angles, you can overlay it perfectly onto a photo of a very similar looking, young Ronald Reagan... And I am sure that I do not need to remind you of the big part that Reagan has already played in this book.

PHOTO U3: Stephen Paddocks class photo

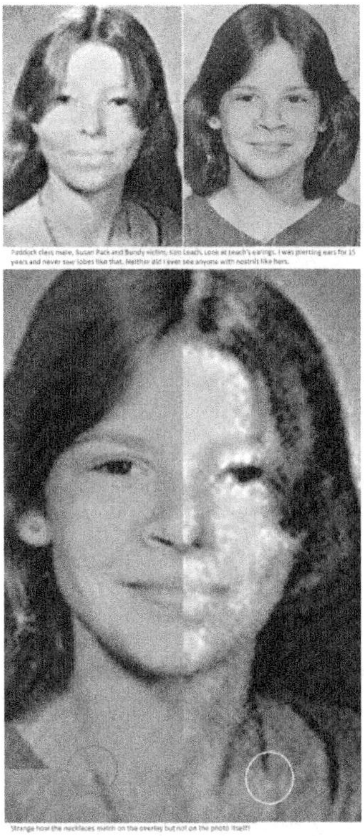

PHOTO U4: Susan Pack & Kim Leach comparison

PHOTO U5: Kevin Page & Stephen Paddock comparison.

PHOTO U6: Kevin Page/ Ronald Reagan comparison.

Chapter 13
The Presidential Collection

Now I can also tell you that you can take that class photo of Stephen Paddock and overlay it - without changing any angles - onto the Ronald Reagan photo that I used in photo U6 (see photo U7).

Nevertheless, I am not saying that young Reagan is young Paddock, because that would be silly since they do not look alike. However, given all of what I have already written, I am indeed saying that the fact that Paddock overlays Reagan perfectly is due to the fact that the source photos have been manipulated to do so in order to form a Satanic connection.

Moreover, I can take a photo of a young John F Kennedy and not only overlay the half face section of the Young Ronald Reagan over it perfectly, but I can also add a half face section of young Stephen Paddock to the mix - without changing any angles and still come up with a perfect photo (see photo U8).

John Fitzgerald Kennedy (May 29, 1917 – November 22, 1963), commonly referred to by his initials JFK, was an American politician who served as the 35th President of the United States from January 1961 until his assassination in November 1963. He served at the height of the Cold War, and the majority of his presidency dealt with managing relations with the Soviet Union. As a member of the Democratic Party, Kennedy represented the state of Massachusetts in the United States House of Representatives and the U.S. Senate prior to becoming president.

Kennedy was born in Brookline, Massachusetts, to Joseph P. Kennedy Sr. and Rose Kennedy. He graduated from Harvard University in 1940 and joined the U.S. Naval Reserve the following year. During World War II, he commanded a series of PT boats in the Pacific theater and earned the Navy and Marine Corps Medal for his service. After the war, Kennedy represented the 11th congressional district of Massachusetts in the U.S. House of Representatives from 1947 to 1953. He was subsequently elected to the U.S. Senate and served as the junior Senator from Massachusetts from 1953 to 1960. While in the Senate, he published his book entitled Profiles in Courage, which won a Pulitzer Prize for Biography. In the 1960

presidential election, Kennedy narrowly defeated Republican opponent Richard Nixon, who was the incumbent Vice President. At age 43, he became the youngest man to be elected as U.S. president as well as being the first (and only) Roman Catholic to occupy that office.

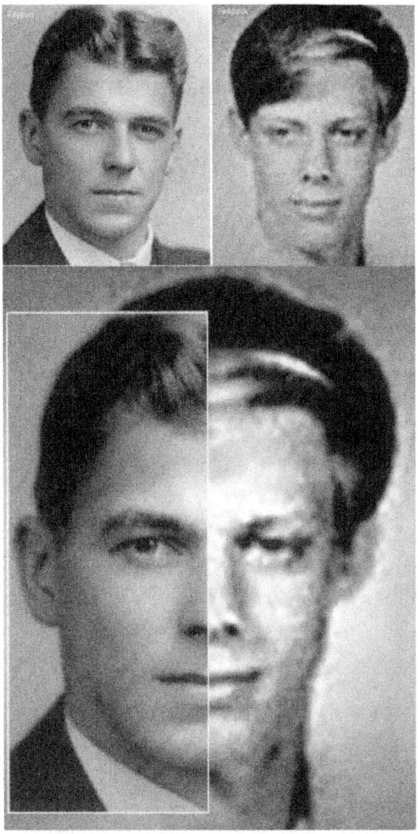

PHOTO U7: Reagan/Paddock overlay

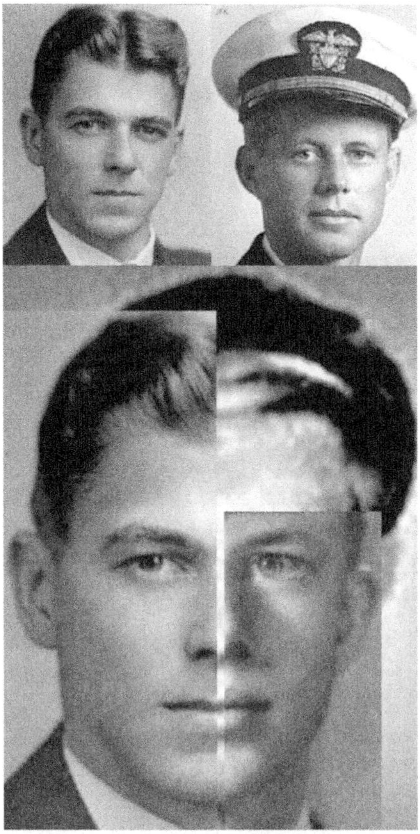

PHOTO U8: Raygun-Paddock-JFK

Kennedy's time in office was marked by high tensions with communist states in the Cold War. He increased the number of American military advisers in South Vietnam by a factor of 18 over President Dwight D. Eisenhower.

In April 1961, he authorized a failed joint-CIA attempt to overthrow the Cuban government of Fidel Castro in the Bay of Pigs Invasion. He subsequently rejected Operation Northwoods plans by the Joint Chiefs of Staff to orchestrate false flag attacks on American soil in order to gain public approval for a war against Cuba. In October 1962, U.S. spy planes discovered that Soviet missile bases had been deployed in

Cuba; the resulting period of tensions, termed the Cuban Missile Crisis, nearly resulted in the breakout of a global thermonuclear conflict. Domestically, Kennedy presided over the establishment of the Peace Corps and supported the civil rights movement, but he was largely unsuccessful in passing his New Frontier domestic policies.

Kennedy continues to rank highly in historians' polls of U.S. presidents and with the general public. His average approval rating of 70% is the highest of any president in Gallup 's history of systematically measuring job approval.

On November 22, 1963, Kennedy was assassinated in Dallas, Texas. Lee Harvey Oswald was arrested for the state crime, but he was never prosecuted due to his murder by Jack Ruby two days later; Ruby was sentenced to death and died while the sentence was on appeal in 1967.

Pursuant to the Presidential Succession Act, Vice President Lyndon B. Johnson was sworn in as president later that day. Both the FBI and the Warren Commission officially concluded that Oswald had acted alone in the assassination, but various groups challenged the findings of the Warren Report and believed that Kennedy was the victim of a conspiracy. After Kennedy's death, Congress enacted many of his proposals, including the Civil Rights and the Revenue Acts of 1964. *Source: Wikipedia.*

Furthermore, I can also do the same using a photo of a young Jimmy carter… Who does indeed look very much like the young Stephen Paddock (see photo U9)... And once again, I do not need to remind you of the huge part that Carter has played in this book. In fact Carter and JFK are very similar in appearance and their photos perfectly overlay each other without changing any angles too (see photo U10)...
Which again is extremely suspicious.

In fact the likeness between JFK and Carter has led many conspiracy theorist to the conclusion that they are one and the same (see photo V1).

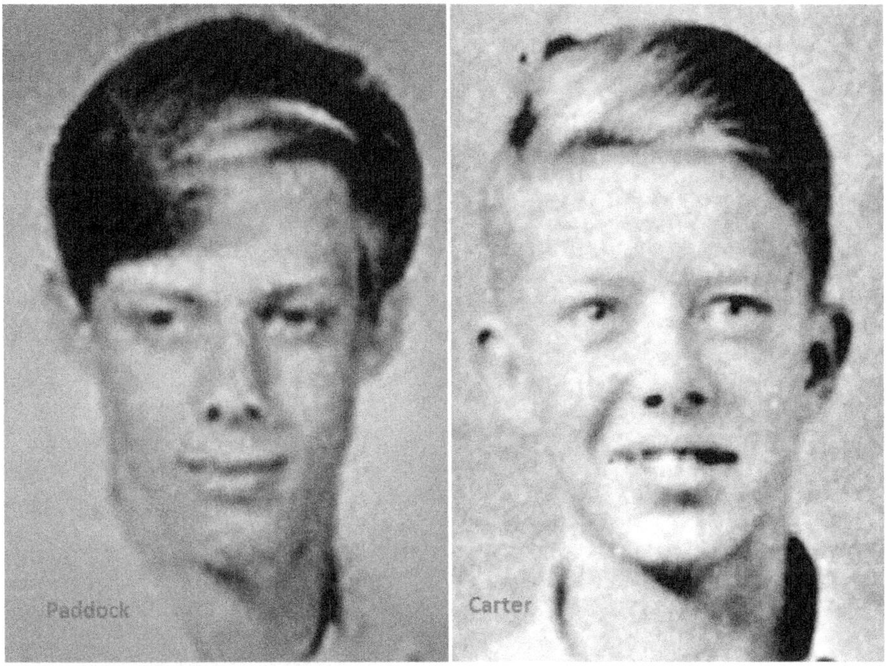

PHOTO U9: Carter/ Paddock comparison

PHOTO U10: JFK/Carter comparison

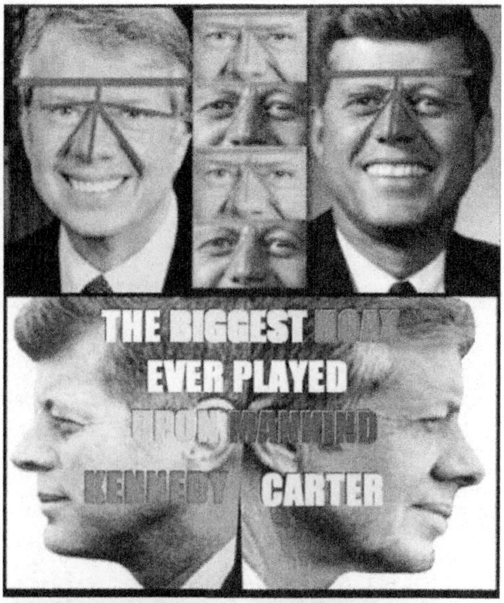

PHOTO V1: JFK/Carter comparison

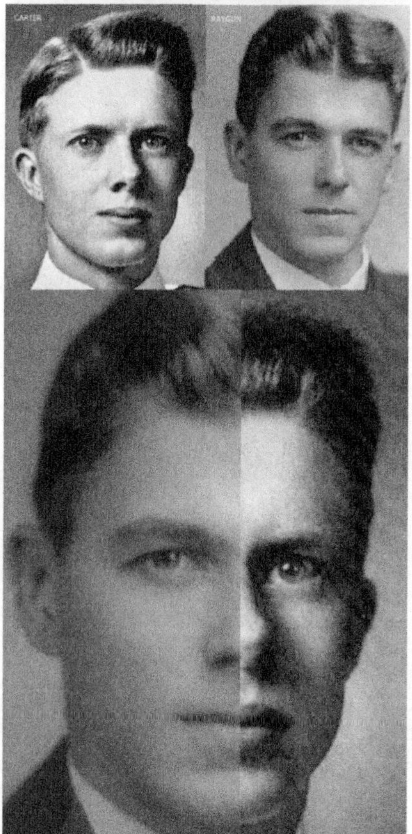

PHOTO V2: Carter/Reagan comparison

Mind you, whilst I do not necessarily buy into that conspiracy theory, you will know if you have read my " ***How The West Was Won*** *" articles, that Lee Harvey Oswald is most definitely a created persona. And of course, the young Carter photo also perfectly overlays the young Reagan photo (see photo V2).*
However, when you take a closer look at all of the US Presidents, you quickly realise that none of them stand up to scrutiny. For instance, President number 3, THOMAS Jefferson was played by a fella called THOMAS Watson (see photo V3).

The following is taken from the New Georgia Encyclopedia:

The public life of Thomas E. Watson is perhaps one of the more perplexing and controversial among Georgia politicians.

In his early years he was characterized as a liberal, especially for his time. In later years he emerged as a force for white supremacy and anti-Catholic rhetoric. He was elected to the Georgia General Assembly (1882), the U.S. House of Representatives (1890), and the U.S. Senate (1920), where he served for only a short time before his death. Nominated by the Populist Party as its vice presidential candidate in 1896, he achieved national recognition for his egalitarian, agrarian agenda.

Although his terms of elective office were short, for more than thirty years his support was essential for many men running for public office in Georgia. In addition to his political achievements, Tom Watson was a practicing lawyer, publisher, and historian. He is remembered for being a voice for Populism and the disenfranchised, and later in life, as a southern demagogue and bigot...

Moreover, there are many famous people walking this earth today who are clones of historical figures (see photos V4, V5, V6).
But I will leave it there for now. Which just leaves two more Markle relatives to do before we get to the main event, Meghan Markle.

PHOTO V3: THOMAS Watson and US President number 3

PHOTO V4: Actor Alec Baldwin & US President number 13, Millard Fillmore

PHOTO V5: John D Rockefeller & Vladimir Putin

PHOTO V6: Donald Trump & General George Patto

Chapter 14
The Sister & The Uncle

Now the first of these last two 'relatives' is Meg's half sister, Samantha Grant…

Although I can find no reason that she should have 'Grant *' as a surname.*

However, to me Sam looks very much like the washed-up actress Melanie Griffiths:

Melanie Richards Griffith (born August 9, 1957) [is an American actress. Griffith began her career as an adolescent in nonspeaking film roles before making her credited debut opposite Gene Hackman in Arthur Penn's Night Moves (1975).

She rose to prominence for her role in Brian De Palma 's Body Double (1984), which earned her a National Society of Film Critics Award for Best Supporting Actress. Griffith's subsequent performance in Something Wild (1986) garnered critical acclaim before she was cast in 1988's Working Girl, which earned her a nomination for the Academy Award for Best Actress and won her a Golden Globe.

The 1990s saw Griffith in a series of roles which received varying critical reception: she received Golden Globe nominations for her performances in Buffalo Girls (1995), and as Marion Davies in RKO 281 (1999), while also earning a Golden Raspberry Award for Worst Actress for her performances in Shining Through (1992), as well as receiving nominations for Crazy in Alabama (1999) and John Waters ' cult film Cecil B. Demented (2000).

Other credits include John Schlesinger 's Pacific Heights (1990), Milk Money (1994), the neo-noir film Mulholland Falls (1996), as Charlotte Haze in Adrian Lyne 's Lolita (1997), and Another Day in Paradise (1998).

She later starred as Barbara Marx in The Night We Called It a Day (2003), and has appeared on the television series Nip/Tuck, Raising Hope, and Hawaii Five-0. After acting on stage in London, in 2003 she made her Broadway debut in a revival of the musical Chicago, receiving celebratory reviews that made it a box office success. *Source Wikipedia*

Now Melanie Griffith left home at the age of 14 to move in with the then 22 year old 80's heartthrob, Don Johnson.

Course, this led to Johnson having to defend the relationship and he later told ***Entertainment weekly*** *that; Melanie was the "* aggressor in the relationship *" and that* "She pursued *" him. So I suppose that makes it ok then ya nonce. Nevertheless, let's compare Griffiths and Grant (see photo V7).*

And that just leaves Meghan's uncle, Fred Markle for us to look at… Or Uncle Fat as he is affectionately known... By no one but me.

Nevertheless, Uncle Fat could be any of the usual suspects so I am not going to dwell on him too much... He is however our old friend Tom Hollander, the structural engineer from Iowa, for instance (see photo V8)... And Thomas Hollander is - as we have already seen - also Thomas, so you work it out for yourself.

PHOTO V7: (main) Samantha Grant (inset) Melanie Griffiths

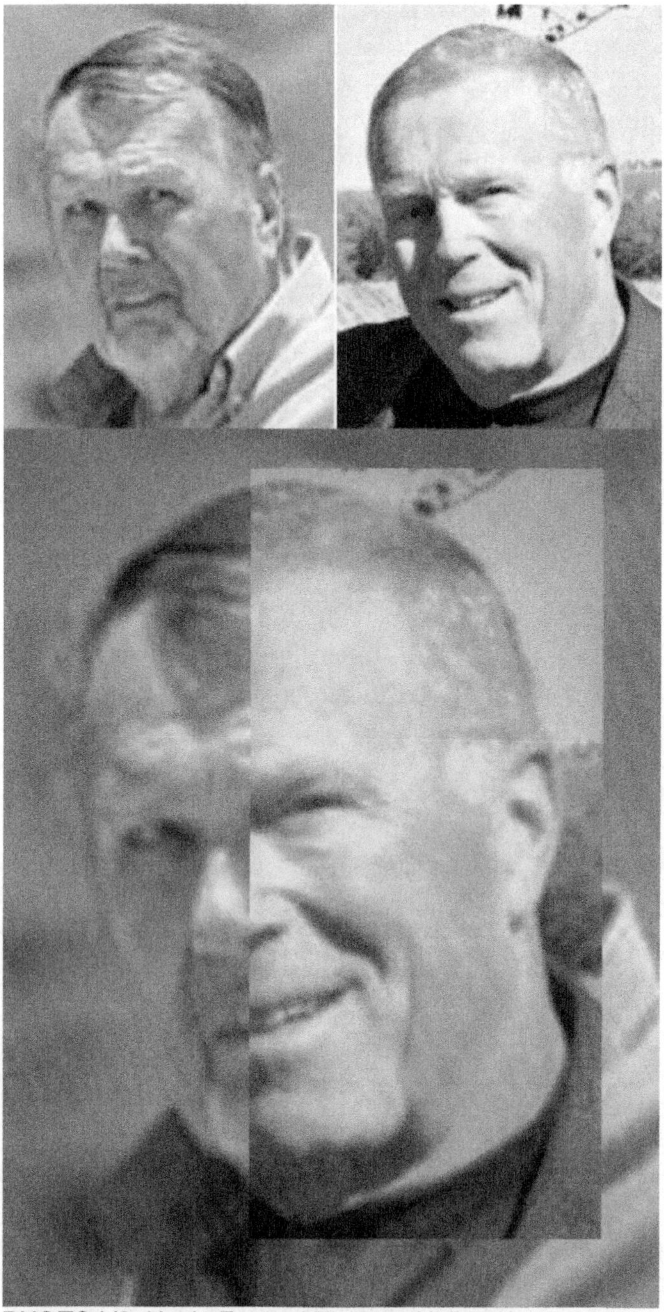

PHOTO V8: Uncle Fat and Thomas Hollander comparison

Chapter 15
Meghan Markle

So who is Meghan Markle?

And the answer to that is she is no one… She is just a made-up persona, invented to give the British royal family some credibility and make it appear that they are moving with the times.

Nevertheless, let us get her 'official' bio out of the way first:

Meghan, Duchess of Sussex (born Rachel Meghan Markle; August 4, 1981), is an American-born member of the British royal family and a former film and television actress.

Meghan Markle was born and raised in Los Angeles, California. During her studies at Northwestern University, she began playing small roles in American television series and films, but found her mixed-race heritage to be an obstacle.

From 2011 to 2017, she played her best-known role, Rachel Zane, on the American legal drama series Suits. As an outspoken feminist, Markle has addressed the issue of gender inequality, and her lifestyle website, The Tig, featured a column profiling influential women. Her humanitarian work in the 2010s saw her represent international charity organizations. She has also received recognition for her fashion and style, releasing a line of clothing in 2016.

From 2011 until their divorce in 2013, Markle was married to actor and producer Trevor Engelson. In 2017, she announced her engagement to Prince Harry, grandson of Queen Elizabeth II, and moved to London. She consequently retired from acting, closed her social media accounts, and started undertaking public engagements on behalf of the British royal family. Following their wedding on May 19, 2018, Markle became known as Duchess of Sussex.
Rachel Meghan Markle was born on August 4, 1981, in Los Angeles, California, at West Park Hospital in Canoga Park.

Her mother, Doria Ragland, a social worker and yoga instructor, as of 2017 lives in View Park–Windsor Hills, California. Markle has often described a very close friendship with her mother. Her father, Thomas Markle Sr., who lives in Rosarito, Mexico, is a retired television director of photography and lighting director, whose profession resulted in his young daughter often visiting the set of Married...with Children.

Markle's parents divorced when she was six years old. She has two older paternal half-siblings, Thomas Markle Jr. and Samantha Markle, from whom she is reportedly estranged.

Describing her heritage in a 2015 essay for Elle, Markle states that her "dad is Caucasian and my mom is African American. I'm half black and half white ...
While my mixed heritage may have created a grey area surrounding my self-identification, keeping me with a foot on both sides of the fence, I have come to embrace that. To say who I am, to share where I'm from, to voice my pride in being a strong, confident mixed-race woman."

Markle grew up in Hollywood. She was educated at private schools, beginning at age two at Hollywood Little Red Schoolhouse.

At age 11, her successful campaign to get a company to change a national television commercial she viewed as sexist was profiled by Linda Ellerbee on Nick News.
Markle attended Immaculate Heart High School, an all-girl Catholic private school in Los Angeles, but was raised as a Protestant. She then attended Northwestern University, where she joined Kappa Kappa Gamma sorority, and participated in community service and charity projects.
She graduated from Northwestern's School of Communication in 2003 with a bachelor's degree and a double major in theater and international studies. She also served an internship at the American embassy in Buenos Aires, Argentina, and studied for a semester in Madrid, Spain. Source: Wikipedia

And that is just total, total bollox.
However, what is interesting is the following hogwash published in the Daily Mail on May 27th 2018:

The Duchess of Sussex was pregnant when she stood in front of the altar. And she was in love — not with her husband-to-be but her cousin.

No, not Meghan, obviously — but the last woman to bear the title Duchess of Sussex.

More than 200 years ago, a red-headed royal prince fell in love with a dark-haired older woman. What followed was a web of love, lies, deceit and royal disgrace which was to last 40 years. She was Lady Augusta Murray, daughter of the Earl of Dunmore.

He was Prince Augustus Frederick, sixth son of 'mad' King George III — and soon to be made the first Duke of Sussex.

So, if that were to be believed then the current Duke of Sussex and the last Duke of Sussex were both ginger haired fellas who married "dark haired, older women"... Or put another way; history repeating itself.

Moreover, and again if the press is to be believed, then Harry & Meghan are related:

An investigation into the lineage of Prince Harry and Meghan Markle has revealed that they are actually cousins. Despite growing up on different sides of the Atlantic, a study has found they are distantly related thanks to a 15th century ancestor of the Queen Mother.

Meghan's father, Emmy-winning cinematographer Thomas Markle, can trace his line all the way back to an Englishman called Ralph Bowes. Ralph was a High Sheriff of County Durham whose family seat was Streatlam Castle and lived from 1480-1518. His estates, through a succession of males heirs, eventually passed down to Sir George Bowes, an MP related to Elizabeth Bowes-Lyon.

Elizabeth would later become the Queen Mother when her daughter became Queen Elizabeth II in 1952. The Queen became Harry's grandmother when he was born 1984.
Meghan can trace her lineage back hundreds of years to when her ancestors first first arrived in America. Sheriff Ralph Bowe's granddaughter married John Hussey of Dorking, Surrey.

Their grandson, Christopher Hussey, moved to America in 1632 and helped to found Nantucket, Massachusetts. Mail Online reported that it was this line of the family that would eventually produce Meghan. Her German ancestors also have their own coat of arms, thanks to grandfather Gordon, husband of Doris, who was related to Abraham Merckel (1630-1698) of Alsace, France. *Source: The Metro, 30 Oct 2017*

But once again, that is just total bollox designed to muddy the waters and give Meghan some credibility.
Moreover, in an effort to strengthen the myth, nude photos of Meghan have recently surfaced (see photo W1). And when you couple that with the now hard to find photos of Meghan giving a fella a blow job in a tv show (see photo W2), do you really believe that the royal family would allow her to join their ranks?

PHOTO W1: Nude Meghan

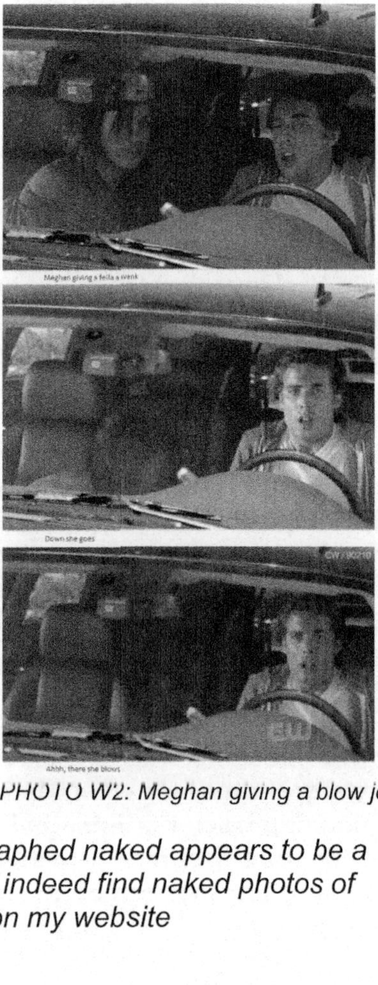

PHOTO W2: Meghan giving a blow job.

Mind you, the Royal Family photographed naked appears to be a clause in their contract and you can indeed find naked photos of nearly every single family member on my website www.chrisspivey.org.

These photos include: Prince Charles, Prince Andrew, Sarah Ferguson, Diana, Kate Middleton, Sophie Wessex, Prince William amongst others. There are also naked photos of Kate Middleton's sister, Pippa.

And Pippa was of course, the first actress to play Meghan.Indeed, such was their likeness that the national press were forced to address the fact.

The following is taken from www.heart.co.uk and just one of many reports on the fact:
Is it just us or does Prince Harry's girlfriend resemble Kate's younger sister, Pippa Middleton...

Ever since we found out that Prince Harry is dating American actress, Meghan Markle, we have been OBSESSED with getting to know her.

The 35-year-old divorcee is known for playing Rachel Zane in the law drama, Suits, is a humanitarian and a lifestyle blogger. Now, eagle-eyed fans are claiming that Meghan bears a striking resemblance to Harry's sister in law's younger sibling, Pippa Middleton.

Aside from having the same big, brown eyes and luscious, brunette locks, their face shapes a very similar. And it looks like they could share a wardrobe too!

Rumours of a romance between Prince Harry, 31, and Pippa Middleton, 32, surface after they both played significant roles in Prince William and Kate Middleton's wedding.

Although we'd like to think that Harry fell in love with Pippa after she wore THAT figure-hugging bridesmaid's dress (dubbing her Her Royal Hotness), we're not sure there was much substantial evidence behind the rumours.

Having said that, he was seen telling Pippa on his way to Westminster Abbey that "you do look very beautiful today - seriously."

The similarities don't stop there: both women are key ambassador for meaningful causes. Meghan is an advocate for

UN Women and Water Aid ambassador, whilst Pippa Middleton is a supporter of the British Heart Foundation.

Perhaps Prince Harry has a type?

Pippa is officially off the dating market, as she plans to tie-the-knot with her hedge-funder fiancé, James Matthews, 41.

Prince Harry and Meghan are said to have met through a mutual friend, Misha Nonoo, over the summer when Harry was in the USA promoting the Invictus Games.

Course, modesty prevents me telling you that I reported on the likeness between the pair months before the press picked upon the fact - or should I say months before the press were ORDERED to report on the fact.

Indeed, it kinda smacks of the way that the press were forced to comment on the ever changing face of Ted Bundy.

Nevertheless, as my old mother always says; the proof is in the pudding (see photos W3, W4 & W5)

(Next Page)

W3

W4

PHOTOS W3, W4, W5: Pippa & Meghan comparisons

PHOTO W6: Meghan & Pippa's moles are in the same place.

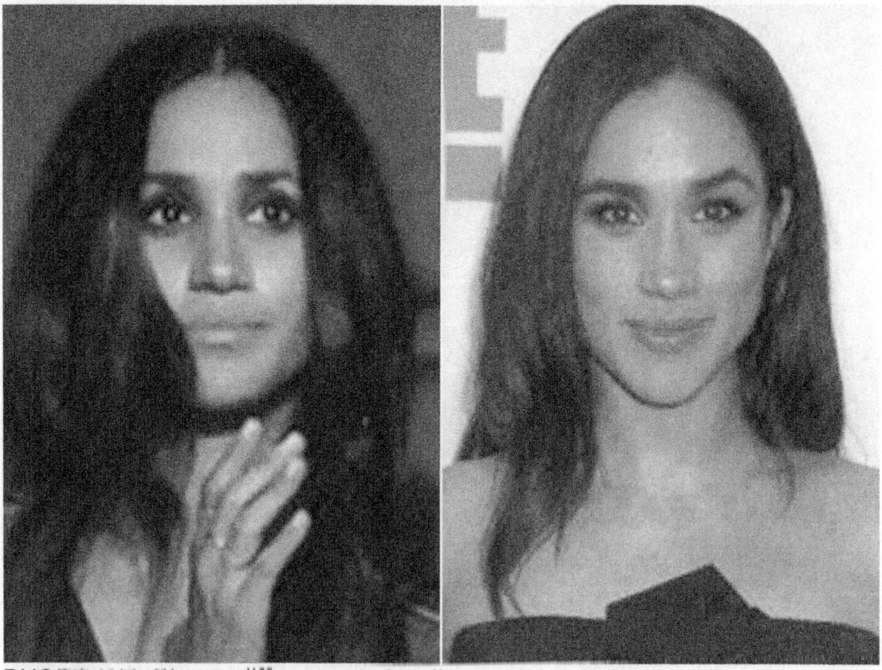

PHOTO W7: Shows difference in jaw lines

Moreover, Meghan has a mole on the right side of her upper lip and Pippa has one on the left side. However, if you reverse Pippa's photos, you can see that her mole sits in the exact same spot as Meghan's (see photo W6).

Which is extremely coincidental. Indeed it is also extremely suspect in the way that Meghan goes from sometimes having a relatively square jaw to sometimes having a very sculpted, thin jaw (see photo W7).
Another of those who plays the part of Meghan is her 'friend' Jessica Mulroney.

Jessica Mulroney (born Brownstein; born 14 March 1980) is a Canadian fashion stylist who regularly does segments for the television show CityLine Mulroney is the daughter of Veronica (Coleman) and Stephen Brownstein. She is a descendant of the founders of Browns Shoes, a niece of Bill Brownstein, writer for the Montreal Gazette, and sister of Harvard Professor John Brownstein.

Mulroney is a graduate of McGill University.
In November 2015 Mulroney styled ensembles for Sophie Grégoire Trudeau, the wife of Justin Trudeau, the Prime Minister of Canada. Her efforts on Grégoire Trudeau's behalf attracted particular attention because Mulroney is the daughter-in-law of former Prime Minister Brian Mulroney, political opponent of Grégoire-Trudeau's father-in-law, Pierre Trudeau. Despite the cool relationship between their parents, the Mulroney and Trudeau children have been friendly with Ben Mulroney being an invited guest at Justin Trudeau's wedding in 2005.

Mulroney and her sisters-in-law Caroline, Katy and Vanessa Mulroney co-founded a charity called The Shoebox Project. The project's goal is to provide makeup to women living in shelters. Donors are asked to fill a shoebox with approximately $50 worth of cosmetics and toiletries.
Both Maclean's and Chatelaine have interviewed Mulroney about the Canadian marketing rights she and her sister Elizabeth acquired for the high-end lingerie lines la Perla and Cosabella Brownstein married Ben Mulroney, the eldest son and second eldest child of Mila Mulroney and former Prime Minister of Canada Brian Mulroney, on October 30, 2008. The couple have three children: identical twins, Brian Gerald Alexander Mulroney and John Benedict Dimitri Mulroney (born August 12, 2010), and daughter Isabel Veronica Mulroney, known as "Ivy" (born June 12, 2013).

Mulroney is considered a close friend of Meghan, Duchess of Sussex (Meghan Markle). In 2018, she and her husband attended Markle's wedding to Prince Harry, and their children participated as page boys and flower girl. Earlier, she and her husband had attended the closing ceremony of the 2017 Invictus Games at the Air Canada Centre, Toronto, on September 30, 2017, where Markle and Prince Harry made a joint public appearance. *Source Wikipedia*

And once again the proof is in the pudding (see photo W8).

PHOTO W8: Meghan and Jessica comparison

PHOTO W9: CJ Franko

What would the chances be?

However, there are also three or four others who step into Meghan's shoes when needed, such as the model, CJ Franko (see photo W9). Nevertheless, the actor who plays the role of Meghan most is Natalie Suliman.

Natalie Denise Doud-Suleman (born Nadya Denise Suleman, July 11, 1975), known as Octomom in the media, is an American media personality who came to international attention when she gave birth to octuplets in January 2009.
The Suleman octuplets are only the second full set of octuplets to be born alive in the United States.

One week after their birth, they surpassed the previous worldwide survival rate for a complete set of octuplets set by the Chukwu octuplets in 1998. The circumstances of their high order multiple birth led to controversy in the field of assisted reproductive technology as well as an investigation by the Medical Board of California of the fertility specialist involved.

Public reaction turned negative when it was discovered that Suleman already had six other young children and was unemployed and on public assistance programs. Suleman conceived the octuplets and her six older children via in vitro fertilization (IVF). Although she initially denied ever having used public assistance, she confirmed in April 2012 on NBC's Today show that she was indeed on public assistance.

Suleman was born in Fullerton, California in 1975, an only child. Her mother Angela Victoria Suleman (born Stanaitis) was a school teacher and her father Edward Doud Suleman was a restaurant owner, and Iraqi army veteran. She attended Nogales High school, where she was known as Natalie Doud, and later California State University in Fullerton Suleman quickly captured the public eye with the birth of octuplets. Within the first week, the media dubbed her "Octomom". Suleman hired the Killeen Furtney Group as her initial public relations company, with Wes Yoder providing a small amount of pro bono advice. Both groups soon ended their involvement after receiving death threats. Her next spokesman was Victor Munoz, who quit on March 6, 2009...

Suleman continued efforts to raise money to support herself and her children. In June 2012, she announced that she would be recording a new single with recording artist Adam Barta after she appeared in an alternate cut of his "Q&A" music video, where she was heard saying, "Let's do a duet, on my new album!" In Summer 2012, Suleman appeared in the adult film Octomom Home Alone produced by Wicked Pictures. The film is solely of Nadya Suleman in solo scenes with the aid of sex toys;

there are no other actors. The film was released on June 20, 2012. (In December 2012, Octomom Home Alone received four AVN Award nominations, and won for Best Celebrity Video.)

She has also begun work as an adult entertainer dancing in men's clubs. She released a single called "Sexy Party" with Adam Barta in September, and caused a controversy when he was seen holding her breasts surrounded by crucifixes on a bed on the compact disc artwork. She stated she was inspired by the work of Madonna. In October 2012, she was paid to participate in the launch of an internet debate site, Deeyoon.com, including doing an online debate on parenting with Michael Lohan. *Source: Wikipedia*

Okay, before we go any further I best show you a comparison of Natalie & Meghan (see photos X1, X2, X3, X4).

PHOTO X1: Octomum Natalie suliman

PHOTO X2: Natalie & Meghan comparison - No angles changed

PHOTO X3: Natalie & Meghan comparison - No angles changed

PHOTO X4: Half face comparison of Natalie and Meghan

Now according to Google the odds of a woman carrying eight babies to birth is one TRILLION to one… Or put another way, damned near impossible.

So, to put that in context; it would take you thirty one thousand, seven hundred years (31,700) to count to a trillion… And that is counting 24 hours a day, 7 days a week without a break!

Therefore, what would the odds be of a woman having eight babies in one pregnancy as well as being a 31 billion to 1 doppelganger of Meghan Markle?

Not that Suliman really had 8 babies in one go. Indeed you only need look at her tits to see that the story is just another in a long line of hoaxes. Yet strangely enough, Meghan doesn't have any children, and I say "strangely enough" because at 38 years old, a twice married woman as beautiful as Meghan - who claims to love children - not having any is extremely strange… Although I doubt we will have to wait long before it is announced that the new Duchess of Sussex is pregnant - although that will be in reality, a hoax too.

Mind you, that no-children-anomaly could be explained away by the fact that there are more than a few researchers who believe that Meghan (Suliman) is a male to female transgender - which is an agenda that I have already touched upon.

And indeed those researchers point to the fact that Meghan has very large hands (men's hands are larger than women's) and her forefingers are much longer than her ring fingers (see photo X5).

You see, it is a fact that 97 percent of women's forefingers are the same length as their ring fingers which would make Meghan in the 3 percent club… Another coincidence?

Course, that could very well be the case but then when you take in to account that Meghan's shoulders are wider than her hips (as are all men's who aren't fat slobs) and women's hips are wider than their shoulders, the very real possibility cannot be dismissed.

There are of course other indicators to suggest that 'Meghan' was once a man, such as the poses that she adopts in order to hide the hip fact and look more feminine as well as her long arms. However, you will have to do that research for yourself.

Nevertheless, the fact is that Meghan simply does not exist.

And that is why ALL of her childhood photos are faked - some of which we saw at the beginning of this book. After all, if Meghan does not exist then she cannot of had a childhood can she?

PHOTO X5: Meghan's big hands and long forefinger and shoulders wider than her hips.

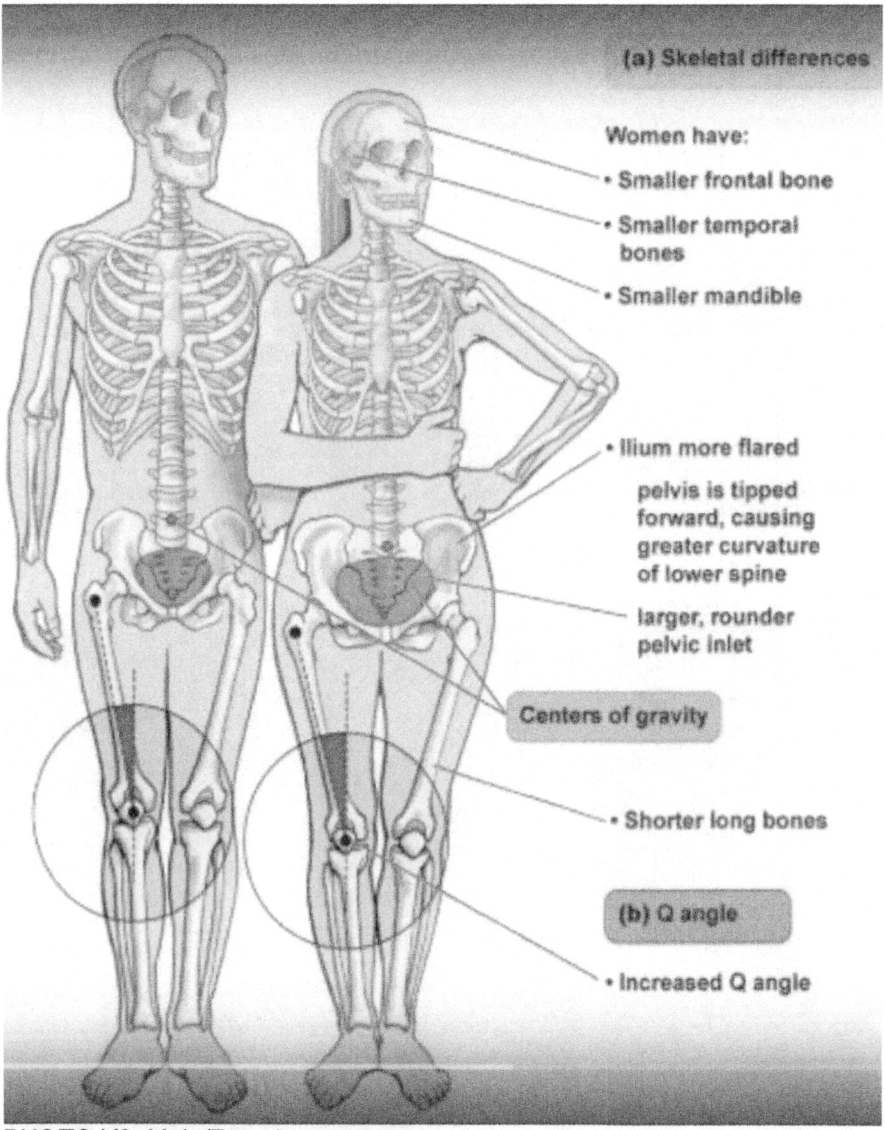

PHOTO X6: Male/Female anatomy

In fact I can tell you that the majority of Meghan's childhood photos are actually photos of Karis Jagger.

Karis Hunt Jagger was on November 4 th, 1970 in London and is the eldest daughter of Mick Jagger - legendary frontman of the 'Rolling Stones'.

Her mother is Marsha Hunt:

Marsha Hunt (born April 15, 1946) is an American actress, novelist, singer and former model, who has lived mostly in Britain and Ireland. She achieved national fame when she appeared in London as Dionne in the long-running rock musical Hair. She enjoyed close relationships with Marc Bolan and Mick Jagger, who is the father of her only child Karis.

According to Hunt, The Rolling Stones ' controversial hit song "Brown Sugar" was based on her. She has written three novels, as well as three volumes of autobiography, which include a frank account of life as a breast cancer sufferer.

Hunt was born in Philadelphia, in 1946 and lived in North Philadelphia, near 23rd and Columbia, then in Germantown and Mount Airy, for the first 13 years of her life. Hunt remembers Philadelphia with affection, particularly the "Philadelphia steak sandwiches and the bad boys on the basketball court".

Hunt's mother, Inez, was her primary parent and worked as a librarian in a local library. Hunt's father, Blaire Theodore Hunt, Jr., was one of America's first black psychiatrists but he did not live with Hunt; she found out when she was 15 years old that he had committed suicide three years previously. Hunt was brought up by her mother, her aunt, and her grandmother; three strong but very different women. Hunt describes her mother Inez as "extremely intelligent and education-minded", her Aunt Thelma as "extremely Catholic but very glamorous", and her grandmother Edna as an "extremely aggressive...ass-kicking" independent Southern woman.

Hunt credits the experience of having been poor with teaching her not to be materialistic. Her family put a great deal of emphasis on academic performance, and Hunt did very well in school. In 1960, the family moved to Kensington, California, which Hunt still regards as home, so that her brother and sister could attend Oakland High School and prepare to attend the University of California, Berkeley. Hunt also went to Berkeley, in 1964, where she joined Jerry Rubin on protest marches against the Vietnam War. In her book Undefeated she recalled that during her time at Berkeley they "were sitting in for the Free Speech Movement, smoking pot, experimenting with acid, lining up to take Oriental philosophy courses, daring to cohabit, and going to dances in San Francisco." *Source: Wikipedia*

Indeed, reading that bio makes me think that the story of Doria Ragland could have been concocted from Marsha's life.

Nevertheless, let's go compare Meghan & Karis (see photos X7 & X8)

PHOTO X7: Meghan (aged approximately 6 months old) and Karis Jagger

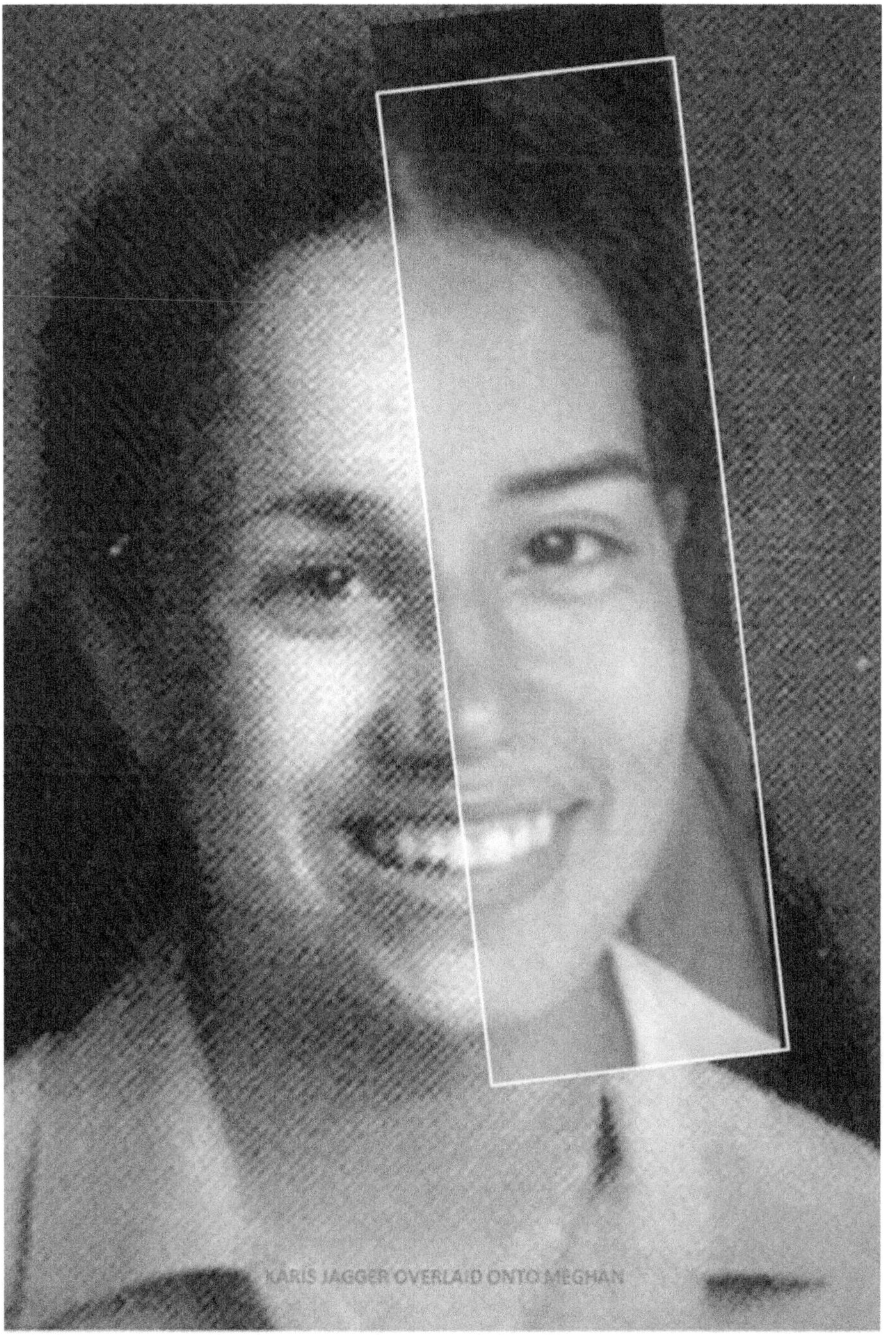

Slight angle change needed

PHOTO X8: Karis overlai onto Meghan photo.

And that is that as they say. However, you can't go on turning a blind eye or burying your head in the sand.

These people are seriously deranged and have to be stopped... You all need to stand up and be counted.

Thank you for reading.

Printed in Great Britain
by Amazon

86020237R00153